NEIL PERRY

THE FOOD I LOVE

BEAUTIFUL, SIMPLE FOOD TO COOK AT HOME

Dedicated to the memory of my father

ACKNOWLEDGMENTS

How do I thank all the people who have made it possible for me to write this book? It all started so long ago, and many people have been instrumental in my life as a cook well before this project started and many have directly helped to put this book together. So I guess it all started with my father; he taught me to care about food — thanks Dad. All the great cooks I have met in my life, thank you. My business partner Trish Richards, you gave me the opportunity to live my dream, run a great restaurant and work with the most fantastic, energetic staff you could imagine. To you, the biggest thanks of all. To all at Rockpool, in particular Khan Danis and Catherine Adams — my food would not be half of what it is without that dynamic duo — a very big thank you. Thanks to all my staff in my restaurants and particularly the Qantas team, all you guys know who you are; you keep the dream alive. Thanks Sarah Kodicek for checking the manuscript and asking 'what did you mean?' countless times: the book will mean more because of it. Thanks also for being the jack of all trades who keeps all the other projects we have going, actually going. Thanks to Kate Barker for all her help through testing and shooting, and keeping Sarah focused. Thanks Belinda Smith, my assistant, for getting me to the right place at the right time and making all these things possible.

Thanks to Juliet Rogers and Kay Scarlett, who commissioned this project and went with it when it was totally out of control. Maybe next time I will stick to the brief. Thanks to Margaret Malone, my editor; you let my voice come through when others in your position would have gone for the scalpel, and thanks for your enquiring efforts — I sometimes forget that I have been cooking for years. Thanks to Marylouise Brammer — your design and excitement over a new font has left me holding a truly beautiful book. Earl Carter, what can I say? I love you, mate. This book is about the energy that we felt at the shoot, and should be called Earl Carter's favourite food photos with words by Neil Perry. Sue Fairlie-Cuninghame, MATE, I love you too, and it is your understanding of what I'm capable of and making me do it that is the reason the book is what it is, but thank you most of all for just being my friend. Lastly to my beautiful wife Samantha and gorgeous daughter Josephine, you both endured long hours of me sitting and typing when I should have been spending time with you. I thank you for your patience, and love you both heaps. The week that I handed in the last of the manuscript my second daughter Macy was born; when you're old enough to read, here is a thank you for bringing so much love into your mother's and your sister's lives and mine.

CONTENTS

INTRODUCTION

My father was a butcher, mad fisherman and keen gardener. He had the most amazing effect on me, though I didn't know it until I was many years into my working life. As with many things in life, I didn't fully understand the impact he had on me until he was gone. It is a great shame that he never got to see the three books that I have written, as he was instrumental in me being able to evolve them. It's not that my mother didn't have a lot to do with it as well, she was and still is a great Mum, and the one who taught me most about loving and caring in the way she created a loving environment not just for her kids, but for all the extended family and beyond. I wouldn't be who I am now without her, so my balance really comes from having a great Mum and Dad. However, this is a cookbook and I have to acknowledge the first cook who had an enormous influence on me and that, as you may have guessed, was my Dad. I cook and feel about food the way I do today because of his great skill, understanding and love of everything that tasted good in this world. He taught me to taste, to question, to care for produce and to develop a palate that is the driving force in my life. He instilled an understanding that eating was for pleasure, not for fuel. I learnt that if food was thought about, then it was remembered, and it is this that makes me who I am today.

If you asked what are the main factors in my life as a cook, I could say skill or technique, understanding and taste. But, while I suspect that they have something to do with my cooking, the main reason I do what I do now is because I am completely committed to sourcing the finest ingredients. They are the only ones I am interested in, and why? Because my father was a butcher, a fisherman and a gardener: what a great start in life. But he wasn't just those things, he was the best at those things. He put the very best quality meat on the table, he caught and handled fish well, and he grew superb fruit, herbs and vegetables in the garden. We picked and dug a lot of our food in the early days. His chooks would lay eggs and we would eat them fresher than you can imagine. We had all this and his desire for food to be pleasurable. I didn't have a good upbringing, I had an exceptional upbringing and at the time I didn't even know it. I thought that everyone ate like that. I now know that I was very privileged and that I would have no hope of being who I am today without that upbringing.

So, with that great start, I have dedicated myself to cooking the food I love, influenced by my father and all the great chefs I have had the privilege to work with and see work, both here and around the world. My cooking has also been shaped by the multicultural nature of Sydney and the wonderful produce that comes in the door at my restaurant, Rockpool. I have, over time, written two other books. Ten years ago, when I wrote my first, the *Rockpool* cookbook, I thought the world probably didn't need another cookbook. I really feel like that now as well, but I also think it is important to communicate something that you haven't said before, so here I am, doing it again. I hope with *Rockpool* that I communicated some of the restaurant's ethos on food, among many other things. I hope with my second book, *Simply Asian*, that I communicated clearly that Asian, or what I called modern Asian, cooking can be achieved at home with simple and delicious results. I hope that I can encourage you to read this book, cook from it, and that I can either give you new simple skills or remind you of how wonderful some of these classic recipes are. I hope that you start to think about what temperature you are cooking at, or when pan-frying a piece of barramundi or a rump steak you think about changing the garnishes to suit the season and availability, so that you don't cook from a recipe, but are simply inspired by one. *Rockpool* was about my love of modern

Australian cooking; *Simply Asian* was about my love of Asian food; and this book is about the great pleasure to be gained from the cooking of the Mediterranean. If you look at all three together, it really does tell the story of what it has been like living in Sydney for the past forty-eight years. Together, they are a true reflection of how multiculturalism in Australia has had a profound effect on not just what I cook in my restaurant, but how I cook and eat in every part of my life.

THE THREE PARTS OF MY LIFE

I'm involved in three different areas of the food industry, each of them just as important as the other. First, I am a cook who loves cooking beautiful produce in my restaurant, surrounded by a group of young, energetic and enthusiastic people from both front and back of house. They keep me inspired and looking forward to cooking each day. The restaurant is where we have the chance to create food that draws on all the influences of my life, and which hopefully inspires customers and other food professionals. Second, I am a food communicator, in books, magazines and on television. In this role I try to encourage people to cook better, spend more time doing it, and hopefully derive pleasure from it. Finally, I am a food producer, with a line of fresh sauce products. I have recognized that people are, in the main, time-poor, particularly during the week, and they may have to throw together pre-prepared dishes to create a quick meal. I felt that it was important to make sure people had a fresh offering at their disposal, which would mean they could create a truly fresh food experience with real restaurant flavours for their family, without compromise. That is why I'm doing it and am very proud of my dedicated team and the way in which Woolworths has supported a little company like mine with a big vision.

QANTAS

Working with Qantas has been one of the most exciting projects I have ever been involved in. In 1997 I was asked by Geoff Dixon's office to be involved in the new Qantas first class. There was major investment in the new sleeper seat, and he wanted the soft product to match this impressive new hard product. For me, being Australian and having grown up with Qantas as the biggest and best Australian ambassador to the world, it was like being asked to pull on a Wallaby jersey; I was incredibly proud and honoured. We have worked together for the last seven years, making sure the food, service and total experience is the best that we can deliver. We work with thirty-three catering centres in Australia and around the world, over four thousand international crew and two thousand five hundred domestic crew. It is a great pleasure working with so many people to try to achieve a great aim. We put together seven hundred recipes a year for first and business class international, and work on product development in other areas as well. The menu development process is difficult but highly rewarding. We need to create food that can be produced by the caterers in different parts of the world, taking on board cultural needs and the strengths and weaknesses of the catering centres. All up, the disciplines learnt have made it easier for me to write this book.

HOW TO USE THIS BOOK

This book has over two hundred recipes. However, it is set out so that in reality there are considerably more recipes than that on offer. I have made each recipe a building block, which you have the freedom to use as you like. I have tried to create a book that is of a certain size and thickness, but which allows you to cook hundreds of different dishes from it. Call it a new space-saving idea, if you like, because it works as a 'how to cook' book, rather than a group of recipes.

Read the chapter introductions and recipes first. Get a thorough understanding of how you will cook the food you have in mind. It is vital to be organized when cooking, but more on that later. Equipment is another thing that is very important; you can, in fact, cook on just about anything successfully, if you try hard enough, but good-quality equipment will give you a head start. For instance, cutting is easier if you have good sharp knives. You need both an oven and a digital meat thermometer for cooking meat and poultry and for checking your oven temperature, as they vary quite a bit. You also need a set of accurate scales, particularly for dessert recipes. Other than that I hope that the recipes will give you great joy. There are, in my opinion, quite a number of dishes that you should be able to produce better than the average restaurant, not because they are difficult, but because they are simple and should be served the moment they are ready, something many restaurants fail to do because of staff or customer constraints. So enjoy, this should be home cooking at its simplest and best.

MISE EN PLACE

This phrase simply means to put in place, a fancy way of saying be organized. In a professional kitchen we always work off a list that is a comprehensive breakdown of all the components of each dish on the menu, what we call the house preparation. At the beginning of each day the kitchen team goes through all the jobs on the list; when they are finished, we are ready for service. If it is important for us to make a good list, then you should consider writing a little one, too, particularly when you are entertaining and cooking a few dishes. It helps with clarity and ensures you do everything you have to. Organization is the key to all good cooking; if you are ready to put everything together when it is needed, you will have great success. If you are in a flap, have forgotten elements of the dish, or are working in a haphazard manner, you will generally be in a mess. What's more, cooking won't be as much fun and you are not assured of a great result.

Before starting a recipe, make sure that you have the right equipment and it is all working properly, that you have all the ingredients, and lastly, that you know what you are supposed to do. The goal is to do as much as possible before the last minute put-together of a dish. If you haven't tried a recipe before, you must at the very least have an understanding of the theory, otherwise you are headed for tears, and we don't want that now, do we? So, before you begin a recipe, imagine how it will end up: know the result you are looking for. For instance, if you have to cook and rest meat, how will you rest it, how will you cook the vegetables, how will you carve and sauce the meat, and what state will the kitchen be in after you have finished? Be in control. That, in essence, is what mise en place means.

HYGIENE AND SAFETY

These are not just the domain of the professional kitchen. It is equally as important to make sure that you at home don't contaminate food and don't use food that could be contaminated. Firstly, it is essential to keep your kitchen, appliances and equipment clean. I have a saying with my guys in the kitchen at Rockpool — you have to learn to clean before you can learn to cook. It is really about taking pride in yourself and your surroundings. I can hear you say, 'wait a minute, I'm not a professional chef', but you will be more organized and will cook better

PRESENTATION OF THE DISHES

Presentation is important; you want to please the eye as well as the palate. I never add gratuitous garnishes just to make the food look good. Good-quality ingredients cooked well always look good. When it comes to the presentation of the meal you may wish to serve the main ingredient simply sauced and the vegetables in side dishes; I like to do that. I also like to serve the main ingredient on a large platter in the middle of the table by itself. You can also play around with the way in which you plate up a main course. For, say, a barbecued tuna steak, you can spoon a sauce (or a vegetable garnish that you want to serve as a sauce) on the plate, then top with the tuna, or you can serve the vegetable garnishes on the side of the plate or in side dishes. You can do the reverse and put the fish on the plate and the sauce over the top. You can place the fish on the side of the plate and add two vegetable garnishes, which would have it looking a bit like twelve o'clock, four o'clock and eight o'clock on the plate. You can place them side by side on the plate from three o'clock, six o'clock and nine o'clock, and so on. So, have fun, but remember that good-quality ingredients will look and taste good if cooked well. One very important point: wipe the plates with tissues before they go to the table. You must serve clean plates, as the food will look much better.

ON SEASONING

The role of seasoning is a simple one: to bring out the best flavour in the ingredients you are using. It is probably the most important thing you can do. It is also the one thing that is done badly by the vast majority of home cooks. Well-seasoned food tastes great and the flavour of most food is dramatically different when it is done well. By seasoning, I mostly mean salting. I always use sea salt, as it has a finer, cleaner taste than other salts. I rarely pepper before and during cooking, as I believe the aromatic quality and fresh bite in pepper is destroyed by cooking. I also believe that when pepper is seared or roasted at high heat on food it becomes slightly bitter. So, pepper for me is always lashings on the food as I plate up or, indeed, when I have plated up.

When seasoning, think about this: salting heightens the natural flavours of food. If I salt a dish at the beginning of cooking, the food ends up tasting of its natural self rather than if I add it at the end, when it tastes

like salt and the food. I do add salt at the end as well, when I want the fresh taste of salt, as well as its wonderful texture. So it is important to season properly to get the most flavour out of your food. Always season meat, poultry and fish before cooking. When using aromatic vegetables for a stew, soup or sauce, salt when you put them in the saucepan as it will help bring out the flavours. The other very important thing to do is taste — taste all your food before serving and correct the seasoning.

When I use pepper I generally use white peppercorns, freshly ground. Peppercorns are the fruits of a tropical, perennial climber and there are over a thousand different species. Black is the most popular and strongest flavoured pepper used, with a warm aroma, slightly sweet flavour and lingering heat. It is picked when the berry is not quite ripe and then dried until it shrivels and the skin turns dark brown to black. Generally, however, I prefer white pepper. It is creamy white in colour, the surface is smoother than that of black peppercorns due to the outer skin being removed and it is more intense but with a finer flavour. Also, it doesn't add colour to most cooked foods. It is very important not to use pre-ground pepper as it loses its qualities quickly.

A last point — with all spices, buy only a small amount at a time and use it quickly. Spices taste the strongest when they are fresh. Also, buy from a spice merchant; you won't believe the difference in quality, and nine times out of ten it is only because the spices are fresher.

Other flavourings or seasonings can be added to food to create more flavour. Unlike salt, which is there to enhance the natural flavour of the food, flavourings add a depth of flavour that, in the main, becomes part of the flavour. Garlic, ginger, onion, wine, spirits, herbs and spices are all at our disposal to add flavour. It is very important to make sure you add lemon and lime juice at the end, and definitely off the heat, as all the wonderful fresh flavour they bring to food is lost when heated.

I nearly always cook with extra virgin olive oil when cooking food from the Mediterranean. You can call me wasteful if you like, but I believe that the food tastes better than if using just olive oil. People will tell you the quality and nuances that make the oil great are lost with heat, but I will tell you that you end up with a better tasting dish. Try it and see.

Parmesan cheese is an important seasoning in this book, so spend your money well and you will be rewarded. I use Parmigiano Reggiano, but you can use Grana Padano as well. The essential thing is to have a hunk at home; never use pre-grated cheese or other cheap Parmesan-style cheeses. Keep the cheese in a large plastic container with a tight-fitting lid and place a damp cloth underneath the cheese to maintain the correct humidity. The perfect container is a cake container with a lift-out tray — the damp cloth can go under the tray and the Parmesan on top. All cheese should be kept in this way.

HERBS USED IN THIS BOOK

Always give herbs a good wash and dry them well before using.

• basil — this very popular and versatile herb originated in India. It has an aromatic flavour reminiscent of mint and cloves. There are more than forty varieties, including sweet Thai basil, purple basil and bush basil, and its uses range from pesto, pastas and salads to curries. Basil leaves will bruise and darken when cut with a knife. Tearing them is the preferred option, though the flavour is not affected by the bruising.

• bay leaf — this herb is available in both fresh and dried form, though fresh is best. Bay is known for its strong aroma, often described as being like tea with a slight menthol fragrance. It is used in casseroles, stews and stocks, and is also an important part of a bouquet garni.

• bouquet garni — the traditional bouquet garni was a group of herbs consisting of 3 flat-leaf (Italian) parsley stalks, 1 thyme sprig and 1 bay leaf, often wrapped in the outside skin of a leek or some cheesecloth, and tied with a piece of string. The herbs are used to flavour simmering foods for the duration of cooking, and are removed before serving. Any herbs or spices (fresh or dried) can be used, depending on the recipe.

• chervil — this native herb of Eastern Europe and Western Asia was introduced to France and England by the Romans more than two thousand years ago. It is used with poultry, seafood and vegetables; in vinegars and soups; and in bouquet garni and fines herbes. Even though it is a member of the parsley family, it is much more aromatic. Its flavour is similar to aniseed, with a hint of sweetness. I love it picked through salads and it makes a great butter to put on barbecued foods.

• **chives** — this member of the onion family has a delicate, peppery, onion flavour. It is used in cheese and cream sauces, dips, potatoes, and as a garnish. Chives are part of the blend fines herbes.

• **coriander** — also known as cilantro, this very aromatic herb belongs to the parsley family. It has a clean, uplifting flavour with a slight aniseed touch. Its flavour has also been described as minty, sweet and citrus-like. Coriander has many medicinal virtues, being both a stimulant and a digestive.

• **dill** — an annual of the parsley family, dill is related to anise, caraway, coriander, cumin and fennel. It is used with fish and shellfish, in Middle Eastern cooking, and as a seasoning for meats and vegetables.

• **fines herbes** — this mixture of very finely chopped herbs traditionally contained chervil, chives, parsley and tarragon but other herbs can be used as part of the blend. The blend should be added to the dish just before serving, otherwise its delicate flavour will be lost.

• **mint** — these green leaves have a pleasant warm, fresh, aromatic, sweet flavour with a cool aftertaste. Mint is used in teas, beverages, jellies, syrups, ice creams, confections and, of course, lamb dishes.

• **oregano** — this herb is generally described as possessing a strongly aromatic, camphoraceous aroma and a slightly bitter, pungent flavour. This pungent flavour is composed of earthy/musty, green, hay and minty notes. The herb imparts a slightly astringent taste and is most often used dried. However, it is wonderful fresh, and doesn't seem to be at all overpowering, as it can be when dried.

• **parsley** — the flavour and aroma of parsley is generally described as being green and vegetative in character. One of the most popular herbs, flat-leaf (Italian) parsley is the variety used exclusively in this book. It is mild and adds a fresh flavour to almost any savoury dish. The stalks contain a lot of the flavour, so don't discard them, but chop and include them in recipes too. Parsley is used in soups, stews and sauces. It is particularly good with fish, and is also used in stuffing, in many garnishes and as a finishing touch to dishes.

• **rosemary** —this hardy plant grows to about 60–90 cm (2–3 feet) tall under harsh mountainous conditions. Rosemary is found in herbes de Provence, bouquet garni and many seasoning blends for lamb. It is used extensively in Mediterranean cuisines. It has a distinctive pine-woody aroma with camphoraceous undertones and a fresh, bittersweet flavour.

• **tarragon** — the slender dark-green leaves of this herb have a pleasant anise-like flavour and aroma. It is characteristically minty, earthy and green. Tarragon blends well with other spices. It is used in sauces, especially Béarnaise sauce, and in tarragon vinegar. In French cuisine it is an integral part of fines herbes.

• **thyme** — this is a small-leaved perennial of the mint family. The plant produces small flowers that are very attractive to honey bees. Thyme is used in stuffing, meats, stews, fish and game, and plays an important part in bouquet garni, herbes de Provence and the Middle Eastern spice blend za'atar, along with jerk and curry blends. Warming and pungent, thyme is characterized by a minty-green, hay-like taste.

SPICES USED IN THIS BOOK

• **cinnamon** — this light brown bark from tropical evergreen trees is related to the avocado and bay laurel trees. Cinnamon can be ground into a powder to be used in spice mixes or desserts, or may be left whole to infuse into liquids or stews, to be removed after cooking. The fragrance is sweet and woody.

• **cloves** — these are the most fragrant of all the spices. They have a powerful flavour and should be used sparingly. Cloves also work as an antiseptic and preservative. They produce a strong numbing feeling.

• **coriander seeds** — these seeds are an important ingredient in spice rubs and marinades for barbecuing. They have a clean flavour that is enhanced by roasting. The small ribbed brown seeds have a sweetly aromatic flavour that is slightly lemony.

• **cumin seeds** — similar in appearance to caraway seeds, cumin seeds have a strong earthy flavour that is enhanced by roasting. Like coriander, cumin seeds are great in rubs and marinades.

• **fennel seeds** — green to yellow-brown in colour, fennel seeds have an intense liquorice flavour that mellows with dry-roasting. Often used as a filler spice, I believe that when used with coriander and cumin the seeds increase the flavour of a blend substantially.

• **nutmeg** — this is the seed of the fruit of a tropical evergreen tree, originally native to Indonesia. Predominantly sweet and aromatic, it is a wonderful addition to gnocchi. Grate nutmeg only as needed, as the fragrance deteriorates after grating.

• **paprika** — there are a number of different types of paprika available. All are from the same family, which is closely related to chilli. Paprika varies in colour and heat, from sweet to hot. Smoky paprika, which is traditionally processed in a smokehouse heated by slow burning oak wood, then ground, lends extra depth of flavour to food.

• **ras el hanout** — roughly translated, this means 'top of the shelf'. A Moroccan spice mix, its contents can vary widely but it usually contains over twenty different spices, resulting in a well-rounded blend that is not at all harsh. However, its effect on dishes is potent. Try this spice blend in marinades, rubs and as a component in chermoula pastes.

• **saffron** — this is the most expensive spice in the world. Each saffron flower produces three stigmas, which are hand-picked and dried. It takes roughly twenty thousand stigmas to make 125 g (4$1/2$ oz) saffron. It must be infused in water before being used in a dish — if it comes into contact with oil first, its flavour will never really be released.

• **vanilla** — a long, thin, black pod containing thousands of tiny seeds, vanilla comes from the fruit of an orchid native to tropical America. The expense of real vanilla beans is due to the labour-intensive and time-consuming process needed to obtain them. To use vanilla beans, slit them lengthways down the centre and scrape out the seeds. These seeds can be added directly to foods such as ice cream, pastry and sauces. Whole beans that have been used to flavour sauces or other mixtures may be rinsed, dried and stored for reuse. Vanilla extract is made by grinding chopped beans in an alcohol–water solution in order to extract the flavour; the mixture is then aged for several months.

TOOLS AND EQUIPMENT

• **knives** — you can go mad with knives. I have about twenty and each has a specific use, but really, the basics can be covered by three knives – a 26 cm (10½ inch) chef's knife, a boning knife and a paring knife. If you intend to have a few others, a fish filleting knife would be good if, indeed, you intend to fillet fish; also a long, sharp knife for slicing raw fish; and an oyster knife, if you want to knock the lids off some fresh oysters. I recommend Japanese mandolins for slicing vegetables very thinly, but take care as they are very sharp and it is easy to cut yourself.

It is important to keep your knives sharp. To do so you really need two implements — a stone and steel. Don't freak out, as sharpening a knife is easy and very therapeutic. I love that time in the evening at Rockpool, when everyone is ready and we are waiting for the first customers to come in: the chefs in the kitchen will be sharpening their knives on stones, ready for the precision cutting that will take place that night.

Make sure you feel comfortable with the knife in your hand. Your thumb can move down towards the blade, or your index finger can slide down to the top of the knife and rest there. Do not grip the knife too hard and remember that you don't need to use brute strength; let the knife glide through and do the work for you. It should feel comfortable. Also, you have two hands; using them properly will stop you from ever cutting yourself. The following is a very important basic cutting technique that you must learn. With the guiding hand, make a bridge and tuck your thumb behind (very important for keeping thumb intact for the length of your life). Use your thumb and little fingers like claws to hold what you're cutting and make the bridge of your hand come forward. The knife blade is always sliding against your knuckles; this will make sure your fingertips and thumb are safe at all times. That's it — you can now slice, dice and cut safely.

• **sharpening stones** — there are a couple of different stones available, some use oil, others water and detergent. I prefer the ones that soak in water and are then ready for use. The three most important things to remember are: always hold the knife at the same angle on both sides; make the movement in one direction; and make the same number of strokes on each side. Press the knife firmly at the tip, just on the stone

and at an angle of 20 degrees to the stone, then slide the knife up the length of the stone in one movement. Repeat this about ten times, then turn the knife over, hold at the same angle and repeat the process. Wash the knife and give it a quiet slide down a steel. It's that easy.

• the steel — this tool is used to help maintain the edge on your knife after sharpening it on the stone. You only need the stone every now and again, depending how often you use your knife, but give the knife a little go on the steel before each use. To use, hold the steel away from your body and put the heel of the knife at the tip of the steel, at a 20-degree angle to the steel. In one fluid motion, take the knife down the steel to the tip of the knife, then repeat the action on the other side of the knife. Make sure the strokes are light and even and make no more than five strokes on each side.

• chopping boards — now that you have a good sharp knife, it is important to have a good chopping board. I like wooden ones with some weight and size so that I can cut and chop all manner of things easily. Mine at home is 40 × 60 cm (16 × 24 inches) and I just love it!

• pots and pans — you need a large saucepan to make stock and soup and boil water for pasta. A pan with an 8 litre (280 fl oz) capacity and a diameter of 28 cm (11 inches) is good. It can also serve as a deep-fat fryer and as a steaming pan for a bamboo steamer. I have two non-stick pans, the smaller one about 22 cm (8 1/2 inches) wide, for cooking single omelettes and pan-frying for two, and the larger one about 28 cm (11 inches), for making large omelettes and cooking four pieces of fish or a couple of crumbed veal chops. I also have a bunch of saucepans that are either straight-sided or sloped, which I use for pan-frying, sautéing and making pasta sauce — smaller ones 22 cm (8 1/2 inches) and larger ones 26 cm (10 1/2 inches) wide. I use high-sided pans for heating things, making small stews and boiling vegetables — larger ones 22 cm (8 1/2 inches) wide, with a 4 litre (140 fl oz) capacity, and the smaller ones about 8 cm (3 1/4 inches) wide. It is also good to have a couple of heavy cast-iron frying pans for pan-frying steaks and chicken — they should be around the same size as the non-stick pans. Finally, I have some large, heavy roasting tins. If you have all this, you will be able to tackle every recipe in this book.

• **thermometers** — you will be able to cook with aplomb with the help of two very valuable, inexpensive pieces of equipment. One is an oven thermometer. You definitely need this to make sure your oven is at the right temperature. Most domestic, and for that matter, even commercial ovens, vary quite dramatically, and with an oven thermometer you can be sure that you have the correct temperature. The second piece of equipment is a digital meat thermometer that will instantly read the core temperature of what you are cooking. Using one of these takes all the risk out of cooking large pieces of meat and will really put you in the driver's seat. It is also a good idea to get a candy thermometer if you decide to deep-fry at home in a pot, as again, this takes all the guesswork out of it. (A good reliable pair of scales is also a worthwhile investment as, particularly with pastry, you need to be very accurate.) On temperature, it is worth reading the meat and poultry and seafood sections well and then trying low-temperature cooking. It does affect the texture greatly, and texture and flavour work hand in hand.

OTHER EQUIPMENT

I love my mortar and pestle. In fact, I have two — one large at 26 cm (10^1/$_2$ inches) and another 22 cm (8^1/$_2$ inches) in diameter. They are granite and are available cheaply from Chinatown. I use them to make pesto and salsas, pound marinades and grind spices, but they are great for lots of uses, easy to clean and look beautiful. I also have a food mill and a potato ricer. They are suitable for many uses, too, and are worth the outlay. I also think a rice cooker is a must. Then, you need stainless steel bowls for mixing, a salad spinner, spoons (solid and slotted), tongs, fish lifters, wooden spoons, rolling pins and things of that nature, a large colander for draining pasta, and a sauce and drum sieve for improving the texture of puréed things. You need a grater for grating cheese on pasta and other dishes and a citrus zester. Have a couple of bamboo steamers that fit the pans you have and make sure you clean them well, as you don't want to introduce flavours to dishes where they are not welcome. Then there is a long list of moulds, cake tins and things you need if you embark on the dessert section.

A food processor, stick blender, blender, spice grinder and electric mixer are great pieces of equipment to collect along the way — or you could just get married and get them all in one go.

LIGHT BREAKFAST

I usually like to start the day with something light. It's not that I don't love bacon and eggs, it's just that I think a glass of freshly squeezed juice and a little muesli is the perfect way to start the day. Or, if one is feeling like it, some roast tomatoes or mushrooms on toast. Yum. But, there is a whole chapter on eggs later on, so when you want to go the whole hog, by all means do.

My wife Sam and I usually start the day with a fresh juice. It makes you feel healthy on the inside, for the very simple reason that it is so good for you. And, yes, you do have to clean the juicer afterwards, but once you get in the habit you will never look back. We vary the fruit and vegetables to reflect the season and that always keeps us looking for the next combination. Here are a few of our favourite blends — all you need to do is start juicing and you will soon discover your own.

- carrot, beetroot, apple, orange and ginger
- pineapple and mint
- grapefruit and orange
- apple, pear, lemon and strawberries
- watermelon and ginger
- watermelon, apple and ginger
- peach, mango, pineapple, passionfruit and orange
- pear, apple and pineapple

OPPOSITE PAGE passionfruit and banana energizer drink and berry energizer drink

ENERGIZER DRINKS

When I first started working with Qantas, I wanted to come up with a breakfast drink that would refresh and invigorate the body after a sleep in an environment of low humidity. These energizers have worked well.

MANGO ENERGIZER DRINK
INGREDIENTS
2 mangoes, chopped

185 ml (6 fl oz/$3/4$ cup) freshly squeezed orange juice

125 ml (4 fl oz/$1/2$ cup) unsweetened pineapple juice

250 ml (9 fl oz/1 cup) low-fat milk

60 g ($2^1/4$ oz/$1/4$ cup) plain yoghurt

1 teaspoon honey

1 teaspoon wheat germ

juice of $1/2$ lime

BERRY ENERGIZER DRINK
INGREDIENTS
225 g (8 oz/$1^1/2$ cups) very ripe strawberries, stems trimmed

60 g ($2^1/4$ oz/$1/2$ cup) raspberries

1 very ripe banana, chopped

125 ml (4 fl oz/$1/2$ cup) unsweetened pineapple juice

375 ml (13 fl oz/$1^1/2$ cups) low-fat milk

125 g ($4^1/2$ oz/$1/2$ cup) plain yoghurt

2 tablespoons honey

PASSIONFRUIT AND BANANA ENERGIZER DRINK
INGREDIENTS
2 bananas, chopped

125 g ($4^1/2$ oz/$1/2$ cup) fresh passionfruit pulp, sieved

500 ml (17 fl oz/2 cups) freshly squeezed orange juice

125 g ($4^1/2$ oz/$1/2$ cup) plain yoghurt

1 teaspoon orange zest, without any pith

METHOD
Put all the ingredients in a blender. Blend until well combined and smooth. If making the berry energizer drink, strain the mixture through a medium sieve to remove the seeds. Pour into chilled glasses and serve immediately. Serves 4

SUPER BIRCHER MUESLI

This muesli is a lot softer and wetter than the original Dr Bircher's muesli. It has a silky texture and more complex taste. The wonderful thing about it is that you can whip it up the night before it is needed. So, if you have guests arriving for a special breakfast, just prepare a fresh juice and serve this for a really nice start to the day. Ross Lusted, one of the great chefs I have had the pleasure of working with over the years at Rockpool, pulled this recipe out of his repertoire. I think it came from his past hotel experience — I can imagine Ross up at the crack of dawn putting this beauty on the buffet.

INGREDIENTS

2 sour green apples, such as Granny Smith

125 ml (4 fl oz/$1/2$ cup) freshly squeezed orange juice

500 g (1 lb 2 oz/2 cups) plain yoghurt

200 g (7 oz/2 cups) rolled oats

125 ml (4 fl oz/$1/2$ cup) pure (whipping) cream, whipped to soft peaks

115 g (4 oz/$1/2$ cup) caster (superfine) sugar

4 passionfruit, pulp sieved

2 tablespoons sultanas

2 tablespoons desiccated coconut, roasted until lightly golden (page 30)

8 dried apricots, diced

1 mango, diced

fresh berries, to serve

METHOD

The night before, grate the apples, with their skin on, into a bowl. Immediately combine with the orange juice and yoghurt to prevent discoloration. Fold in the oats and cream, then add the remaining ingredients and mix well. Cover and refrigerate overnight.

Spoon the muesli into four bowls and top with fresh berries or other seasonal fruit. Serves 4

THE ORIGINAL DR BIRCHER MUESLI

A good friend, Greg Fraser, passed this recipe on to me many years ago, and now Sam and I have it almost every day. It is very simple and good for lowering cholesterol levels. You can have any fruit you like with it; we tend to have fresh berries in summer, and either poached quinces or pears during the rest of the year. A really good yoghurt, such as a sheep's milk yoghurt, will make the muesli taste even better, though taste as you go and adjust the lemon juice a little to balance the yoghurt's sharpness.

HOW TO ROAST NUTS — Hazelnuts can be roasted by simply cooking in a preheated 180°C (350°F/Gas 4) oven until golden brown. To remove their skins, allow the nuts to cool, then put them in a clean tea towel, fold it in half and rub the nuts inside the towel on the bench. Tip the nuts into a strainer and allow the skins to fall to the bottom. To roast nuts such as almonds and walnuts, you must first blanch them in boiling water for 2–3 minutes to loosen their skins. Strain, then peel away the skin. Put the nuts on a tray and roast in the centre of a preheated 150°C (300°F/Gas 2) oven. Shake the tray often to ensure an even roast. The nuts will continue to cook on removing from the oven so take them out when they are a light brown colour. Desiccated or shredded coconut may be roasted in the same way.

INGREDIENTS

200 g (7 oz/2 cups) rolled oats
juice of 2 lemons
2 sour green apples, such as Granny Smith
500 g (1 lb 2 oz/2 cups) plain yoghurt
150 g (5^{1}/2 oz/scant ^{1}/2 cup) honey
poached fruit, such as poached pears (page 432), or fresh fruit, to serve
40 g (1^{1}/2 oz/^{1}/3 cup) roasted hazelnuts, skinned and crushed, to serve

METHOD

The night before, mix the oats, lemon juice and 125 ml (4 fl oz/^{1}/2 cup) water together in a bowl. Cover and soak overnight.

In the morning, grate the apples, with their skin on, and add to the bowl of soaked oats. Add the yoghurt and honey and mix together well. Divide the muesli among four bowls, top with your fruit selection and sprinkle with the hazelnuts. Serves 4

FRUIT SALAD WITH SOUP

This is a perfect soup for any fruit salad. It adds an extra dimension to the salad, and helps to protect it from drying out and oxidizing, which means you can make it a little in advance. Use any combination of seasonal fruit you like and cut the fruit precisely. You need good knife skills for this recipe.

INGREDIENTS

1 lemon grass stem

1 pineapple, peeled, cored and juiced

250 ml (9 fl oz/1 cup) freshly squeezed orange juice

60 ml (2 fl oz/$1/4$ cup) freshly squeezed lime juice

2 tablespoons caster (superfine) sugar

1 cm ($1/2$ inch) piece fresh ginger, peeled and sliced

1 vanilla bean, split lengthways and seeds scraped out

1 star anise

4 mint leaves

fresh seasonal fruit, to serve

METHOD

Trim 5 mm ($1/4$ inch) from the end of the lemon grass and remove the coarse outer leaves. Using the side of a large chef's knife, carefully push on the lemon grass to bruise it and release the flavours. Combine all the ingredients in a saucepan and simmer, covered, for about 15 minutes. Cool the soup in the refrigerator, then pass it through a sieve and discard the lemon grass, ginger, vanilla bean and star anise.

To serve, choose an array of the freshest seasonal fruit available. In summer try mango, sugar banana, pineapple and strawberries. Cut the fruit into even dice and add them to the soup. Leave to macerate for 30 minutes before serving. Add a dollop of yoghurt to make it a more substantial breakfast dish, or serve with a really good ice cream for a truly sophisticated dessert. Serves 4

ROAST TOMATOES ON TOAST

Tomatoes are one of the truly great ingredients to use as a chef. The balance between sweet and acidic is superb. Although they are really a fruit, most cooks use them like a vegetable. Tomatoes are one of a number of marvellous gifts introduced to European cooking from the Americas. I could never imagine Italian cooking without them, but they didn't arrive there until the sixteenth century and did not really become a table item until the seventeenth century. Back then, many thought them poison, and believed that consuming them could cause madness. But imagine pasta without tomato sauce, or pizza without tomato.

A very important thing to remember with tomatoes is that these fruit are in season from mid to late summer. As a matter of fact, there is nothing to compare with the taste of a sun-kissed tomato straight from the vine. In summer, many varieties will be in peak form: I love ox hearts and Roma (plum) tomatoes, and you will notice how sweet some of the cherry tomatoes become at this time. During winter, use vine-ripened tomatoes if you must; they will be from a hydroponic hot house, but at least they will be ripe and have some flavour. Roasting helps intensify the flavour of tomatoes and will render a fairly ordinary tomato palatable, but it will only ever be a limp imitation of a ripe summer one.

INGREDIENTS
8 vine-ripened tomatoes
2 tablespoons extra virgin olive oil
sea salt
freshly ground pepper
4 slices sourdough bread or 4 long slices of baguette, cut on the diagonal

EGGS

If you have an egg in the house you have a meal. No truer phrase has been spoken; however, I think I would have to add 'wonderful and delicious' to that statement. In years gone by in Australia, the egg was mainly confined to the breakfast table. As we now know, it is delicious at all times of the day, whether as the main player in a dish or as a sidekick in a great salad.

An egg mainly consists of yolk and white, and, of course, a shell. Though both the white and yolk are protein, they set at slightly different temperatures, the white at about 60°C (140°F) and the yolk at 65–70°C (149–158°F). This allows us to set the white and still maintain a runny yolk, which is an integral part of many good salads, not to mention boiled eggs and toast soldiers. The white is made up of two parts, a thick white substance that surrounds the yolk and the thinner, more liquid part on the outside, closest to the shell. It is this part that flies away and becomes wispy when you are poaching an egg, and the bad news is that the older the egg, the larger that part becomes. In general, you should cook eggs gently because of the low setting point of protein, otherwise they will easily become rubbery, especially the whites when shallow-frying.

When cooking with eggs it is obvious, but I will say it: a really fresh egg is best, and a free-range or organic egg will lift the result and be worth the extra cost. The easiest way to tell whether an egg is fresh or not, if you're concerned, is to submerge it in cold water. It should sink to the bottom and stay there. The egg will start to rise from the broad round end, and the older it is, the more steeply it will rise. As I said before, an egg is mainly white and yolk, but it also has a little air in it when fresh. Because the shell is porous, over time the inside loses moisture and air replaces it. That is why the egg floats when no longer fresh.

HOW TO COOK THE PERFECT SOFT-BOILED EGG

There are many methods for boiled eggs. Some start with the egg being put in boiling water and then simmered for enough time to render it anywhere from soft to hard. Others start with the egg being placed in cold water, brought to the boil, and simmered for a shorter time to reach the same final result. I prefer to simmer for a short time and rest the egg in the hot water for a period of time. I believe this results in a softer-textured white. But it's your choice as to which method works best for you — they will all give a similar result.

When boiling eggs it is important to use the freshest eggs available. Eggs should be stored in the refrigerator, as they last much longer than in the pantry. However, allow them to come to room temperature before cooking to prevent them cracking from the sudden temperature change.

INGREDIENTS
    fresh eggs
    sea salt

METHOD
    Bring a saucepan of water to the boil. Add a pinch of sea salt. The saucepan needs to be big enough that the eggs won't bump each other and crack, and should hold enough water to cover the eggs when you add them without any danger of it overflowing. Don't have the water boiling too fiercely, as this will cause the eggs to jump about and also add to the likelihood of cracking. When placing the eggs in the water, use a large slotted spoon to lower them gently one at a time, or if you have a wire basket you can lower them together. Cook the eggs for 1 minute on a gentle simmer, then remove the pan from the heat, cover and allow to sit for 4 minutes. This allows the eggs to cook while retaining the whites' creamy texture. Remove the eggs from the water immediately and serve with toast.

    To make hard-boiled eggs, simmer the eggs gently for 2 minutes, then remove the pan from the heat, cover and allow to sit for 10 minutes. If using the eggs for salads, refresh immediately in iced water once fully cooked, then peel.

BOILED EGG WITH VEGETABLE SALAD

This is a combination of a few different little vegetable salads that makes a nice starter. At home I like to serve them on one large platter, set in the middle of the table, though individual plates are good too. Any combination of salads can be used, but by all means, just eat the egg with one and it will still taste great. Make the celeriac remoulade once and you'll make it many times throughout the celeriac season. It is great with fish straight off the barbecue, especially tuna.

INGREDIENTS

6 soft-boiled eggs
Parmesan
extra virgin olive oil
freshly ground pepper

FOR THE TOMATO SALAD
4 small vine-ripened tomatoes, quartered
1 red onion, sliced
2 tablespoons extra virgin olive oil
a few drops of balsamic vinegar
sea salt and freshly ground pepper

FOR THE CARROT SALAD
40 g (1^{1}/2 oz/^{1}/3 cup) raisins
250 ml (9 fl oz/1 cup) cold Earl Grey tea
2 small carrots, peeled and grated
4 tablespoons chopped flat-leaf (Italian) parsley
80 ml (2^{1}/2 fl oz/^{1}/3 cup) extra virgin olive oil
1^{1}/2 tablespoons red wine vinegar
sea salt and freshly ground pepper

FOR THE CELERIAC REMOULADE
^{1}/2 small head of celeriac
60 ml (2 fl oz/^{1}/4 cup) mayonnaise (page 351)
2 teaspoons Dijon mustard
1 tablespoon finely shredded flat-leaf (Italian) parsley
sea salt and freshly ground pepper

BASE
1 radicchio, leaves pulled apart, washed and torn

METHOD

To make the tomato salad, put the tomato and onion in a bowl and mix with the extra virgin olive oil, balsamic vinegar and seasoning. To make the carrot salad, soak the raisins for 20 minutes in the cold Earl Grey tea, then drain. Put the carrot, raisins and parsley in a bowl. Add the extra virgin olive oil, red wine vinegar and seasoning and mix together. To make the celeriac remoulade, peel the celeriac, cut into very fine strips and immediately blanch in boiling water to avoid discoloration. Combine the blanched celeriac with the mayonnaise, mustard, parsley and seasoning in a bowl.

Arrange the radicchio leaves on four plates. On each plate, place some of the tomato salad on one-third of the radicchio, the carrot on the second third, and the celeriac on the remaining third. Peel the eggs and cut in half. Carefully put the halves on top of the salads. Finish with freshly shaved Parmesan, a little splash of extra virgin olive oil and some freshly ground pepper. Serves 4

VARIATIONS

• For a simple salad Niçoise, combine braised or canned tuna, some green beans, potatoes, olives, tomatoes, anchovies and boiled eggs, and dress with lemon juice, extra virgin olive oil and seasoning.

• Chop up some cooked king prawns (shrimp). Add chopped hard-boiled eggs and sliced iceberg lettuce and mix with a little mayonnaise. This makes a great salad or terrific sandwich filling.

• A boiled egg also makes a welcome addition to potato salad.

• Try making your eggs really soft-boiled, then just knocking the top off and scooping out the runny egg onto toast with a good soft blue cheese — a fantastic lunch snack.

FOLLOWING PAGES boiled egg with vegetable salad, left, and poached eggs with yoghurt and burnt sage butter, right

HOW TO POACH AN EGG

Poaching an egg is, in principle, like boiling an egg, but without the shell. There are various things to keep in mind: you are trying to cook the white; keep a nice texture; and just set the yolk. You are also trying to keep the egg in a nice compact shape, reminiscent of its egg shape, and not break the yolk. Easier said than done.

There are a number of rules that I use to help, however, as with all egg cooking, there are many different approaches. As I said before, if your method works for you, keep doing it.

1   Use the freshest of eggs. If the eggs are fresh they will coagulate well and not run through the water, and you also won't need to add vinegar and salt to the water. So, when poaching, more than any other type of cooking with eggs, fresh is best. Sorry for saying fresh so often, but it needs to be done.

2   Don't have your saucepan filled too deeply with water. No deeper than about 4 cm (1 1/2 inches).

3   Don't have the water boiling too fiercely or your eggs will blow apart. Just barely simmering is perfect.

4   Don't try to cook too many eggs at one time. As you become more proficient, you can be a little bolder and fill the pan.

5   Gently spoon water from the pan over the eggs as they cook. This helps to cook the tops so you don't have to turn them over.

6   Carefully remove the eggs with a slotted spoon when set to your liking. Dry on paper towels.

VARIATIONS

• A poached egg on any salad adds an extra dimension: just blanch green beans, add some roasted slivered almonds and top with an egg. Dress with extra virgin olive oil, lemon juice and seasoning.

• In autumn make a salad from cooked globe artichokes, roasted fennel and celeriac, blanched peas and broad (fava) beans and some lightly fried and warm lardons. Top with a poached egg and sprinkle with croutons, then dress with walnut oil, fresh lime juice and seasoning.

• One poached egg dish that I love is another bistro classic. In Burgundy, meurette sauce is served with eggs on toasted brioche. It is essentially a red wine butter sauce and is quite easy to prepare at home.

The sauce is made by sweating a finely chopped mixture of 1 onion, 1 carrot, 80 g (2^3/4 oz) ham, 1 celery stalk and 2 garlic cloves in 50 g (1^3/4 oz) butter and 60 ml (2 fl oz/^{1}/4 cup) olive oil (it is good at this stage to add a little sea salt). Slowly cook for 20 minutes, then pour a good-quality bottle of red wine on top. Add a bouquet garni and reduce until there is 250 ml (9 fl oz/ 1 cup) left (this will take about 30 minutes). Remove the bouquet garni. Whisk in 125 g (4^1/2 oz) softened unsalted butter, making sure you don't boil the sauce or it will split.

Place your poached egg on a square of toasted brioche or good-quality crusty bread. Pour the sauce over, season with sea salt and freshly ground pepper and serve. Yum! Some lardons, baby onions and button mushrooms sweated in butter until soft are a welcome addition to this dish. This amount of sauce is perfect for four starters. Also, try this sauce on a piece of barbecued fish or minute steak.

FOLLOWING PAGE poached eggs with pancetta and frisée   47

HOW TO FRY AN EGG

There are two ways to fry an egg, either shallow- or deep-fry. I use deep-frying when cooking Asian-style dishes, mostly. To my mind, that is when crispy egg whites really work, with a spicy sauce and some steamed rice. Shallow-fried eggs are usually a breakfast preparation and with greasy bacon and toast are a classic hangover cure, or so they say. So, here I shall discuss shallow-fried eggs.

The best way to shallow-fry an egg is to use a small non-stick frying pan. Add a little butter, olive oil or bacon fat, depending on your preference. Heat the fat until just bubbling. Add the egg, either by cracking it into the pan or the more cautious approach of breaking it first into a cup and then sliding it into the pan. Once in the pan your objective is to cook the white through but leave the yolk warm and runny. This can be done in three ways. You can spoon hot butter over the egg, helping to set the top of the white and warm the yolk; you can turn the egg over easy; or you can cook the egg for a minute in the pan and then place the pan under the grill (broiler) for 30 seconds, just long enough to set the top of the yolk.

VARIATIONS

• Fried eggs slot in really well with any of the salads discussed in this chapter.

• My father used to feed me fried eggs when I was little, and I still have them the same way. He would place some crisp bacon on a piece of toast, spread strawberry jam over the bacon, then place the egg on top with a big grind of pepper. This dish is so good — don't knock it till you've tried it. I bet you'll love that wonderful salty, sweet and creamy combination as much as I do.

• Don't underestimate a fried truffled egg on toast either, and if you happen to find yourself with a fresh truffle or two, try a fried truffled egg with some pasta. To make, store the eggs and a truffle in a jar for one day (use 4 eggs per truffle). As the eggshell is porous, the fats in the eggs will absorb the smell of the truffles and you will have wonderfully aromatic fried eggs.

FRIED EGG WITH RATATOUILLE

This is another full-flavoured dish that is very rustic but simple to prepare. I love to put a big dollop of aïoli on top of the egg, but that is very indulgent. This also works very nicely as a picnic dish with boiled eggs.

INGREDIENTS

4 eggs
toasted bread, to serve

FOR THE RATATOUILLE
400 ml (14 fl oz) extra virgin olive oil
1 small eggplant (aubergine), cut into 1 cm (^{1}/2 inch) dice
1 mixed large handful flat-leaf (Italian) parsley and basil
^{1}/2 brown onion, cut into 1 cm (^{1}/2 inch) dice
2 garlic cloves, chopped
sea salt
1 red capsicum (pepper), seeds removed and cut into 1 cm (^{1}/2 inch) dice
1 green capsicum (pepper), seeds removed and cut into 1 cm (^{1}/2 inch) dice
2 zucchini (courgettes), cut into 1 cm (^{1}/2 inch) thick rounds
4 vine-ripened tomatoes, peeled, deseeded and cut into 1 cm (^{1}/2 inch) dice
  (page 66)
freshly ground pepper

METHOD

To make the ratatouille, heat half the extra virgin olive oil in a large saucepan until hot (it will be starting to shimmer). Add the eggplant and fry until golden brown. Remove with a slotted spoon and drain on paper towels. Add the herbs, taking care to avoid the oil splashing, and fry until crisp. Remove and drain on paper towels. Let the oil cool slightly, then add the onion, garlic and sea salt and sauté for about 5 minutes. Add the remaining oil, then add the red and green capsicum and zucchini and stew for a further 10 minutes. Add the tomato and cook for 5 minutes, then return the fried eggplant and herbs to the pan and cook for a further minute. Check the seasoning and add some freshly ground pepper. Meanwhile, fry the eggs as explained opposite.

Divide the ratatouille among four bowls. Top each serving with a fried egg and serve with toasted bread. Serves 4

HOW TO MAKE AN OMELETTE

I love omelettes — they are so versatile. They can be as simple as the one opposite, or as luxurious as you can imagine. If you add a freshly sliced truffle to eggs and cook a simple omelette you have a meal that is fit for a king, and doesn't everyone deserve to be treated like royalty some days? I love to rustle one up on a Sunday lunch and serve with a green salad, some crusty bread and a good glass of red. Nothing is as simple and satisfying.

I find the easiest way to cook for two, three or four people is to make a large omelette in a big non-stick pan and cut it into generous wedges. It looks so good, and it is just as easy to quickly cook another, if need be. Nothing is quicker to make than an omelette. Remember that the secrets to a good crust are bubbling hot nut-brown butter and keeping the omelette runny and soft in the centre. This is a lush self-saucing dish. If you cook it perfectly it will be one of the yummiest things you eat. As with all things, you can cook an omelette ever so slowly, to create a solid melting texture, or cook it quickly at high heat. That is how I prefer it — I love a firm crust and a delicious wet interior.

Like risotto, whatever filling you add to an omelette should be cooked and ready to go, just warming through as you serve it. Finally, add the salt after the omelette starts to cook. I find it makes the omelette more tender, as the salt can toughen the protein in the egg if added when mixing at the beginning.

SANDWICHES

I love a good sandwich. When made properly, there are very few things as satisfying or delicious. Unfortunately, they can be few and far between. Many people forget the most basic rule when making simple things: use good-quality ingredients and the results will be assured.

Sandwiches can be closed, open or toasted. In their truest form, they are simply bread and fillings, so we must focus on the quality of the bread and the freshness of the fillings. A delicious bread roll with good-quality cheese will be a memorable cheese sandwich. The same may not be said of a mass manufactured roll and a processed cheese slice.

For the bread, you can choose from white, sourdough, wholemeal (wholewheat), rye and flatbreads. There are a few others but in the main these are the most popular. They will come in a variety of sizes and shapes, so you can either have single-serve style rolls, or slice from a larger loaf yourself. Generally speaking, this will be more satisfying than a pre-sliced loaf.

As for fillings, there are as many combinations as there are ingredients in this beautiful world. All smallgoods and cheeses make wonderful sandwiches, as do all roasted, pan-fried and barbecued meats, poultry and seafood. Vegetables, both cooked and raw, work well, and there are countless condiments. So go forth, remembering that you'll get out of your sandwich what you put in. The sky's the limit.

One of my favourite sandwiches is nothing more than two thin layers of rye bread holding slim linings of sliced hot salami, a quality Swiss cheese and a veil of pickled cucumbers, the sandwich being no more than 1 cm (1/2 inch) thick. For me this is a perfect transfer of flavour with each of the individual tastes detectable, yet coming together as a force to create a delicious combined end result.

A few classics, all very simple sandwiches indeed, are listed below. Just choose your bread, use butter very lightly if you wish, or olive oil, or even mayonnaise, if you like. Layer the fillings and make sure you season the sandwich with sea salt and freshly ground pepper.

- mortadella and provolone
- hot salami, Gruyère and pickled cucumbers
- pastrami and horseradish cream
- smoked ham, Cheddar and mustard
- roast beef with roast tomatoes and mustard
- roast leg of lamb with roast garlic spread
- tomato, fresh mozzarella and basil
- roast chicken mixed with Waldorf salad
- barbecued zucchini (courgette), eggplant (aubergine) and tomato with ricotta
- canned tuna, egg and mayonnaise
- Gorgonzola, pear and walnut
- vegetable omelette and aïoli

STEAK SANDWICH WITH CHEDDAR, ROCKET AND TOMATO JAM

This is a quick steak sandwich that we have served on Qantas as a refreshment since 1997. There is nothing like the simple things in life to make you feel good and this certainly fits into that category. Make sure you season your meat well with sea salt before you cook it — that is where the enhancement of the natural flavours is to be found. You can either quickly grill (broil) or pan-fry the steak, or cook it on the barbecue for a slightly smoky flavour. Put the cheese on the resting meat to soften slightly.

INGREDIENTS

4 x 125 g ($4^1/2$ oz) slices beef rib or scotch fillet
extra virgin olive oil
sea salt
8 thin slices good-quality Cheddar
4 rolls or baguettes
tomato jam (page 376)
rocket (arugula) leaves
freshly ground pepper

METHOD

Using a meat mallet, pound the beef until it is about 3 mm ($^1/8$ inch) thick. Brush with extra virgin olive oil, sprinkle with sea salt and barbecue it quickly on both sides until medium rare. This will only take a couple of minutes in all. Place the cheese on the beef and allow to rest for 5 minutes in a warm place. Meanwhile, cut the rolls or baguettes and toast until crispy. Sprinkle with a little extra virgin olive oil.

To assemble, layer the beef and cheese on the baguette, followed by the tomato jam and rocket. Season and serve. Serves 4

PANINI OF ROAST CHICKEN, BACON, LETTUCE, TOMATO AND AIOLI

This is a classic and has been on and off the Qantas menu for some time. We first started making it at the MCA café in The Rocks in Sydney, back in 1991. It was very popular for lunch, but it does make a good Sunday night dinner when you just feel like something light to go with a good movie. It was originally served on wholemeal (wholewheat) baguettes, but I like it now on a panini, which is an Italian elongated roll, as it is easier to handle. Toasted focaccia is another winner.

INGREDIENTS
    1 roast chicken (page 242)
    4 panini or other good-quality rolls
    4 bacon rashers, grilled (broiled)
    4 vine-ripened tomatoes, roasted but not peeled (page 34)
    sea salt and freshly ground pepper
    extra virgin olive oil
    balsamic vinegar
    1 baby cos (romaine) lettuce, washed and shredded
    aïoli (page 352)

METHOD
Shred the roast chicken flesh with a spoon or fork. Cut the panini in half and put on a chopping board. Put the shredded chicken on the bread, add the warm bacon rashers and the roast tomatoes and season. Drizzle with the extra virgin olive oil and vinegar, top with the shredded lettuce and place a dollop of aïoli on top.

Serve the panini on a plate with the top either on the panini or placed next to it. Cut in half or leave whole: your choice. Serves 4

VARIATIONS
• You can buy a good-quality roast chicken if you don't have time to cook one, or, if you wish, it's also fine to just pan-fry some chicken thigh fillets or breasts and add them to the sandwich.

• A slice of roast beef, or a minute steak will also taste great with the bacon, tomato and aïoli.

• For a great brunch sandwich fry an egg, or make a quick omelette, and add it to the roll with the bacon, tomato and aïoli. If you don't like mayonnaise, a tomato and chilli relish (page 377) will work fine.

METHOD

First butterfly the chicken breasts. Put the fillets on a chopping board, with the side that is cut from the bone towards the board, and the pointy end facing you. Using a sharp knife, cut from where the wing would be (at the thickest part) and slide the knife towards you, making sure you don't cut through to the other side. You should now have a chicken breast almost completely sliced through its thickness, but still joined where the breastbone would be. When you open it up you will have a large thin piece of chicken that will cook quickly. Another way of doing this is to put the chicken between greaseproof paper and gently bash with a rolling pin until you achieve the desired thickness.

Combine the breadcrumbs, Parmesan and a little sea salt in a shallow bowl and mix well. Beat the egg and milk until combined and tip into a second shallow bowl. Put the flour in a third shallow bowl. Dip the first chicken breast, on both sides, first in the flour, then in the egg mix, then finish with the breadcrumbs and shake to evenly coat. Repeat with the remaining chicken breasts. Heat some olive oil and butter in a large non-stick frying pan and shallow-fry the chicken in batches for 3 minutes on the first side, or until golden. Turn over and cook the other side for 2 minutes. Remove and drain on paper towels.

To make the coleslaw, combine the vegetables in a bowl and dress with aïoli.

Cut the baguette into four 18 cm (7 inch) lengths and cut each piece in half horizontally. If you wish, drizzle with a little extra virgin olive oil. Cut each chicken breast into three pieces and lay along the baguette. Top with the coleslaw and season with sea salt and freshly ground pepper. Serves 4

VARIATIONS

• If you feel like a change of course, pork or veal schnitzel will be just as good. I also like to grate cheese such as Gruyère or Montasio into the coleslaw, which gives it a great kick along.

• For a real treat, cut the bones from lamb cutlets, crumb and pan-fry them, leaving them pink and juicy inside, and place on a baguette. Top with mint jelly and some cos (romaine) lettuce, season, and you'll have a great sandwich. Equally yummy is lamb with roast tomato and some chilli sauce for a bit of fire.

• Try this variation and I promise you will love it. Boil some kipfler (fingerling) or pink eye potatoes in salted water, with their skin on. When done, remove and drain. While still hot, crush the potatoes gently with a potato masher. Drizzle with extra virgin olive oil and sprinkle with sea salt and freshly ground pepper. Mix together a little sheep's milk yoghurt, some sea salt, freshly ground pepper, crushed garlic and freshly squeezed lemon juice in a bowl. Add the potato to the yoghurt mixture. Place the chicken schnitzel on a bread roll, top with cos (romaine) lettuce and add a little of the potato salad. This is a great sandwich.

THE HAMBURGER

There is nothing more satisfying than a good burger, especially if a glass or two of red wine accompanies it. The problem is, of course, that for a dish that is cooked in so many fast food joints, cafés and restaurants around the world, it is still bloody hard to get a good one! I find the problem especially frustrating in Australia, and that is why I love having one or two every time I go to the United States, if I know the café has the right approach. But here is the good news: it is easy to make great burgers at home, and thus never have to suffer that fast food boring taste again. Hamburgers should taste of the meat, so there is the starting point. We must use the freshest, best-quality meat. We also don't need to use too much in the way of filling, which makes sense, because if the meat tastes clean, succulent and delicious, why mask it? So I love a little cheese, a rasher of bacon, some barbecue sauce and a thin layer of pickled cucumbers. In the States, I may stretch it to a little mustard as well. The bun must be fresh and I like it toasted on both sides.

In terms of the meat, you need fat in a burger to give it great texture and taste — about 20 per cent is perfect — and, like so many American chefs, I have found chuck steak the best cut to use. It has great flavour and texture and the right fat content. The meat must be fresh with a bright red bloom and white fat. It will be much better if it has not been cryovaced (vacuum-packed — discussed in detail in the meat chapter), as this destroys the taste and can add an unpleasant odour. This means it will be hard to satisfy the guidelines by buying pre-minced (ground) beef. If you want to raise a burger meal to a gourmet experience, get to know your butcher and ask him to mince (grind) your chuck steak for you, as you wait. Go to this effort and I promise you will never look back. The other factor is seasoning; a patty needs nothing more than salt added as freshly ground steak has the gelatinous ability to bind by itself without the addition of egg, something you see in other recipes.

Judy Rodgers, in her cookbook named after her San Francisco restaurant, *The Zuni Cafe*, talks about salting the chuck steak the day before mincing (grinding) the meat. At Rockpool, we had always salted large roasts the day before cooking, but had never tried it on smaller pieces of meat. Try it. The flavour of the salt is more even and Judy says the patty will be more moist. The best way to cook the patties is to barbecue them. This adds a lovely smoky flavour. But on those nights when you don't want to venture out to the barbecue, a heavy-based frying pan works well too. You need a nice crust and a melting interior: this is really the start and finish to a great burger, the rest just helps.

INGREDIENTS

700 g (1 lb 9 oz) freshly minced (ground) chuck steak

$1/2$–$3/4$ teaspoon sea salt

extra virgin olive oil

4 slices Gruyère

4 rashers bacon

4 hamburger buns or focaccia squares, halved horizontally

tomato or barbecue sauce, or mustard, or any combination you like

a few thin slices of pickled cucumber

freshly ground pepper

lettuce and tomato, to serve

METHOD

Put the meat in a bowl and sprinkle with the sea salt. Gently mix together, then divide into four patties. Move each patty from hand to hand for 2 minutes, to make a firm but not overworked patty, then shape into a ball. Gently flatten to form 2 cm ($3/4$ inch) thick patties. If making the patties the day before, cover and store in the refrigerator. However, if you do, make certain you take them out of the refrigerator well before cooking to allow them to be closer to room temperature when you cook them. This will ensure an even temperature for cooking and help the patties retain the heat from the barbecue or pan.

Prepare a barbecue or heat a frying pan until very hot. Brush some extra virgin olive oil over the patties and cook on one side, then turn over to finish the cooking (see notes, below). Rest the meat for 5 minutes. At this stage, if you want it plain, just place on a bun, sauce and serve. If you are adding other flavours, while the meat rests, place a slice of cheese on the meat to soften and cook the bacon on the barbecue. Toast the buns on both sides.

Place the bun bottoms on four plates. On each bun, place a patty with the cheese, bacon and chosen sauce and, if you wish, some pickled cucumber. Add a grind of fresh pepper. Top with the bun lid and serve. I like to serve the hamburger with lettuce and tomato on the side, but by all means, place them on the burger if you like. Serves 4

NOTES

If you like it rare, cook the burger for 5 minutes on each side. If you like it medium rare, cook for 6 minutes on each side, and if you like it well done, cook the burger for 7–8 minutes on each side. Don't forget to rest the meat for at least 5 minutes; it will taste better.

BRUSCHETTA

Bruschetta originated in the middle of Italy, but quickly spread to the rest of the country and now the world. And why not? It is the original garlic bread and still to this day the best. Bruschetta in its purest form is good-quality firm bread, usually a couple of days old, sliced about 1 cm (1/2 inch) thick, grilled over an open fire, rubbed with garlic, drizzled with extra virgin olive oil and sprinkled with a little sea salt. So, when guests come over, or you just feel like a snack, make bruschetta and serve with these topping ideas. To make the bruschetta, you can cook the bread under the grill (broiler), on a barbecue or just use the old family toaster. Then cut some garlic, rub it on the bread, and drizzle with the oil. The better quality the oil, the better the taste.

You can treat bruschetta just as a little bite with a glass of wine before lunch or dinner, as a course in itself, or as a meal. Anything that is an antipasto, salad or braise sits well on bruschetta.

The simplest recipe is, in summer, to peel, deseed and dice some vine-ripened tomatoes, add seasoning, drizzle with good oil and spoon them onto the bruschetta. This is the dreamiest form of tomatoes on toast.

HOW TO PEEL TOMATOES — Remove the stalk and cut a small cross 2–3 mm (1/16–1/8 inch) deep on the opposite end. Bring a saucepan of water to the boil and add enough salt to make it taste like seawater. Blanch the tomatoes for 10 seconds, then refresh in iced water. Once cooled, remove the tomatoes from the water and peel off the skin —it should come away easily from the cross — while the flesh is still firm.

FENNEL AND PARMESAN SALAD
INGREDIENTS
    1 baby fennel bulb
    extra virgin olive oil
    juice of 1 lemon
    sea salt and freshly ground pepper
    4 bruschetta
    Parmesan

METHOD
    Trim both ends of the fennel, cut in half lengthways and slice very thinly. A mandolin does this job well. Dress the sliced fennel with a little extra virgin olive oil and the lemon juice and season to taste. Arrange the dressed fennel on the bruschetta and top with freshly shaved Parmesan. Serves 4

TOMATO AND ANCHOVIES

INGREDIENTS

1 vine-ripened tomato

4 bruschetta

4 anchovies, roughly chopped

extra virgin olive oil

sea salt and freshly ground pepper

METHOD

Slice the tomato and place it on top of the bruschetta. Lay the anchovy slices across the top, drizzle with a little extra virgin olive oil and sprinkle with sea salt and freshly ground pepper. Serves 4

MUSSELS, SMOKY BACON AND OLIVES

INGREDIENTS

200 g (7 oz) mussels

extra virgin olive oil

1 garlic clove, sliced

$1/2$ small red onion, finely sliced

2 rashers smoky bacon, cut into 1 cm ($1/2$ inch) thick strips

$1/2$ teaspoon smoked paprika

6 green olives, pitted and chopped

1 small handful chopped flat-leaf (Italian) parsley

4 bruschetta

METHOD

Pull the beard out from the mussels and wash away any sand and mud. Heat a medium to large saucepan and add a little extra virgin olive oil. Add the garlic, onion and bacon and fry for 30 seconds. Add the mussels and paprika. Cover with a tight-fitting lid and steam until the mussels open, stirring a couple of times. Add the olives. Remove the pan from the heat and when cool enough to handle, remove the mussels from their shells. Discard the shells and return the mussels to the sauce. Stir through the parsley. Spoon the mussels and sauce over the bruschetta and serve. Serves 4

FOLLOWING PAGES mussels, smoky bacon and olives and fennel and parmesan salad on bruschetta

SALADS

Let's start by discussing what a salad is. Salads are generally either side salads, composite salads (these can be starters or main courses) or fruit salads. It will have a body (the main ingredient) and a base and garnish — these can be one and the same, or a mixture of different things. It is most often bound together by a dressing, which will usually be thin (vinaigrette style) or thick (mayonnaise style). It is usually cold, but since the days of *nouvelle cuisine*, warm is also on the agenda.

The green salad is the king of side salads. A big statement, but true. There is nothing like the crisp crunch of lettuce and the balance of olive oil and acid. After eating my main course I love nothing more than forking some leaves onto my plate and dressing them with the juices left on the plate. A green salad will either be delicious or ordinary; there is no middle ground. The reason: it has so few elements to it. Very fresh, well washed and dried leaves and a well-balanced dressing made with quality ingredients are all you have to hide behind, so failure is easy. So here is my favourite green salad, the one I make at home, and please forgive me, I know radicchio is red, but I choose not to see it that way.

Carefully pull the leaves off a baby cos (romaine) lettuce, throwing away the large dark green outside leaves, and wash them in the sink in lots of fresh cold water. Do exactly the same with a radicchio lettuce, then a curly endive, and then pull the leaves off a witlof (chicory/Belgian endive) and tear all the leaves into bite-sized pieces. Now, using a salad spinner, gently dry the leaves. Place the leaves in a container and chill.

To make the dressing, mix 100 ml (3 1/2 fl oz) extra virgin olive oil with 1 tablespoon good-quality red wine vinegar and season with sea salt and freshly ground pepper. Seasoning well is very important. If I feel like going to the effort, I pick a number of herbs and add them to the salad just before dressing. This could include coriander (cilantro), flat-leaf (Italian) parsley, dill, chives, mint or chervil. Remove the lettuce from the refrigerator and put in a bowl. Toss with the dressing and serve. Tossing the salad is very important; if you just drizzle the vinaigrette over the leaves in the bowl, you won't get a really even coating.

SOME POPULAR TYPES OF LETTUCE

- cos (romaine) — crisp textured, sweet flavoured
- curly endive or frisée — narrow curly leaf, slight bitter flavour
- green and red oak — soft textured, sweet flavoured
- iceberg — crisp textured, neutral in flavour
- radicchio — red leaves, pronounced bitter flavour
- treviso — elongated radicchio, crunchy textured, slightly bitter flavour
- witlof (chicory/Belgian endive) — crisp white leaves, slightly bitter flavour

DRESSING INGREDIENTS

My two favourite oils for dressing salads are extra virgin olive oil and walnut oil. I like to mix these with a variety of acids, the most popular being balsamic, red wine, sherry and cider vinegar, verjuice and fresh lime and lemon juice. Generally, a mix of three parts oil to one part acid is about right, but it will depend on the strength of the acid used, so always take a little taste from both the oil and the acid before mixing, to get an idea of their strength and to see how they will balance. Don't forget to season with sea salt and freshly ground pepper.

Many of the salad dressings in this chapter are made with red wine vinegar as the acid component. Feel free to exchange it for any of the other acids, but you may have to change the ratios slightly. It won't be long before you'll be whipping up all sorts of vinaigrettes. You can also add a little mustard, chilli or some fresh herbs.

- **extra virgin olive oil** — this is extracted from olives solely by mechanical methods under the right temperature conditions. Other oil that is classified as olive oil is extracted with heat and sometimes chemicals. The first pressed oil will then be classified. If it has less than one per cent acidity then it can be called extra virgin. This type of oil is the one that we use most in the kitchen and that has the best flavour. Olive oil, like wine, is a product of its surroundings: different soils produce oils of different flavours. The great thing about that is that it allows us to have oils that we will use for different dishes — for salads, on raw fish, to drizzle on barbecued meats and so on.

- **walnut oil** — this is a fantastic oil for making dressings for salads and starters that have seafood in them. I particularly like it with crab. My favourite use is in combination with fresh lime juice. It is expensive but worth it. You should also buy as small a can as you can, as it needs to be stored in the refrigerator after opening and goes rancid very easily.

• **balsamic vinegar** — a wonderful, complex, sweet condiment. This incredible vinegar begins life as a white grape, but through years of reducing down in different wood-flavoured barrels becomes dark, mysterious and sticky. With balsamic you get what you pay for. The cheaper ones are imitations only. As the good ones age, they become incredibly intense, so just use a few drops and you will get really flavoursome rewards.

• **red wine vinegar** — made from fermented red wine, this vinegar is usually high in acid. If the vinegar is made from good-quality wine, it is one of the best all-rounders.

• **sherry vinegar** — this is made from fermented sherry, with the rich sherry flavours evident. I like to use it in combination with red wine vinegar for salad dressings.

• **cider vinegar** — made from fermented apple cider, this vinegar has a sweet mild flavour and is a welcome addition to salad dressings and sauces and in simple pan deglazing.

• **verjuice** — this is the sour juice of unripe grapes. Its sourness comes from the natural high acidity of the grapes, not from fermentation. It lends itself to all sorts of dressings and in the cooking of seafood, meat, poultry and salads.

• **lemon and lime juice** — both of these have a wonderful soft fresh taste. These juices will bring cooking to life and I always have a lemon in the house — from dressings to barbecues, they are so versatile. The following recipes can be served as salads with a main course, as a separate starter-style salad or as a garnish to a main plate.

BOILED LEEKS WITH VINAIGRETTE

Leeks are sometimes unfairly called the poor man's asparagus. Unfairly, because they are so wonderful to eat on their own. Leeks are often among the aromatic vegetables that I sweat off to bring flavour to soups and braises, and they are also an important part of a bouquet garni as they wrap all the herbs together. This dish below, as part of an antipasto spread, is sublime, and is such an easy recipe to make.

Pick young medium-sized leeks that are straight and have a generous white part. It is important to dress the leeks while they are hot as this helps the flavour of the vinaigrette to soak in.

INGREDIENTS

4 small–medium leeks, washed
80 ml ($2^1/2$ fl oz/$^1/3$ cup) extra virgin olive oil
$1^1/2$ tablespoons red wine vinegar
sea salt and freshly ground pepper
10 g ($^1/4$ oz/$^1/2$ bunch) chives, finely snipped with scissors, to serve

METHOD

Bring a large saucepan of salted water to the boil and add the leeks. Gently simmer for 8–10 minutes, or until tender.

Remove the leeks and drain on paper towels. Carefully cut the first layer of skin from each leek and discard. Cut the leeks in half lengthways. While still warm, dress with extra virgin olive oil, red wine vinegar, sea salt and freshly ground pepper.

Either place on four individual plates or on one large serving dish. Sprinkle with the chives and serve. Serves 4

VARIATIONS

• You can transform this dish from the humble to the most sophisticated by adding fresh truffles to the vinaigrette when they are in season. Simply chop the truffles or shave them over the hot leeks and serve warm.

• Leeks braise well with water just to cover and seasoned with sea salt, whole peppercorns, thyme, a fresh bay leaf, parsley stalks, carrot julienne and onion, some garlic and a little olive oil. By the time they are tender, the nage (the broth liquid) in which they have cooked makes a delicious dressing.

• Any of the dressings mentioned on the previous pages work well with leeks that have been boiled in salted water until soft.

ROASTED CAPSICUMS WITH VINAIGRETTE

This is a simple classic salad that gives you a few options for preparing capsicums (peppers). These days you can choose from red, green or yellow capsicums, as well as banana peppers and chillies, which can all be served singly or as a mixture, as the colours look quite beautiful. I like to grill (broil) or barbecue them until the skin is nice and blackened. Then I put them in a bowl and cover them with plastic wrap; this allows the capsicums to continue cooking and soften in the trapped steam. When they are cool enough to handle, I peel and deseed them. Try to do this without running water over them as that takes away some of their lovely intense flavour. Cut them into large slices, about 3 cm (1 1/4 inches) thick, and arrange them on a plate in alternate colours, if using different ones. Douse them with a vinaigrette made of garlic, red wine vinegar, extra virgin olive oil, sea salt and freshly ground pepper. The capsicums can be embellished with fresh herbs — mint, coriander (cilantro), chives, flat-leaf (Italian) parsley, chervil or tarragon; use just a couple or all of them, chopped together and sprinkled over the dish.

This dish can also be made by rubbing the capsicums with extra virgin olive oil and roasting them in the oven. Put them in a bowl, cover with plastic wrap and proceed as above. The other alternative is to cut the capsicums in half, deseed them and cut them into thick strips. Put some extra virgin olive oil in a heavy-based frying pan and add the capsicum strips. Sear them over high heat until the skin starts to blister. Don't worry if the skin colours; that simply adds to the flavour. Put in a bowl and cover, so that they will continue cooking and soften, then serve with the vinaigrette. I don't bother skinning the capsicums when I do them this way; again, it adds another interesting texture.

Don't limit yourself to the dressing that I have explained here, you can add your own favourite one and it will work well.

POTATO SALAD

There are as many recipes for potato salad in the world as there are mothers who claim to serve the very best. I will explain a few of my favourites. I must say that I do like to use small potatoes that are sweet and waxy and I love to cook them whole and leave the skin on. Not only does it add wonderful texture, but there are also more vitamins in the skin than in the potato flesh.

I usually allow 100 g (3^1/2 oz) potato per person. I like the potatoes to be the size of a thumb; they are so cute. My favourite varieties for this salad are kipflers (fingerlings), pink eyes, Jersey royals, Dutch creams or Yukon golds.

Wash the potatoes under running water, then simmer in a saucepan of salted water until tender. Drain. Now, while they are still warm, crush them slightly with a potato masher and drizzle with extra virgin olive oil, red wine vinegar, sea salt and freshly ground pepper. This allows the potatoes to soak up some of the dressing. When you serve them, drizzle a little more dressing over and add a sprinkling of fresh herbs.

The potatoes are also great mixed with yoghurt and finely chopped garlic, especially if you don't like mayonnaise. If you do, simply allow the potatoes to cool, then mix with aïoli and serve.

A yummy way of dealing with larger potatoes is to boil them with the skin on, then slice the potatoes into rounds and put in a bowl. Make a warm vinaigrette by sautéing diced bacon with chopped onion and a little finely chopped garlic. Transfer to a bowl, season and add some extra virgin olive oil and red wine vinegar. The bacon fat will mix with the vinaigrette and enliven the taste. Pour the dressing over the potato, allowing it to soak in, and add freshly chopped herbs. Serve on a platter.

CHERRY TOMATO, PEA AND POTATO SALAD

I love peas and potatoes, so I really love this salad. The more anchovies the better and I like to add some chilli flakes to the oil when I'm braising the peas, but that's just me. I'd add chilli flakes to everything if I could.

Peas are a vegetable that need to be eaten young and fresh. They start to lose their sweetness from the moment they are picked and can get quite woody and rather bitter when they are too mature. For this reason it is often far better to use frozen peas, which have been frozen within hours of being picked in season, than dubious old large peas that will yield no sweetness. Frozen ones will be sweet and tender to the tooth. I have used them many times in soup recipes and for braises when doing Qantas recipes. They give me incredible consistency, so I can vouch for them. They haven't let me down over the last seven years. In this salad, the peas are braised, which simply means to cook slowly in a small amount of liquid. Don't rush it, or you won't get the best flavour.

INGREDIENTS

4 medium pink eye potatoes
30 ripe cherry tomatoes, about 300 g (10^1/2 oz)
85 g (3 oz/1 large bunch) mint
150 g (5^1/2 oz/1 cup) fresh or frozen peas
4 anchovies
60 ml (2 fl oz/^{1}/4 cup) extra virgin olive oil
2 tablespoons balsamic vinegar
sea salt and freshly ground pepper

METHOD

Boil the potatoes in a saucepan of salted water for 20—25 minutes, or until tender. Allow to cool, then peel. Cut into chunks and put in a bowl. Slice the cherry tomatoes in half and add to the potato. Roughly slice the mint and transfer to the bowl.

In a heavy-based frying pan, gently braise the peas and anchovies in the extra virgin olive oil for 30 minutes, or until they are well cooked and starting to lose their colour. Add the balsamic vinegar and season to taste, carefully, as the anchovies will be salty. Pour the pea mixture over the potato and tomato mixture and combine. Transfer to a serving platter or bowl and serve. Serves 4

BEETROOT, CARROT AND BLUE CHEESE SALAD

Root vegetables have a natural sweetness that works well with blue cheese. This salad works best with a creamy blue. The beetroot is roasted, but you can boil it. If you do, boil it with the skin on. It tends to hold its colour better as the water doesn't leach into the cell wall of the cut beetroot. I quite like the skin's texture and taste, especially when the beetroot is roasted, so often I don't bother to remove it after cooking.

INGREDIENTS

2 medium beetroots

3 medium carrots, peeled

150 g (5^1/2 oz/1 bunch) flat-leaf (Italian) parsley

185 ml (6 fl oz/^{3}/4 cup) extra virgin olive oil

60 ml (2 fl oz/^{1}/4 cup) red wine vinegar

sea salt and freshly ground pepper

100 g (3^1/2 oz) blue cheese such as Gorgonzola, crumbled

1 tablespoon freshly grated ginger

METHOD

Roast the beetroots with their skin on in a preheated 180°C (350°F/Gas 4) oven for 1^1/4–1^1/2 hours, or until soft when pierced with the tip of a knife. Allow to cool, then peel, if you wish, and cut into wedges. Meanwhile, bring a saucepan of salted water to the boil, add the carrots and gently simmer for 10 minutes until they are just cooked. Drain and cut into 3 cm (1^1/4 inch) lengths.

Put the parsley, beetroot and carrot in a bowl. Dress with the extra virgin olive oil and vinegar. Season with sea salt and freshly ground pepper and add the blue cheese and ginger. Gently mix to ensure the dressing fully coats the ingredients. Spoon the salad onto individual plates or one large platter. Serves 4

VARIATIONS

• You can simplify this salad by removing the cheese. For the beetroot you can substitute any vegetable that can be boiled; try snowpeas (mangetout) or beans.

• The bistro classic of blue cheese, pear and walnut is a fantastic starter. You need a slightly crumbly but still creamy blue such as Roquefort, some creamy sweet pears like beurre bosc, some roasted walnuts and a few leaves of rocket (arugula). Add a little dressing and away you go.

• Instead of roasting the beetroots, you can boil them in 500 ml (17 fl oz/ 2 cups) water with 125 ml (4 fl oz/^{1}/2 cup) red wine vinegar, 55 g (2 oz/^{1}/4 cup) caster (superfine) sugar and some sea salt. Boil for 40 minutes, or until soft.

SALAD OF BRAISED BEETROOT, YAM, PEAS AND BEANS

This salad started life as a tagine of vegetables when Sam and I would eat only vegetables for a week, but then I started serving it for friends with chicken tagine or braised meat and Moroccan salads. Being lazy, I'd make it in advance and let it come to room temperature while other things went on the stove. I realized that it tasted better when cool and it made things even easier. Now isn't that what entertaining is all about?

INGREDIENTS

2 medium beetroots, peeled and quartered
2 small yams, peeled and cut into 4 rounds
2 medium carrots, peeled and cut into 4 rounds
150 g (5^1/2 oz) baby beans
250 ml (9 fl oz/1 cup) chermoula (page 372)
150 ml (5 fl oz) extra virgin olive oil
115 g (4 oz/^{1}/3 cup) honey
juice of 2 lemons
sea salt
300 g (10 oz/2 cups) shelled peas, about 700 g (1 lb 9 oz) unshelled
8 fresh dates, pitted
80 g (2^3/4 oz/^{1}/2 cup) blanched almonds

METHOD

Put the beetroot, yam, carrot and beans in a bowl and loosely coat with the chermoula. Transfer to a tagine or large saucepan that has a lid, set over high heat and add the extra virgin olive oil. Fry, covered, for 2 minutes. Add enough water to the vegetables to come halfway up their side, then add the honey, lemon juice and some sea salt. Bring to the boil, reduce the heat to a simmer, cover and cook for about 30 minutes. Add the peas and cook for 30 minutes, then add the dates and almonds and cook for another 10 minutes. Remove the tagine from the heat and bring to room temperature. Serve it in the tagine or, if using a saucepan, transfer the vegetables to a bowl and serve. Serves 4

VARIATIONS

• It's easy to pan-fry some chicken thighs until coloured and cook them slowly with the vegetables to create a delicious meal; just serve with couscous or rice. By the same token, you can add braised lamb or beef, or even add some pieces of fish to the vegetables about 15 minutes before the dish is finished.

• Pumpkin, parsnip, artichokes, fennel or potato can all be used, as can Treviso or radicchio (both types of red chicory), cut in half and cooked for the full amount of time. It all goes soft, melting and slightly bitter. Yum!

ITALIAN-STYLE COLESLAW

I love this simple preparation. It showcases the brilliant taste of fresh produce, and gives a lovely clean salad that goes well with barbecued meat, poultry and fish, and all crumbed food. As well, it is beautiful as a simple starter or, as I have it at least every couple of weeks at home, as part of a Mediterranean-style shared meal. Don't forget that it's not just Asian food that can be shared. Roast some chickens and carve onto a large plate, serve this coleslaw, some roast pumpkin, a green salad and some potatoes and you have a wonderful meal that can be passed around the table and shared with good bread, wine and conversation. Finish with cheese or fruit and you have the simplest meal at home. If you use good-quality fresh produce your friends will marvel at the great cook and, more importantly, the great host you are.

Italian coleslaw differs from the regular in its simplicity. It is only finely shaved cabbage, cheese and dressing, so the finer you shave the cabbage, the better. I find the best tool for this is a Japanese mandolin. It is very sharp so watch your fingers, but once you get used to it you'll use it for all kinds of vegetable preparation.

METHOD

Finely shred 1 baby cabbage or half a Savoy cabbage. Put in a large bowl and season with sea salt and freshly ground pepper. Drizzle extra virgin olive oil and red wine vinegar over at a ratio of three parts oil to one part vinegar. Start to toss the cabbage. Don't add so much dressing that it becomes wet, just enough to moisten. Toss through as much freshly shaved Parmesan as you like. I like a lot. Place on four small plates and serve as a starter, or place on a large platter and serve as a shared starter or salad with the main. Serves 4

VARIATIONS

• The vinegar can be changed to balsamic with great success. A really old one, just drizzled over the top, is gorgeous.

• Slice and julienne some celeriac, then quickly blanch and dress as you would the cabbage. This makes a fine garnish for poultry and seafood. Red cabbage can also be used. I just sprinkle over a little sea salt to allow it to soften and release some of its water, then give it a quick rinse. Just dress and serve.

• Once you have purchased your mandolin, you can easily make all manner of shredded vegetable salads. Try shredding fennel really finely, marinating it in lemon juice for a while, then seasoning and adding some extra virgin olive oil. You now have a light and refreshing starter.

FATTOUSH

This salad is a Middle Eastern version of panzanella, the Italian bread salad. I love it with hummus and tabbouleh as a starter before a Turkish pizza, or with roast chook rubbed with a few spices and some chilli.

You can just tear the bread and mix it through, but it is really good when fried. It adds another dimension. It is also really important to use fresh lemon juice, as the acid is soft and allows the other flavours in the salad to shine through.

INGREDIENTS

1 piece fresh pitta bread
125 ml (4 fl oz/^{1}/2 cup) extra virgin olive oil, plus extra
12 cherry tomatoes, cut in half
1 small red onion, roughly chopped
1 teaspoon sumac
1 Lebanese (short) cucumber, cut in half, deseeded and diced
1 handful mint
2 handfuls flat-leaf (Italian) parsley
1 handful coriander (cilantro) leaves
sea salt and freshly ground pepper
2 garlic cloves
juice of 1 lemon

METHOD

Slice the pitta bread horizontally through the middle, then heat a little extra virgin olive oil in a saucepan and fry the pitta bread until crisp. Remove and allow to cool. Tear the bread into pieces and put in a bowl. In a separate bowl, put the tomato, onion, sumac, cucumber, mint, parsley, coriander and some sea salt and freshly ground pepper.

In a mortar with a pestle, pound a pinch of sea salt together with the garlic. Add the lemon juice and extra virgin olive oil.

Mix the tomato salad well, add the dressing and fold through the bread. Divide among four plates or spoon the salad onto one large platter. Serves 4

VARIATION

• As this is essentially a salad with bread mixed through, you can change the salad to have anything in it you wish; just look for balance of flavours and interesting textures.

BUFFALO MOZZARELLA AND CAPSICUM SALAD

If you live in Europe or the USA you have long been able to get fresh buffalo milk mozzarella from Italy. Thank goodness it is now available in Australia. As this salad is very simple, it relies on the quality of the cheese and dressing. This is a variation of the classic Caprese salad.

INGREDIENTS
2 large red capsicums (peppers)
150 ml (5 fl oz) extra virgin olive oil
60 ml (2 fl oz/1/4 cup) red wine vinegar
sea salt and freshly ground pepper
6 small fresh buffalo mozzarella balls
60 g (2^1/4 oz/1/2 bunch) basil

METHOD
To prepare the capsicums, rub the skins well with some of the extra virgin olive oil and put on a hot barbecue. Keep turning the capsicums as they cook until they are well blackened on all sides. Put the capsicums in a bowl and cover with plastic wrap. Leave them to steam for about 30 minutes, then peel, deseed and slice into thin strips. Dress the capsicums with the remaining extra virgin olive oil, red wine vinegar, sea salt and freshly ground pepper.

Cut each mozzarella ball into thick slices and place on four plates or arrange on a large serving platter. Spoon over the dressed capsicum and tear the basil leaves roughly over the top. I like to drizzle some more extra virgin olive oil on top and give another grind of pepper for the cheese. Serves 4

VARIATIONS
• The capsicums (peppers) can be roasted in the oven and peeled in the same way, but you won't get that slight smoky flavour. For even more smokiness, you can blacken the capsicums a little less, allow to soften in the covered bowl, then deseed and slice, leaving the charred skin on.

• It is also really nice to cut the capsicums in half, deseed and cut into strips, then cook in a medium hot pan with some extra virgin olive oil until soft and the juices are released. When you put the capsicums in the pan, add sea salt.

• The salad can be changed into the traditional Caprese by simply replacing the capsicums with beautifully ripe summer tomatoes. I sometimes like to peel the tomatoes, as that provides a slight textural change. On other occasions I have also added roast tomatoes instead of fresh ones, added olives, and used balsamic vinegar in place of red wine vinegar.

FOLLOWING PAGES buffalo mozzarella and capsicum salad, left, and moroccan eggplant salad, right

MOROCCAN EGGPLANT SALAD

You can use olive oil for this dish, but the flavour of extra virgin olive oil is worth the extra money. I first started making this salad in the eighties and to this day it is still one of the most satisfying flavours I know. We serve it at the restaurant with barbecued seafood mainly, but it is great as one of the dishes you can serve with a Moroccan-style shared lunch. Make chicken tagine, eggplant (aubergine) salad, fennel salad and the braised beetroot and yam salad in this chapter and then all you have to do is decide whether it's rice or couscous and you are serving fabulous food. The best thing is you can make it all in advance and serve at room temperature. Nothing could be tastier or easier.

INGREDIENTS

3 eggplants (aubergines), sliced into 1 cm ($1/2$ inch) thick rounds
extra virgin olive oil
1 handful flat-leaf (Italian) parsley
4 vine-ripened tomatoes, peeled, deseeded and diced (page 66)
1 tablespoon ground cumin
sea salt
juice of 1 lemon
freshly ground pepper

METHOD

In a large frying pan, heat enough extra virgin olive oil — about 1 cm ($1/2$ inch) deep — to shallow-fry the eggplant. Add the eggplant and fry, in three or four batches, until dark brown all over. Remove to a bowl when done. Carefully add the parsley to the hot oil — it will spit a fair bit. Add the tomato, cumin and some sea salt and toss with the parsley for 1–2 minutes over low heat (trying not to burn the cumin). Add the eggplant and cook for a further 5 minutes. Add the lemon juice, check the seasoning and finish with a grind of pepper.

Spoon the eggplant salad into a pretty bowl. The salad itself is not that attractive, but it sure does taste great. Serves 4

VARIATIONS

• If you like less oil, roast the whole eggplants (aubergines) in the oven until soft, then remove the skin and chop the flesh. Fry the parsley, tomato and cumin and add the chopped eggplant. The salad will have a slightly different taste, as it won't have the caramelization from the initial frying.

• You can also barbecue the eggplant to add a smoky flavour, and then start at the parsley frying stage again.

TABBOULEH

This salad makes a great first course with a number of dishes, creating a delicious mezze table. Think antipasto, only Middle Eastern. It is also, of course, a wonderful accompaniment to many barbecued and roasted foods. Try sitting slices of roast chicken on top of the tabbouleh, or some barbecued lamb chops and a big dollop of garlic yoghurt. This is really a recipe that you can play around with. This version has more parsley than is traditional, but I love the taste of the fresh herb, so feel free to take some out, or add more burghul wheat as you like. You would usually see the herbs chopped; however, at the restaurant we finely shred them into strips. It gives the salad a different texture and is worth the effort. So this is how we make it at Rockpool, when we serve it with seafood.

INGREDIENTS

175 g (6 oz/1 cup) burghul (bulgur)
3 handfuls flat-leaf (Italian) parsley, finely shredded
1 handful mint, finely shredded
1 small red onion, finely diced
3 spring onions (scallions), sliced into fine rounds
3 vine-ripened tomatoes, peeled, deseeded and finely diced (page 66)
125 ml (4 fl oz/1/2 cup) extra virgin olive oil
juice of 2 lemons
sea salt and freshly ground pepper

METHOD

Soak the burghul in cold water for about 20–25 minutes, or until soft. Don't oversoak it as it will make the salad soggy. Remove from the water and drain in a colander lined with muslin. Bring the top of the muslin together and squeeze well. The burghul must feel dry at this point. Put the burghul in a bowl and add all the remaining ingredients, except the extra virgin olive oil, lemon juice and seasoning. Mix well, then add the dressing and mix through thoroughly. Check the seasoning.

Place on a large platter to serve as part of a mezze table, or spoon onto a plate and serve with roasted or barbecued meat or seafood. Serves 4

VARIATION

• Another simple salad can be made by replacing the burghul with couscous. To add more body, remove a lot of the herbs and just add the vegetables and dressing to the couscous. It is also possible to add other herbs, such as dill, and I have also added quite a bit of rocket (arugula) on occasions.

SOUP

Soup would have to be one of the oldest and simplest dishes known to humans. I can imagine hunters and gatherers sitting around the fire throwing whatever was available into a pot, adding water and boiling the ingredients until palatable. These days, soup is often served as a simple starter but we can still sit down to a hearty meal of soup, bread and, now that we're out of the Dark Ages, a bowl of salad.

Richard Olney tells us in the Time-Life *Good Cook Series* that restaurant chefs have reason to acknowledge the culinary influence of soups. The first eating establishment to be known as a restaurant was opened by a soup vendor in Paris, a M. Boulanger, in 1765. Inscribed above the entrance to his shop was *Venite ad me omnes qui stomacho laboratis et ego restaurabo*, which means 'come to me all of you whose stomachs cry out and I will restore you'. I think a few chefs have forgotten about the restore, and let the ego run away with them instead…

Soups are generally either broth-based, with any number of ingredients in them (stocks and consommés fall into this category), or purées. Most of the compound broths make great one-bowl meals and the purées are thickened by the vegetables that are cooked in the broth, or by bread, egg yolks, cream or flour (but let's not go there with the flour).

Compound broths can be made from many ingredients. They can be based on chicken, beef, fish or vegetable stock, but generally speaking, it is easy to just start them off with water, especially the slow-cooked ones. All types of meat, simmered slowly with all manner of vegetables, herbs, pulses and grains, can be used. Minestrone is a classic example.

There are few rules to soup making; however, it is best to cook soups slowly, making sure they don't stick to the bottom of the saucepan and burn. A tasty addition to a compound broth can be a dollop of sauce such as pistou, pesto, aïoli or rouille; equally as welcome are garlic croutons. With puréed soups, a blender or stick blender will make the soup quite smooth, but for a really silky finish, pass the purée through a fine sieve after blending it. It will take all your soups to the next level.

SPICY TOMATO SOUP

This soup is easy to make and tastes great. Don't let the fact that you have to make a little paste stop you. You can also add a couple more spices if you wish to increase the complexity of the flavour. If you want, you could add chicken stock instead of water — it may add a little more body, but not much extra flavour. You can also use good-quality canned tomatoes (you will need 1.25 kg/2 lb 12 oz). The taste isn't quite as good, but maybe in the dead of winter and for convenience. Whatever you do, don't use insipid, out-of-season tomatoes.

INGREDIENTS

1.5 kg (3 lb 5 oz) very ripe tomatoes, peeled, deseeded and chopped (page 66)

125 ml (4 fl oz/$1/2$ cup) extra virgin olive oil

2 celery stalks, trimmed and finely chopped

1 small carrot, peeled and finely chopped

2 tablespoons red wine vinegar

1 teaspoon sea salt

freshly ground pepper

1 tablespoon chopped coriander (cilantro) leaves

FOR THE PASTE

4 garlic cloves, finely chopped

$1/2$ small red onion, finely chopped

1 handful flat-leaf (Italian) parsley, chopped

1 handful coriander (cilantro) leaves

1 teaspoon smoked paprika

$1/2$ teaspoon hot chilli powder

2 teaspoons ground cumin

METHOD

To make the paste, combine all the ingredients in a food processor and purée. Remove and set aside.

To make the soup, put the tomato in the cleaned food processor and purée. Set aside. Put the extra virgin olive oil in a large saucepan and heat until hot (it will be starting to shimmer). Add the celery, carrot and the paste and cook over low heat for about 10 minutes. Stir constantly to avoid burning the spices. Add the tomato purée, the vinegar, seasoning and 500 ml (17 fl oz/2 cups) water. Simmer slowly for 30 minutes until the vegetables are soft. Return to the food processor and purée until thick and smooth.

Check the seasoning and divide the soup among four bowls. Sprinkle with the chopped coriander leaves. At this stage, you could drizzle a little extra virgin olive oil on top, but only if it takes your fancy. Serves 4

VARIATIONS

• This soup makes a great sauce, especially with meat. You will need to reduce the soup down until you have about half the original amount. Try the following:

Take a leg of lamb and butterfly it (page 266), or have your butcher do it for you, if you don't want to go to the trouble. Season the lamb leg with sea salt and splash it liberally with balsamic vinegar. Allow to marinate for 2 hours. Get the barbecue nice and hot and cook the flattened leg for about 10 minutes on each side. Don't worry if you char the outside too much, as it adds flavour. Transfer the lamb to a plate and allow to rest in a warm place for 10 minutes. Meanwhile, cook some sliced zucchini (courgettes) and red capsicums (peppers) on the barbecue.

Pour the reduced tomato soup/sauce onto a large platter and top with the barbecued vegetables. Slice the meat and place it on top, sprinkle with a little chopped coriander (cilantro) leaves and add a grind of fresh black pepper. Mix the juices from the rested lamb with a little extra virgin olive oil and pour over the meat. Serve with a big bowl of couscous and a salad and you have a cracking good Saturday night barbie. Just get your mates around. If you like it spicy, offer a side dish of harissa (page 374).

• The easy way out with this lamb dish is to simply throw some lamb cutlets on the barbecue, instead of the leg. You won't get that heavy charred flavour and the melting interior of the larger cut of lamb, but it is still delicious.

GAZPACHO

I love gazpacho in summer when tomatoes are at their peak. The combination of spice and olive oil is so seductive. Gazpacho is a soup that requires no cooking. You can make it in a mortar with a pestle if you like the really rustic look; you will also be able to taste every ingredient. Many purists would say that that is the only way to do it, but I think the easiest method is to purée it and add diced tomatoes and different coloured capsicums (peppers). Little croutons add a nice crunch and you can serve ice in it if you wish. Whichever way you make gazpacho, you must serve it really cold.

HOW TO MAKE CROUTONS — Preheat the oven to 180°C (350°F/Gas 4). Cut four 1 cm (1/2 inch) thick slices sourdough bread. Remove the crusts, then cut the bread into 1 cm (1/2 inch) dice. Put on a roasting tray, drizzle with 2 tablespoons extra virgin olive oil and season with sea salt and freshly ground pepper. Roast in the oven until very light brown, shaking the tray every few minutes to colour the bread evenly. For extra flavour, add 1 minced garlic clove to the oil.

INGREDIENTS

400 g (14 oz) vine-ripened tomatoes, peeled, deseeded and roughly diced (page 66)

1 Lebanese (short) cucumber, peeled and roughly diced

2 red capsicums (peppers), roughly diced

1/2 green capsicum (pepper), roughly diced

2 large red chillies, split, deseeded and chopped

1 garlic clove, finely chopped

1/2 small brown onion, chopped

1 tablespoon red wine vinegar

60 ml (2 fl oz/1/4 cup) extra virgin olive oil

sea salt and freshly ground pepper

Tabasco sauce

croutons, to serve

FOR THE CONFETTI

1 vine-ripened tomato, peeled, deseeded and very finely diced (page 66)

1/2 small Lebanese (short) cucumber, deseeded and very finely diced

1 red capsicum (pepper), very finely diced

1/2 green capsicum (pepper), very finely diced

1/2 small red onion, very finely diced

METHOD

Put all ingredients, except the extra virgin olive oil and seasoning, in a blender, and add 125 ml (4 fl oz/1/2 cup) water. Pulse, taking care not to overheat or purée the gazpacho. Push the mixture through a coarse sieve into a bowl. Add the oil, some sea salt and freshly ground pepper and stir through. Check the seasoning, and add a little Tabasco if you like it hot. Chill for at least 2 hours. Gently mix all the confetti ingredients together and set aside.

Ladle the soup into four soup bowls, sprinkle with the confetti and croutons and serve immediately. Serves 4

VARIATIONS

• You can embellish this soup by adding freshly cooked seafood to it just before serving — crab meat, lobster and king prawns (shrimp) are great. These would also make a delicious salad, with the soup served as a sauce. Add one type of seafood or a combination. What a summer treat!

• We also use the soup at the restaurant as a sauce. You don't need as much, about 100 ml (3 1/2 fl oz), and you could make it more garlicky, with 2 cloves. Pour the sauce onto the centre of a plate, mix together some fresh herbs like flat-leaf (Italian) parsley, mint and coriander (cilantro), or perhaps a little frisée, radicchio and baby cos (romaine) lettuce, and add a dash of extra virgin olive oil and lemon juice. Place the herb salad on the sauce and put freshly cooked yabbies on top. You can then sprinkle the sauce with the confetti and a few croutons. Finish by seasoning with sea salt and freshly ground pepper and you have a very sophisticated little salad indeed.

• There is also a white gazpacho, which is not only a great soup, but a wonderful sauce as well. It is incredibly simple to make, apart from the fact that it is garnished with green seedless grapes, which need to be peeled, but that's not really that hard either.
    To make, put 40 g (1 1/2 oz/1 cup) chopped old bread, crusts removed, in a bowl. Add milk to soften it. Put the bread in a blender and add 150 g (5 1/2 oz/ 1 cup) blanched almonds and 3 garlic cloves and blend. With the motor running, slowly add about 185 ml (6 fl oz/3/4 cup) extra virgin olive oil, then drizzle in 375 ml (13 fl oz/1 1/2 cups) very cold water. Add 2 tablespoons sherry vinegar and season with sea salt and freshly ground pepper. Traditionally, the gazpacho is poured into a bowl, the peeled grapes added, a little extra virgin olive oil drizzled over and then served immediately. As with red gazpacho, this makes a wonderful summer sauce with things like lobster, crab and prawns.

MINESTRONE

Minestrone is a homely, hearty mixture of vegetables with white beans, rice, pasta or barley. There is usually a mixture of starchy and leafy vegetables and either stock or water. Quite often pesto is added at the end, as it really heightens the flavour. I think when making this at home, it is easiest to make the soup with water and add flavour from either smoky bacon or speck. The soup cooks until all the vegetables are well done and I think that the water base allows the vegetables to taste very much of themselves, yet allows all the players to create a wonderful complex flavour.

The mixture of vegetables in this soup is by no means fixed. Add different vegetables at will. The most important thing is to cook all the vegetables until well done and melted into the soup. Don't get caught in the trap of adding quick-cooking vegetables near the end. They must all braise together and the texture of all the vegetables should be melting. Cook the beans slowly, as this will allow them to become creamier inside without splitting, and don't salt the water, as this toughens the skin and makes the difference between the texture of the outside and the inside too great. Remember, every component of this soup should be melting. This dish is about comfort and the healing power of soup.

INGREDIENTS

60 g (2^1/4 oz/^{1}/3 cup) dried cannellini beans, soaked overnight
2 tablespoons extra virgin olive oil
60 g (2^1/4 oz/^{1}/4 cup) finely diced smoky bacon or speck
1 large red onion, finely diced
2 garlic cloves, crushed
1 leek, white part only, washed and finely diced
4 celery stalks, finely diced
2 carrots, peeled and finely diced
1 tablespoon sea salt
2 tablespoons tomato paste (purée)
12 baby green beans, cut into 1 cm (^{1}/2 inch) long pieces
25 g (1 oz/^{1}/2 cup) shredded silverbeet (Swiss chard) leaves and stalks
400 g (14 oz) can chopped tomatoes and their juices
1 fresh bay leaf
2 flat-leaf (Italian) parsley sprigs, leaves roughly chopped
freshly ground pepper
Parmesan or pesto (page 366), to serve

METHOD

Drain the cannellini beans and put in a large heavy-based saucepan. Cover with water and simmer very gently for about 1 hour, or until tender. Drain and set aside.

Heat the extra virgin olive oil in a deep heavy-based saucepan and sweat the smoky bacon or speck until it releases its fat, and therefore flavour. Add the onion, garlic, leek, celery, carrot and salt and sweat over low heat for 8 minutes, without colouring. Add the tomato paste, beans and shredded silverbeet and cook for a further 2–3 minutes. Add the tomatoes and their juices, the herbs and 2.5 litres (87 fl oz) water. Bring to the boil and gently simmer for 1 hour. Add the reserved cannellini beans and simmer for a further 5 minutes. Check the seasoning, adding more sea salt, if necessary, and freshly ground pepper.

Remember to remove the bay leaf before serving. Pour the soup into four bowls and add a fresh grind of pepper to each. Serve with freshly grated Parmesan or pesto. Serves 4

VARIATION

• Don't add quite so much water and braise the vegetables together. Instead of adding beans, toss in freshly cooked pasta, either penne or orecchiette, and grate some fresh Parmesan over it. This really is a fantastic pasta sauce.

A FEW THOUGHTS ON PUREED SOUPS

Puréed soups can be made out of just about anything. Vegetables, pulses, chicken and seafood are the usual suspects. They are usually thickened with the naturally occurring starch from the vegetables or ingredients such as bread or rice. Purées can be enriched by cream and, of course, a small amount of butter adds a tremendous amount of flavour. Don't forget that seasoning properly at the start helps to bring out the natural flavours in the vegetables and will give you a superior result. You can add lots of different vegetables to any one soup, but it is generally accepted that a couple of main players will result in a soup of greater definition. Let's face it, we want to be able to tell what the soup is, so it does need to reflect the flavour of the vegetables used.

The way to go about making one of these soups is to start with the usual flavourings — garlic, onion or leek, or perhaps all three. Next, add the spices if you are using them. Sweat them off with sea salt in a little extra virgin olive oil. Add the one or two main ingredients and cook for a few moments. Next, add stock or water and perhaps some fresh herbs and slowly cook at a bare simmer until the ingredients are soft. The amount of stock or water left, and the starchiness of the vegetables will determine the thickness of the soup. You can work that out as you go along. Most are pretty consistent. On that note, it is probably better to be thinning a soup than having it too watery to start with. You can add cream or butter, or both, or neither, if you are keeping an eye on your weight, but don't forget that fat is flavour. You can purée the soup completely or leave it a little bit on the rustic side. I recommend that you push the purée through a sieve if you want a smooth finish. Check the seasoning and always finish with fresh pepper. The soup can then be served with perhaps a drizzle of extra virgin olive oil or a sprinkle of cheese that has an affinity with the main ingredient. Pulses cooked and then finished in the soup will make the texture even creamier.

A FEW CLASSICS

- potato and leek
- pumpkin
- sweet potato
- red capsicum (pepper) and tomato
- tomato
- mushroom
- cauliflower and Gruyère
- asparagus
- Jerusalem artichoke
- globe artichoke
- fennel
- celeriac
- sugar snap pea
- pea

ITALIAN-STYLE ZUCCHINI AND PARMESAN SOUP

This is my favourite puréed soup; it always has a good clean taste of zucchini (courgette). Just make sure you wash them very well as sometimes they can be a little mouldy tasting. If they are not plump, shiny and firm, don't use them. Don't fall into that old trap of thinking soup is the garbage can of the kitchen. As with everything, fresh is best. This is one of those purées that you can leave with texture intact, or blend and sieve for a smooth finish.

INGREDIENTS

750 g (1 lb 10 oz) green zucchini (courgette), cut into 1 cm (^{1}/2 inch)
    thick pieces
extra virgin olive oil
6 garlic cloves, finely chopped
3 handfuls basil, chopped
sea salt
1.5 litres (52 fl oz/6 cups) chicken stock
125 ml (4 fl oz/^{1}/2 cup) pure (whipping) cream
40 g (1^1/2 oz/^{1}/3 cup) grated Parmesan, plus extra, to serve
freshly ground pepper

METHOD

Heat a little extra virgin olive oil in a heavy-based saucepan and add the zucchini, garlic, basil and a good pinch of sea salt. Cook over medium heat for about 10 minutes, stirring occasionally. The zucchini will start to soften.

Add the stock, bring to the boil, then reduce the heat to low and simmer, uncovered, for about 8 minutes. Pour the soup into a blender and pulse until well puréed, but not completely smooth, if you want the soup to have a bit of texture. Return the soup to the pan and stir in the cream and Parmesan.

Divide the soup among four bowls, give a good grind of fresh pepper and sprinkle with the extra grated Parmesan. Serves 4

VARIATIONS

• All soups, but especially the vegetable purée types, make delicious sauces and this one is no exception. I love it with whole roast chicken or barbecued chicken breast.

• This soup is also an absolute cracker served cold in summer. Not only is zucchini in peak season, but the flavour is enhanced by the chilling.

PASTA AND RICE

Pasta is one of the great staples of life, and although Dr Atkins may frown on it, it is important to note that a balanced diet with regular exercise is the best diet in the world, as it is a diet that you can live on for your entire life. It also allows the enjoyment of all the pleasures that one encounters in life, only not to excess. Moderation is the key word.

So that's enough about diets and here is a little bit more about pasta. The two ways you can have it are fresh or dried. After that, however, there are myriad different grains pasta can be made from and many different shapes and sizes it can come in. The ones I will concentrate on are either high-quality hard wheat (durum) dried pastas or fresh pastas that you can make yourself. I'm not a big fan of either mass-produced dried pastas that display little flavour, or fresh pastas that are carried in many delis and supermarkets that have the same issue. The reason is simple: pasta is not the vehicle for the sauce. Pasta is the hero, the sauce a friend, an added flavouring that supports the taste of the pasta. If you would not eat the pasta cooked and dressed only with extra virgin olive oil or a little melted butter, then don't eat it at all. The sauce shouldn't drown the pasta, but should be integrated into it. This is a relationship that needs to be a beautiful one and there must be harmony. So use good-quality pasta; if using cheese, freshly grate it; and if the sauce has a lovely balance, then you won't have a bowl of food, you will have a gorgeous dish that will rise above most of the pasta dishes cooked in cafés and restaurants.

Below is a recipe for making your own pasta. Try it once and you will make it many times; it is such a fun and gratifying thing to do. This is what the love and passion for cooking is all about. By making your own pasta, you can cut fettucine, tagliatelle or any shaped hand-cut pasta. You can even roll your pasta through the machine a little thicker and cut it at that point, to create a really chewy texture. All the sauces in this chapter will go with your home-made pasta.

With dried pastas, make sure when your packet of pasta tells you to cook it for 10 minutes, that you only cook for 8–9 minutes and then mix it through the sauce in the pan and serve. It is important for the pasta to have that slightly resistant feel to the tooth, to be 'al dente'. Fresh pasta will take only half that time, or less, to be cooked to this point. This is what really elevates a pasta dish to greatness. It must have texture.

When cooking pasta, the standard portion size is 100 g (3^1/2 oz) dried pasta for each serving or, if cooking fresh pasta, use a little more, say 125 g (4^1/2 oz) per person. You need less dried pasta as it absorbs more water during the cooking process and thus expands more.

BASIC PASTA

The simplest pasta is made from flour, eggs and salt. All fresh doughs are best hand-made; I find pasta made in a food processor of inferior quality, and no one has yet been able to convince me otherwise. The dough must not be overworked and it is essential that it is rested for at least 30 minutes before continuing with the recipe. Get ready to really fall in love with pasta making.

INGREDIENTS
 400 g (14 oz) high gluten flour
 a pinch of sea salt
 4 x 55 g (2 oz) eggs
 plain (all-purpose) flour

METHOD

Put the high gluten flour and sea salt on a clean bench and make a well in the middle. Break the eggs into the well and whisk with a fork. Start incorporating the flour as you whisk, bringing the flour from bottom to top and over on itself to form a rough dough.

Using your hands, start to bring the dough together, incorporating the flour with a metal pastry scraper or blunt knife. The dough will start to form a rough ball. Push it together with your hands and knead for 1–2 minutes, no longer. At this point the dough will feel quite hard, but as it rests the moisture will soften the flour. Wrap the dough in plastic wrap and allow to rest on the bench for at least 30 minutes before using. At this point it can be refrigerated, but I believe it is best used fresh.

Flatten the dough and roll out with a rolling pin to the width of the pasta machine. Working in small amounts (usually about 200 g (7 oz) at a time for a domestic machine), roll the dough through the machine on the widest setting. Feed it through in one motion to prevent 'stop' marks on the pasta.

Use a little plain flour to lightly flour one side of the rolled pasta and fold the sheet into three: fold the bottom third into the centre and then the top third over, with the floured side on the outside. Press the seam of the dough together and roll the pasta through the machine four or five times, lowering the setting each time you pass the pasta through. Feed the pasta seam side first into the rollers, and flour the sheet lightly between each roll. The pasta should be smooth and elastic. Allow the pasta sheets to dry slightly before cutting, but don't leave them too long or they will become too dry and brittle.

You have a choice of cutting the pasta with the pasta cutters provided with your machine, or rolling the sheets up gently and cutting the sheets with a sharp knife as thick as you like. At the restaurant we also roll the pasta down to the second-last setting and create a thicker noodle; this has great texture and works really well with the thick ragù-style sauces. You can also leave an egg out and replace its volume with different purées or additives like saffron water and squid ink. This is how we make coloured noodles. Use spinach for green, red capsicums (peppers) for red, and so on. It is also fun to take the eggs out and replace that volume with egg yolks (about three yolks to one egg); you get a really silky dough and therefore a delightfully silky pasta. This makes enough for 4 servings

SPAGHETTI WITH CHERRY TOMATO VINAIGRETTE

This is essentially a cherry tomato dressing on pasta and it works really well in summer. Which is exactly when tomatoes are at their peak. You can place the pasta in the bowl and dress with the vinaigrette, but it is much better to finish the sauce and the pasta together in the saucepan, as the sauce will adhere to the pasta and really improve the flavour.

INGREDIENTS

400 g (14 oz) dried spaghetti
150 ml (5 fl oz) extra virgin olive oil
3–4 small red chillies, deseeded and finely chopped
250 g (9 oz/1 punnet) sweet cherry tomatoes, quartered
60 ml (2 fl oz/$1/4$ cup) red wine vinegar
freshly ground pepper
2 tablespoons roughly chopped basil, plus extra
2 tablespoons roughly chopped flat-leaf (Italian) parsley, plus extra
Parmesan

METHOD

Bring a large saucepan of salted water to the boil and cook the pasta for about 8 minutes. Drain. Heat the extra virgin olive oil in a saucepan. Add the chilli and sauté for 30 seconds. Remove the pan from the heat and mix through the tomato, red wine vinegar and some freshly ground pepper. Add the basil and parsley and finally the pasta. Toss to mix through. Transfer to a serving bowl and finish with some freshly grated Parmesan and more fresh herbs. Serves 4

VARIATION

• Ronnie Di Stasio, a true friend and mentor of mine, cooks great pasta, and why not — he's Italian and runs one of Australia's best restaurants. Sam and I have sat in his kitchen watching as he cooks wonderful pasta that goes like this:

Take a bowl of cherry tomatoes, wash them and cut a little crisscross on the bottom. Heat some extra virgin olive oil in a large saucepan and cook some garlic, onion and a little chilli. Add sea salt and the tomatoes and cook for 10–15 minutes depending on their ripeness, or until the tomatoes start to split and emulsify with the oil or, as Ronnie puts it, they become creamy. At this stage the aroma of the sweet tomatoes will be quite heady. Add basil leaves and the spaghetti, which has been cooked with that crunch still evident, to the tomato sauce and toss the pan to mix. Add a good grind of pepper. Place in bowls and grate fresh Parmesan over, serve with a lovely glass of wine and some strong bread and you have a magnificent lunch.

SPAGHETTI ALLA CARBONARA

This is the one pasta that I never eat at a restaurant, mainly because it is so badly done most of the time. All too often, the golden rule of pasta as the hero and the sauce as support act is forgotten. The pasta drowns in a creamy sauce, and a real carbonara doesn't even have cream in it. Why do so many make that mistake? Carbonara is simply a sauce of egg and cheese that coats the spaghetti, with little flavour hits supplied by garlic and pancetta, and white wine adding the finishing touch. Nothing could be simpler, so why is it so hard? The reason is, there are a couple of vital steps that make the dish work really well, but you will see them in few cookbooks. Generally, the attitude is: this is so easy, everything just gets chucked together, then the pasta tossed in and Bob's your uncle. Well, that is the first mistake. The pancetta must be added after the egg and cheese mixture has coated the pasta so it will stick to each thread of spaghetti, not find its way to the bottom of the bowl, which generally happens when you toss them all together. The cheese is also important; you need about two-thirds Parmesan to one-third pecorino. The ratio of cheese, eggs and pasta is also important; you don't want lots of sauce left hanging around on the bottom of the bowl and you want the butter and oil you cook the bacon in to really flavour the dish, but not dominate it. So, once you have mastered all of these simple steps it's time to get in the zone and be a Zen master of carbonara. You will not fail as many have done before you.

INGREDIENTS

- 400 g (14 oz) dried spaghetti
- 60 ml (2 fl oz/$1/4$ cup) extra virgin olive oil
- 20 g ($3/4$ oz) unsalted butter
- 4 garlic cloves, peeled and crushed
- 100 g ($3^1/2$ oz) pancetta or smoky bacon, cut into lardons (batons)
- 80 ml ($2^1/2$ fl oz/$1/3$ cup) dry white wine
- 3 eggs
- 70 g ($2^1/2$ oz/$2/3$ cup) freshly grated Parmesan
- 30 g (1 oz/$1/3$ cup) freshly grated pecorino
- sea salt and freshly ground pepper

METHOD

Heat a small frying pan over medium heat. Add the extra virgin olive oil and the butter and cook until the butter foams. Add the garlic and cook until golden brown. Remove the garlic from the pan. Add the pancetta or smoky bacon to the pan and cook until it begins to turn crisp. Add the wine and cook for about 2 minutes, or until reduced by half, then remove the pan from the heat.

Bring a large saucepan of salted water to the boil. Add the spaghetti and cook for 8 minutes, or until al dente. Meanwhile, in a small bowl, lightly beat the eggs and add the cheese, sea salt and lots of freshly ground pepper. Heat the large bowl you are going to toss and serve the pasta in. Drain the pasta in a colander and quickly tip into the heated bowl, then add the egg and cheese mixture and toss together. Add the bacon mixture and toss again. Add some more freshly ground pepper.

Divide the pasta among four pasta bowls or, more traditionally, leave it in the large bowl, place in the middle of the table and go for it. Most importantly, this pasta waits for nothing; it must be served immediately if it is to be at its best — perhaps that is why it is so ordinary in restaurants. Serves 4

VARIATION

• This will sound really bizarre I know, because I have been telling you how to make the perfect carbonara, and saying that most get it wrong and the only good one is the one that you make yourself (unless you live in Italy). Well, if you promise not to tell anyone, this pasta is fantastic with either pan-fried prawns (shrimp) or pan-fried scallops: just toss them through when you add the bacon. I really will get into trouble saying this because Italians think cheese and seafood don't mix, so I have no idea what they think about seafood and eggs together. However, trust me, this really is delicious. I love living in the new world, no rules! That is, unless they come from me, of course.

SPAGHETTI VONGOLE

This is one of my very favourite pastas and one of the simplest seafood pasta dishes you can make. I love shelling the little clams (vongole) and slurping the pasta, coated with lots of garlic, parsley and clam juice. I had eaten this dish many times on the Italian Riviera, so when a supply of Tasmanian clams started to arrive in Sydney in the early 1990s I was more than pleased. I like to add some chilli flakes to give it a slight hit.

INGREDIENTS

400 g (14 oz) dried spaghetti
1 kg (2 lb 4 oz) live clams (vongole)
125 ml (4 fl oz/$1/2$ cup) extra virgin olive oil
4 garlic cloves, finely chopped
4 French shallots, finely chopped
$1/2$ teaspoon chilli flakes
60 ml (2 fl oz/$1/4$ cup) dry white wine
35 g ($1 1/4$ oz/$1/4$ bunch) flat-leaf (Italian) parsley, chopped
sea salt and freshly ground pepper

METHOD

Clean the clams by giving them a quick rinse in water. Heat the extra virgin olive oil in a large saucepan that has a tight-fitting lid. Add the garlic, shallots, chilli flakes and white wine and bring to the boil. Add the clams and cover. Steam over high heat for 3–4 minutes, shaking the pan, until the shells open. Meanwhile, cook the spaghetti in plenty of boiling salted water until al dente (about 8 minutes), then drain well.

Add the spaghetti and chopped parsley to the saucepan and toss through. Season with sea salt and freshly ground pepper and serve in four deep pasta bowls. Serves 4

VARIATIONS

• This combination of pasta, garlic, chilli and parsley works well with all seafood. You can replace the clams with mussels, pippies or fresh crab meat. Or, you can sauté some prawns (shrimp), rest them on a plate while you make the sauce, then, when ready, add the prawns and pasta and toss together.

• Another good combination is to sauté some squid, perhaps even adding a little squid ink, and toss through the pasta. The addition of the ink makes the pasta slightly black and accentuates the flavour of the sea.

SPAGHETTI WITH MUSSELS, TOMATO AND CHILLI

This is a nice preparation of a fresh tomato sauce mingled with the wonderful taste of the sea from the mussel juice. For this sauce I don't peel the tomatoes, as I like the tomato dice to stay separate throughout the dish. The large red chillies give the sauce body, but don't render it too hot as they are deseeded. This dish can be made even simpler by leaving the mussels in their shells; just add the mussels, tomato sauce and pasta, toss together and serve with bowls for the shells on the side.

INGREDIENTS

400 g (14 oz) dried spaghetti
125 ml (4 fl oz/$1/2$ cup) dry white wine
1 kg (2 lb 4 oz) large black mussels, scrubbed and debearded (page 106)
10 basil leaves, torn
freshly ground pepper

FOR THE TOMATO AND CHILLI SAUCE
2 garlic cloves, thinly sliced
10–12 large red chillies, deseeded and chopped
sea salt
60 ml (2 fl oz/$1/4$ cup) extra virgin olive oil
5 vine-ripened tomatoes, deseeded and chopped

METHOD

To make the sauce, sweat the garlic, chilli and a little sea salt in the extra virgin olive oil. Add the tomato, sauté for 2 minutes and remove from the heat.

Put the wine in a saucepan over medium heat and add the mussels. Cover and steam the mussels in the wine for 4–5 minutes until they open, then remove from the pan once opened. Strain off the mussel juice and reserve it. Remove the mussels from their shells and discard the shells. Add the mussels and the reserved juice to the tomato sauce and return the sauce to the heat.

Cook the spaghetti in plenty of boiling salted water for about 8 minutes, or until al dente. Drain and mix through the mussel and tomato sauce. Check the seasoning and add the basil. Finish with some freshly ground pepper. Spoon the sauce and pasta into four pasta bowls and serve immediately. Serves 4

VARIATIONS

• Make the sauce and add it to penne. As I said earlier, you could leave the mussels in their shells and make this a really easy dish.

• Sautéed prawns (shrimp) or scallops are also a nice variation, and you can, of course, have a combination of several different types of seafood.

BUCATINI ALL'AMATRICIANA

This is a classic pasta dish that is so easy to cook at home. It is usually made with guanciale, cured pig's jowl, which is not always easy to get. You can substitute pancetta, which works really well, or you can do as I like to do and make it with smoky bacon. It really comes to life (although it is not exactly authentic). As the dish also relies on the quality of the canned tomatoes used, make sure you get some sun-kissed Italian ones.

INGREDIENTS
400 g (14 oz) dried bucatini
125 ml (4 fl oz/$1/2$ cup) extra virgin olive oil
1 medium red onion, sliced
sea salt
2 garlic cloves, sliced
$1/2$ teaspoon chilli flakes
70 g ($2^1/2$ oz) smoky bacon, roughly chopped
400 g (14 oz) can Italian tomatoes, roughly chopped
pecorino and Parmesan
freshly ground pepper

METHOD
Heat a frying pan and add the extra virgin olive oil. Add the onion and some sea salt and fry for 1–2 minutes. Add the garlic, chilli and bacon and cook for 3–4 minutes. Add the tomato and simmer for a further 10 minutes.

Meanwhile, cook the pasta in plenty of boiling salted water for about 8 minutes until al dente. Drain well. Add the pasta to the sauce and toss the pan until it is well incorporated. Grate the pecorino and Parmesan over the pasta and toss again. Spoon the pasta into four deep pasta bowls and grate some more of both cheeses on top. Add a grind of pepper and serve immediately. Serves 4

VARIATIONS
• You can make a very simple version of this dish by omitting the bacon and cooking just the tomato sauce. Quite often at home I make tomato sauce with garlic, chilli and anchovy, and it is a more than delicious partner to the pasta.

• My favourite tomato-based sauce includes sausages and goes like this: Cut up 6 Italian-style pure pork sausages. Put in a pan some extra virgin olive oil, anchovies, sea salt, garlic and chilli flakes. Add the sausages and slowly cook for about 5 minutes. Add two 400 g (14 oz) cans chopped Italian tomatoes and stew gently for 1–1$1/2$ hours. The sausage will melt into the sauce. Simply toss with penne and add some freshly grated Parmesan. It is truly delicious.

TAGLIATELLE WITH TUNA AND TOMATO

This is a variation on spaghetti puttanesca. It is based on a simple tomato sauce and is great to put together when you haven't got much in the refrigerator. It is well worth always having a can of good-quality tomatoes, a can of tuna and some capers and anchovies around. These ingredients come together in minutes to make a truly delicious meal. I also like to do the unthinkable with this seafood dish: I grate cheese on it. This is enough to give an Italian a heart attack. But this is one of the great things about being Australian; I'm not bound by rules — I happen to really like cheese with this one, so I serve it that way. I haven't had complaints from any of my friends.

INGREDIENTS

400 g (14 oz) dried tagliatelle
125 ml (4 fl oz/^{1}/2 cup) extra virgin olive oil
6 anchovies
3 garlic cloves, thinly sliced
1 tablespoon salted baby capers, well rinsed and drained
^{1}/2 teaspoon chilli flakes
400 g (14 oz) can Italian tomatoes, roughly chopped
sea salt
185 g (6 oz) can tuna preserved in oil, drained
2 tablespoons roughly chopped flat-leaf (Italian) parsley
freshly ground pepper
Parmesan

METHOD

Put the extra virgin olive oil in a saucepan and heat. Add the anchovies and garlic and cook slowly until the anchovies start to melt into the oil. Add the capers, chilli, tomato and some sea salt and cook for about 10 minutes over medium heat. When the sauce has thickened and the flavours combined, break the tuna up and fold it through the sauce to warm.

Meanwhile, cook the pasta in plenty of boiling salted water for 7–8 minutes, or until al dente. Drain well and add to the sauce, tossing to mix. Add the parsley and a little freshly ground pepper. Spoon into four deep pasta bowls and finish with freshly grated Parmesan. Serve immediately. Serves 4

VARIATION

• This sauce is wonderful without the pasta; try serving it on soft polenta. It also makes a great starter to a meal, served over bruschetta.

BRAISED OCTOPUS WITH PENNE

I started making this sauce back in 1989 when my restaurant Rockpool first opened. I used to serve it with large hand-cut noodles that we made at the restaurant. Now, at home, I usually serve it with penne. It is very simple, as it only requires you to slowly braise the octopus. What I love about this is that the octopus actually takes on quite a meaty taste. That may sound strange but it tastes great.

INGREDIENTS

400 g (14 oz) dried penne
450 g (1 lb) baby octopus
125 ml (4 fl oz/$1/2$ cup) extra virgin olive oil
2 medium carrots, peeled and cut into 1 cm ($1/2$ inch) thick slices
1 medium leek, white part only, cut into 1 cm ($1/2$ inch) thick slices
1 medium brown onion, cut into 1 cm ($1/2$ inch) dice
3 garlic cloves, crushed
$1/2$ teaspoon chilli flakes
sea salt
125 ml (4 fl oz/$1/2$ cup) red wine vinegar
500 ml (17 fl oz/2 cups) red wine
1 teaspoon salted baby capers, well rinsed and drained
1 large handful flat-leaf (Italian) parsley
freshly ground pepper

METHOD

First clean the octopus. Cut the tentacles away from below the head, remove and discard the beak. Cut the tentacles in half. Cut the head just above the eyes, remove all the internal organs, then cut in half. Wash the octopus pieces thoroughly. Heat the extra virgin olive oil in a heavy-based saucepan and add the carrot, leek, onion, garlic, chilli flakes and a little sea salt, stirring for 5 minutes. Add the octopus and cook for a further 5 minutes.

Add the vinegar and wine and simmer slowly, uncovered, for 1 hour. Add the capers and parsley, fold through and check the seasoning. Meanwhile, cook the penne in plenty of boiling salted water for 8 minutes, or until al dente. Spoon the pasta into bowls and spoon the braised octopus over the top. Serves 4

VARIATION

• This is another classic dish that is fantastic on either soft polenta or spooned onto bruschetta as a starter. You could also use squid; braise it for the same amount of time, so it can take on the wine's flavour and become

DUCK RAGU WITH PAPPARDELLE PASTA

Pappardelle is the daddy of pastas. It is a thick-cut noodle that you can buy or very easily make yourself. I have had the duck ragù on and off the Qantas menus for a number of years. I love the rich taste of the duck with the firm-textured large noodle. This is bolognaise with a twist.

INGREDIENTS

400 g (14 oz) dried pappardelle
60 g (2^1/4 oz) unsalted butter
60 ml (2 fl oz/^{1}/4 cup) olive oil
2 rashers bacon, finely chopped
1 celery stalk, finely diced
1 carrot, peeled and finely diced
1 small brown onion, finely diced
3 garlic cloves, finely chopped
sea salt
450 g (1 lb) duck Marylands (thigh and leg attached), bones removed, flesh
  and skin finely chopped
500 ml (17 fl oz/2 cups) full-bodied red wine
60 ml (2 fl oz/^{1}/4 cup) good-quality sherry vinegar
2 x 400 g (14 oz) cans Italian tomatoes, chopped and juice reserved
freshly ground pepper
Parmesan

METHOD

Heat a large heavy-based saucepan over medium heat and add the butter and olive oil. Add the bacon, celery, carrot, onion, garlic and some sea salt, stir and sauté over low heat for 15 minutes. Increase the heat to high, add the duck and cook, stirring, for about 5 minutes, or until the meat is lightly browned. Add the wine and vinegar, reduce the heat and simmer, uncovered, for about 10 minutes, or until reduced by half.

Stir in the chopped tomatoes and their juice and simmer, covered, for about 20 minutes, or until the duck is completely tender and the sauce is rich. Check the seasoning and add a grind of pepper. Meanwhile, cook the noodles in a large saucepan of boiling salted water for about 8 minutes, or until al dente. Drain the noodles and add to the duck ragù. Gently toss together.

Using a pair of tongs, divide the noodles among four deep pasta bowls. Spoon the remaining sauce over and sprinkle over some shaved or grated Parmesan. Serves 4

VARIATIONS

• As this is essentially a bolognaise or ragù, you can substitute the duck for minced (ground) pork, veal or beef. Follow the recipe as it is and it will work perfectly. You can also use minced (ground) duck, just make sure the minced duck contains some skin.

• Remove the celery and carrot and add a couple more small onions and a few more garlic cloves. Add $1/2$ teaspoon chilli flakes and replace the bacon with chopped salami and the duck with some minced (ground) pork. This makes a fantastic sauce for spaghetti that reflects a southern Italian style of cooking.

FETTUCINE WITH TOASTED BREADCRUMBS

This is without a doubt the simplest pasta you could imagine. As a matter of fact, if someone told you that you were going to love a dish that was mainly pasta and breadcrumbs you would think that person was mad. However, having said that, I know that once you try this it will be on your menu forever. The herbs make a big impact, so make sure they are lovely and fresh. I can hear you saying, 'he said it's easy but it has lots of ingredients.' Well, it's easy because you blend it all together and toss it through the pasta, and what could be easier than that?

INGREDIENTS

400 g (14 oz) fettucine
175 g (6 oz/2 cups) fresh breadcrumbs (page 278)
250 ml (9 fl oz/1 cup) extra virgin olive oil
sea salt
10 g (1/4 oz/1 small bunch) tarragon
2 handfuls flat-leaf (Italian) parsley
1 garlic clove
2 tablespoons salted baby capers, well rinsed and drained
3 anchovies
60 ml (2 fl oz/1/4 cup) red wine vinegar
freshly ground pepper

METHOD

Preheat the oven to 200°C (400°F/Gas 6). Put the breadcrumbs on a roasting tray or baking sheet and toss with 2 tablespoons of the extra virgin olive oil and a little sea salt. Cook for 10–15 minutes, or until golden.

Put the herbs, garlic, capers, anchovies, vinegar and the remaining extra virgin olive oil in a food processor and blend until smooth. Correct the seasoning. Bring a large saucepan of salted water to the boil, cook the pasta for about 8 minutes, or until al dente, and drain.

Put the pasta, herb mixture and three-quarters of the breadcrumbs in a bowl and toss well to mix.

Divide the pasta among four pasta bowls and sprinkle with the remaining breadcrumbs. Give a good grind of pepper and serve immediately. Serves 4

VARIATION

• This sauce works well with spaghetti or penne, and you can also vary the herbs; mint makes a nice change. I also like to blend up a couple of fresh chillies.

PENNE WITH ZUCCHINI, BROCCOLINI AND CAULIFLOWER

This would be the most-consumed pasta dish in my house. We love the simple combination of well-braised vegetables in olive oil, anchovies and chilli, and, of course, a good whack of garlic. This dish is inspired by those countless numbers of pasta dishes the Italians create that rely on the wonderful natural flavour of vegetables. This is no place for crisp vegetables; they all need to be well braised (see page 284) and melting. Parmesan is, of course, the king when it comes to using with pasta but don't hesitate to use pecorino, as it is wonderful too.

INGREDIENTS

400 g (14 oz) dried penne
4 large zucchini (courgettes)
100 ml ($3^1/2$ fl oz) extra virgin olive oil, plus extra
12 anchovies
5 garlic cloves, sliced
$1/2$ teaspoon chilli flakes
sea salt
200 g (7 oz/1 bunch) broccolini, cut into 3 cm ($1^1/4$ inch) lengths
125 g ($4^1/2$ oz/1 cup) small cauliflower florets
Parmesan
freshly ground pepper

METHOD

Grate the zucchini and reserve. In a large frying pan, heat the extra virgin olive oil and add the anchovies, garlic, chilli flakes and sea salt. Fry for 3 minutes, stirring continuously, until the anchovies start to melt into the oil. Add the zucchini, broccolini and cauliflower and a dash more oil. Braise the vegetables slowly for about 20 minutes, or until the vegetables are well cooked and soft.

Meanwhile, bring a large saucepan of salted water to the boil. Add the pasta and cook for 8 minutes, or until al dente. Toss the pasta through the sauce and cook for a further minute. To serve, spoon into four deep pasta bowls. Grate Parmesan over the top and finish with a grind of fresh pepper. Serves 4

VARIATIONS

• You can make any number of pastas with vegetables. It is easy to cook either one type of vegetable or a combination, as above.

• I sometimes just slice the zucchini (courgette) rather than grate it, or sometimes use a combination of both, which gives the dish a rather nice textural variation.

• As well as zucchini, beans, peas, any squash, artichokes, fennel and broccoli work well. I always start off by melting the anchovies, garlic, sea salt and chilli flakes together, then I add the vegetables and braise away. This dish can also be served on bruschetta or over soft or grilled (broiled) polenta. It also makes a great vegetarian meal. Try it... the mature flavours of well-cooked vegetables are very seductive indeed.

• Sam and I love eating at the restaurant of a friend of mine, Armando Percuoco. Buon Ricordo is the best Italian place in Sydney, but the best thing about it is the level of hospitality that he and his staff always deliver, as well as the food being beautiful, of course. One of the dishes we really love is his pea pasta, and quite often on Sundays, when his restaurant is not open, this is what we will have. So, here is my version of Armando's dish — a humble imitation, but delicious all the same.

Slice a small amount of onion and dice some smoky bacon. Heat some extra virgin olive oil in a saucepan and add the onion, bacon, a little garlic, some chilli flakes and sea salt. Cook for 5 minutes, without colouring, then add some peas and a couple of glasses of water and stew for 40 minutes, adding more water, if necessary. When the peas are soft, sweet and washed out in colour, add some cooked penne or other pasta that is on hand, season with freshly ground pepper and grate some Parmesan over. It is simply a matter of then dressing the salad, cutting the bread and opening the wine, and you will be eating as well as you could wish.

RIGATONI WITH ARTICHOKES AND PANCETTA

This is another variation on vegetables braised in extra virgin olive oil. It has quite a component of pancetta, but you can also use smoky bacon or prosciutto. I love artichokes when they are in season and use them for all manner of things. The method we use to clean and cook them is on page 324. If you like, you can use drained good-quality preserved artichokes in olive oil (a 280 g/10 oz jar will do); just don't use the ones that come in brine, as they will be too strong for this dish.

INGREDIENTS

400 g (14 oz) dried rigatoni
150 ml (5 fl oz) extra virgin olive oil
100 g (3 1/2 oz/1 cup) roughly chopped pancetta
sea salt
1/2 small brown onion, finely sliced
2 garlic cloves, finely sliced
1/2 teaspoon chilli flakes
4 cooked globe artichokes, quartered and stem roughly sliced (page 324)
grated zest and juice of 1 lemon
Parmesan
2 tablespoons chopped flat-leaf (Italian) parsley
freshly ground pepper

METHOD

Heat a large frying pan and add the extra virgin olive oil. Add the pancetta and sea salt and fry for 2 minutes. Add the onion, garlic and chilli flakes. Reduce the heat a little and cook for about 10 minutes. Add the artichokes and lemon zest and cook for a further 3 minutes. Meanwhile, bring a large saucepan of heavily salted water to the boil. Cook the pasta for about 8 minutes, or until al dente. When the pasta is cooked, drain, add to the sauce and toss through.

Add the lemon juice, some freshly grated Parmesan, the chopped parsley and a grind of fresh pepper to the pasta and fold through. Spoon into four deep pasta bowls and serve immediately. Serves 4

GNOCCHI WITH BRAISED VEAL AND PARMESAN

This is a rich, melting braise of veal that is so simple to make, once you have it on, it cooks itself. The use of flour as a coating helps to colour the veal, and also slightly thicken the juices. This sauce goes well with any pasta, of course, not to mention soft polenta, or it can be thickened with a little more flour and it makes a truly fantastic pie filling (but that's another story). If you wish, you can purchase ready-made commercial gnocchi, but do me a favour, make this once and see how you like it, it is truly a lot of fun.

GNOCCHI
INGREDIENTS
> 750 g (1 lb 10 oz) bintje, pink eye or Yukon gold potatoes
> 2 egg yolks
> 60 g (2^{1}/4 oz/^{1}/2 cup) plain (all-purpose) flour, plus extra

METHOD
Put the whole unpeeled potatoes in a saucepan of boiling salted water and cook for about 25 minutes, or until tender. Drain. When cool enough to handle, but still warm, peel the potatoes and pass them through a food mill or potato ricer. Work quickly, as it is important for the potatoes to be warm when they go through the food mill.

Put the riced potatoes on a clean work surface and add the egg yolks and flour. Fold the mixture together, working towards the centre, gradually adding more flour if the mixture is too wet. Be careful not to add too much flour, as the more flour added the firmer the gnocchi will be. Once the gnocchi mixture has come together, allow it to rest for 5 minutes.

Cut the gnocchi mixture into four and on a lightly floured surface roll each piece into a sausage shape about 2 cm (^{3}/4 inch) in diameter, then cut into 3 cm (1^{1}/4 inch) pieces. Put the gnocchi on a wooden board or floured tray. At this stage the gnocchi can be covered with a damp tea towel and left for 1–2 hours. I generally don't bother to press each of the gnocchi pieces against my thumb and then use a fork to make the classic shape, although I think it works fine that way, particularly if you fry them.

TO COOK
Bring a large saucepan of salted water to the boil and add the gnocchi, being careful not to overcrowd the pan. When the gnocchi come to the surface, allow them to cook for 30 seconds longer, then remove. Drain well and serve immediately. Makes 500 g (1 lb 2 oz)

BRAISED VEAL

INGREDIENTS

800 g (1 lb 12 oz) veal shanks

30 g (1 oz/^{1}/4 cup) plain (all-purpose) flour

100 ml (3^1/2 fl oz) extra virgin olive oil, plus extra

60 g (2^1/4 oz) unsalted butter

1 brown onion, finely diced

1 leek, white part only, washed and finely diced

4 celery stalks, cut into 5 mm (^{1}/4 inch) thick diagonal slices

1 large carrot, halved and cut into 5 mm (^{1}/4 inch) thick diagonal slices

2 garlic cloves, finely chopped

2 fresh bay leaves or 1 dried bay leaf

375 ml (13 fl oz/1^1/2 cups) dry white wine

500 ml (17 fl oz/2 cups) chicken stock

400 g (14 oz) can Italian tomatoes, chopped

2 tablespoons roughly chopped flat-leaf (Italian) parsley

sea salt and freshly ground pepper

400 g (14 oz) gnocchi

Parmesan

METHOD

Dust the veal shanks in the flour and shake away any excess flour. Heat the extra virgin olive oil and the butter over medium to high heat in a frying pan large enough to hold the veal and vegetables quite snugly. Brown the veal in batches in the pan, then remove from the pan. Add a little extra oil to the pan and then add the onion, leek, celery, carrot and garlic. Cook over medium heat for 10 minutes, or until the vegetables are soft but not coloured. Add the bay leaf, white wine and chicken stock to the pan and stir to release any pieces stuck to the bottom of the pan. Add the chopped tomato and half the parsley.

Return the veal to the pan and cook, covered, stirring occasionally, for about 30 minutes. Remove the lid and cook for a further 1^1/2 hours, or until the veal is very tender and falling off the bones. Remove the veal with a slotted spoon and allow to cool slightly. When cool enough to handle, remove the meat from the bones and tear it into 2 cm (^{3}/4 inch) pieces. Return the veal to the sauce and check the seasoning. Keep the sauce warm while you cook the gnocchi.

Stir the remaining parsley into the veal sauce. Spoon the gnocchi into pasta bowls and top with the sauce. Grate Parmesan over and serve. Serves 4

VARIATION

• For added complexity, bring some butter and oil to the simmer and, just before it turns nut brown, add the cooked and drained gnocchi. Fry the gnocchi; it will colour and form a crisp crust. Put in the bowls and top with the sauce.

MACARONI CHEESE

This is such a great dish to make. You can have a mac and cheese (as the Americans say) all by itself or as a side dish. I once had a roasted guinea fowl for two with truffled macaroni cheese at the legendary Joel Robuchon restaurant in Paris — now that is pure indulgence — but there is nothing stopping you from roasting a chook and throwing together a side of macaroni cheese to go with it. The most important thing is to use good-quality cheese and bacon and you can't fail.

INGREDIENTS

400 g (14 oz) dried macaroni
extra virgin olive oil
3 rashers smoky bacon, diced
500 ml (17 fl oz/2 cups) pure (whipping) cream
125 g (4^1/$_2$ oz/1 cup) grated good-quality Cheddar
250 g (9 oz/2 cups) grated good-quality Gruyère
1 garlic clove, crushed
2 teaspoons Dijon mustard
^{1}/$_2$ teaspoon paprika
sea salt and freshly ground pepper
80 g (2^3/$_4$ oz/1 cup) fresh breadcrumbs (page 278)
100 g (3^1/$_2$ oz/1 cup) finely grated Parmesan

METHOD

Put the macaroni in a saucepan with plenty of boiling salted water and cook for 8–10 minutes, or until al dente. Drain and refresh in iced water, then drain again and pat dry with a cloth or tea towel. Heat a little extra virgin olive oil in a saucepan over medium heat. Add the bacon and cook until golden. Remove and drain on paper towels. Add the cream to the same pan, bring to the boil, then reduce the heat to a simmer. Add the cheeses, garlic, mustard and paprika and simmer for 5 minutes, stirring, until the cheese has melted and the sauce is thick. Season and add the macaroni and bacon. Preheat the grill (broiler).

Place the macaroni mixture into four bowls or one large gratin dish. Mix the breadcrumbs with a little oil. Sprinkle the Parmesan over the macaroni, then the breadcrumbs. Grill (broil) until golden brown and with a crisp crust. Serves 4

VARIATION

• Add flavourings to the macaroni: assorted mushrooms, sautéed in butter, oil and garlic, are nice; as is braised cabbage, mixed through and the whole thing gratinéed. Vary the cheeses — there are lots of choices and they are all yours.

RISOTTO

Risotto is one of those things that you can make at home better than most restaurants can. Unfortunately, because of either staff restraints or customer impatience, most restaurants and cafés seem hell bent on cooking the risotto first and then finishing it off when ordered. It is very hard to achieve the right texture using that method. However, at home you are in the driver's seat. You can stir and add stock on a gentle simmer and have everyone take a seat just as the rice is ready. A good risotto should pour into a bowl and be creamy as well as al dente. Like pasta, when it is ready — it is ready and waits for no one. There are a few important things to remember when making risotto: use arborio, carnaroli or nano rice; use fresh rice, so check the use-by date; and use a lively, clean tasting stock, as it is as influential as any of the main players in the final dish. Don't make the flavours too complicated, as one of the wonderful things about this dish is its simplicity. Make sure you reduce down all the wine before adding the stock, and don't have the stock boiling away on the back jet as it will reduce too much, just keep it warm, and simmer the rice gently, don't blow it apart. Other than that, all risotto making is simply a pleasurable experience.

PEA AND PUMPKIN RISOTTO

This is simple and gratifying. Peas and pumpkin have a special affinity. You can use chicken stock, and I do quite often; however, it is easier to boil the pumpkin in water and keep that to cook the risotto in. As with nearly all risottos the last lot of ingredients are added already cooked, and are simply reheated. Don't worry about using fresh peas. If they are not young and fresh, frozen peas are a good substitute, as I have said before. Conventional wisdom says to use a high-sided saucepan when making risotto. However, I like to use a frying pan to cook out the rice. Armando Percuoco from Buon Ricordo restaurant first showed me this method and, from that time onwards, I have always used it. I think it is because the rice is less likely to sink to the bottom and stick, while the top goes dry. Anyway it works for me, so try it, if you don't like it, simple, go back to the old way and follow the rest of the recipe.

INGREDIENTS

325 g (11^1/2 oz/1^1/2 cups) arborio rice

600 g (1 lb 5 oz) butternut pumpkin (squash), peeled, seeded and cut into 2 cm (^{3}/4 inch) dice

150 g (5^1/2 oz/1 cup) fresh or frozen peas

1.25 litres (44 fl oz/5 cups) pumpkin stock (see method) or chicken stock (page 384)

2 tablespoons extra virgin olive oil

^{1}/2 small red onion, finely diced

1 garlic clove, crushed

sea salt

60 ml (2 fl oz/^{1}/4 cup) dry white wine

25 g (1 oz/^{1}/4 cup) grated Parmesan, plus extra, to serve

60 g (2^1/4 oz) unsalted butter, at room temperature

3 tablespoons chopped flat-leaf (Italian) parsley

freshly ground pepper

METHOD

Put 1.75—2 litres (61—70 fl oz/7—8 cups) slightly salted water in a saucepan and add the pumpkin. Simmer for 10—15 minutes, or until just soft. Drain and reserve the water. (You should have about 1.25 litres (44 fl oz/5 cups) pumpkin-flavoured water to use as stock.) Set the cooked pumpkin aside.

Cook the peas in plenty of boiling salted water. If using fresh peas, cook for about 3 minutes; if using frozen, remove as soon as they rise to the surface. Refresh the peas in iced water and set aside.

Put the pumpkin or chicken stock in a saucepan on the back of the stove and keep warm. Heat the extra virgin olive oil in a large heavy-based frying pan. Add the onion, garlic and a little sea salt and sweat over low heat until soft. Add the rice and cook, stirring, for about 3 minutes, or until the starch starts to come out of the rice. The rice will start to stick and become opaque. Add the wine and simmer, stirring constantly, until the wine is completely absorbed. Add enough stock to cover the rice and simmer slowly, stirring occasionally. As the rice absorbs the stock, add more to keep it moist, but don't drown the rice. If you do, the risotto will lose some of its unctuous quality, but if it is too dry it will stick and retard the creaminess of the finished dish. It is important to continue stirring at this early stage or the rice will sink to the bottom and stick. After 15–18 minutes most of the stock should be used and the rice tender. At this point, add the reserved pumpkin and peas, along with the cheese, butter and any remaining stock. Cover, remove from the heat and rest for 2 minutes.

Remove the lid, stir in the parsley and check the seasoning. Spoon into four bowls and sprinkle with extra Parmesan. Serve immediately. Serves 4

VARIATIONS

Using this same formula, you can cook a variety of yummy risottos, just change the pumpkin and peas as the main players and use chicken stock. Below are a few classic flavour combinations. Remember, in the most part, you would cook whatever needs cooking beforehand and simply add to the risotto at the end, at room temperature or warm, to heat up before serving.

• Try pan-frying field mushrooms and then slicing them up; a little garlic during cooking helps bring out the flavour. You can add any type of mushroom you like and even add some dehydrated ones for a really big flavour. You can also grate some pecorino over instead of Parmesan, or use a combination; if you want some greens add cooked English spinach or peas.

• Pork seems to work well in this dish: fold through sliced ham or prosciutto at the end, or add pancetta at the start with the onion. Cooked sausage also goes well but make sure it's a pure pork style with good texture and flavour. Pan-fry or grill (broil) them, then slice. Add at the end with some fresh herbs.

• Of course, all manner of vegetables work well... sliced cooked green beans, spinach, nettle, radicchio that has been grilled (broiled), stewed red or yellow capsicums (peppers), braised red or green cabbage... the list goes on. (See page 284 for a detailed explanation of stewing and braising.)

SQUID INK PAELLA

I include this recipe because it really is very simple, but the taste and texture could only be described as divine. So, for divine, it is well worth lining up some ingredients, chucking them in a pan and letting them simmer away to find that 20 minutes later you have a slice of heaven.

First, I must point out that the word paella has nothing to do with the food, but is the pan itself. This follows along the theme of casserole, tagine and so on. However, once you get over that everything seems fine again. The paella pan is important because it is usually made with a flat bottom of thin metal and has a handle on each side. The thinness is needed so the rice gets a good crust on the bottom and the handles are usually there so you can remove the pan from the fire, which is how paella is normally cooked. They also help when the pans get bigger, as two people usually remove them from the heat. The pan is also always the right size for the amount of people you are cooking for, so they are available in sizes ranging from two to hundreds of servings. Having said that, it is possible to make a good paella using a heavy-based frying pan. The important thing is, once the stock and rice mix, don't stir — this is how the all-important crust forms — and it must be a frying pan, as the depth is important. You don't want the paella to be more than 4 cm (1 1/2 inches) deep. The other vital element is that the rice must be a short-grain rice like risotto rice. There are many brands grown in Spain. We use calasparra brand. Finally, you can make really good paella at home for the very same reason that you can make risotto of high quality. You can cook it to order and serve it when it is ready.

Don't worry about the squid overcooking. Because you braise it, it comes out really tender.

INGREDIENTS

450 g (1 lb/2 cups) paella rice

extra virgin olive oil

1 red onion, finely chopped

4 garlic cloves, finely chopped

sea salt

8 small squid tubes, cleaned and cut into 5 mm (^{1}/4 inch) thick slices (page 186)

1 teaspoon chilli flakes

1 teaspoon smoky hot paprika

2 tablespoons squid ink

1 tablespoon tomato paste (purée)

1.75 litres (61 fl oz/7 cups) chicken stock (page 384)

4 tablespoons chopped flat-leaf (Italian) parsley (optional)

freshly ground pepper

aïoli, to serve (page 352)

METHOD

Heat a paella pan or a heavy-based frying pan with a good dash of extra virgin olive oil added. Add the onion and garlic and a little sea salt and gently cook for a couple of minutes. Add the squid and stir through for 3–4 minutes. Add the chilli flakes, paprika, squid ink and tomato paste, stir through, then add the rice and chicken stock at the same time. Stir through and bring to a simmer, then leave to cook for 20 minutes, or until the liquid has evaporated. Remove the pan from the heat, cover with a tea towel to keep warm and allow to rest for 5 minutes.

Sprinkle with the parsley, if using, and give a good grind of pepper. Now, everyone will want a bit of the crust, so divide the paella into quarters, scoop out the rice and place on a plate. This should be done at the table by the host, which is you. Pass each of your guests a plate and serve with a big dollop of super garlicky aïoli — this is no time to hold back. Crusty bread, a killer green salad and a glass of red and your friends will think you're a magician. Serves 4

VARIATION

• Squid ink can be used for more than just paella. Black ink risotto is also a wonderful thing. Boil some ink in chicken stock, cook some smoky bacon with a little chopped onion, add a few chilli flakes and some squid at the beginning of the risotto and some more squid just before it's ready. This is truly one of my favourite risottos.

SEAFOOD

My father always loved fishing. He would spend hours out in the boat or standing on the beach just fishing. And, although he would more often than not have a good catch, he would sometimes come home with nothing. This phenomenon didn't seem to diminish the experience for him, indeed, I think it was the fishing more than the fish that Dad enjoyed. Those hours of tranquillity spent outside with nature and the lure of a sport that not only relaxed him, but nine times out of ten helped feed the family, was, I think, what my father most enjoyed in his life (apart from loving his wife and children, of course).

The one thing that Dad never tried was fly-fishing. The last time I was in New Zealand I went fly-fishing for trout and really loved it. I know that Dad would have loved it too, standing in those crystal clear cool rivers hunting the clever trout, surrounded by some of the best nature in the world. However, we did do a lot of things together that certainly did have that great combination of sport, fun and nature. We would drift and fish for blackfish with rods and floats, the next morning we would surface fish for garfish, then at night we'd go hunting for prawns (shrimp) and the very next afternoon we'd be beach fishing for whiting; all of this done on holidays down the south coast about three hours out of Sydney. We also went up the north coast, fishing at Yamba for snapper. A couple of holidays we went to the Great Barrier Reef and fished for reef fish. At home Dad would head out on the weekends, chasing eddies in the tide to get some good flathead and we'd gather oysters off the rocks: yes, back in those days you wouldn't risk death doing that. He'd go crabbing in Sydney for blue swimmer, or head up the coast for mud crabs. We really did get to eat a wonderful array of fresh seafood. I guess it was that background that made me totally comfortable with fish at a time when seafood was not often on the table in many Australian homes.

In Australia there has always been a certain reluctance, even suspicion, about fish, which many are getting over only now. One reason for this reluctance is that, of all the proteins we eat, seafood is the most fragile, with a very short shelf life. Fortunately, more and more people are now realizing that good-quality seafood can be delivered fresh to their local supermarkets and markets. You just need to trust your local supplier and start eating more seafood to discover a great treasure trove of delicious food out there. Seafood is an excellent source of omega-3 fatty acids, vitamins and minerals, and, along with fresh fruit, vegetables and meat, makes up a balanced diet.

I have to say that if you take the freshest seafood, treat it well and cook it well, then you will have a fantastic taste experience. The wonderful thing about seafood is the great joy that can come of the simplest preparations. So, rather than just give you a set of recipes to blindly follow, I am also going to tell you how to create for yourself the freshest and best seafood dishes. That means you will work for it. I will tell you how to fillet a fish, and why that is important, and I will tell you how to steam a mud crab and pick the flesh, and so on. In most cases, if you can't get the fish I'm talking about then by all means substitute it with one that works for you and, of course, that is available to you. So you may buy crab meat, or fish already filleted, and you may even use frozen seafood (if it has been caught and handled well and frozen by mechanical freezing that brings the temperature down so quickly that ice doesn't form in the cells of the fish before it freezes). But I could not in all good conscience fail to tell you that if you put a bit of effort in, your reward will be tenfold.

Something to be aware of is that with the right knowledge and skills, you will be able to cook fish at home better than most restaurants can. This is partly because most restaurants find it cheaper to buy in already filleted fish rather than employ someone to expressly handle the fish. I will discuss the pros and cons of filleting your own fish a bit later, but you'll see that there are a lot of pros.

A BRIEF WORD ON THE STATE OF THE WORLD'S SEAFOOD

The world's seafood is a diminishing resource and it needs to be valued more. There is an urgent need for everyone to develop a better understanding of where it comes from, what is happening to it and whether it is farmed or wild-caught.

Since the middle of the twentieth century, when large vessel net fisheries emerged, the world's wild fish stocks have been steadily depleted. This is occurring at a rate that is not only alarming, but is also going to have irreversible consequences, if we don't take the time to see how we might develop sustainable fisheries based on best-practice wild-caught fishing and aquaculture. The Marine Stewardship Council, an international non-profit, independent charity, has been working since 1997 to do exactly that: investigate and award fisheries the right to brand the MSC label on their products as a result of the fisheries' good sustainability practices. This is not only important, it is imperative. The Western Australian rock lobster fishery was the first to be awarded this certificate. It would be really fantastic if, as consumers, we started a campaign to encourage fish markets, retailers and supermarkets around the world to promote and support these sustainable fisheries that are now emerging. If we couple that with making sure that the push to aquaculture is done with a thought for the environment, and that the quality and integrity of the product is intact, then we will be able to enjoy great seafood for a long time to come. Don't take it for granted, however — at the moment the world is at a point where the balancing act is not looking as good as it should. Let's do what we can for the future and our children.

HANDLING OF SEAFOOD

Fish are cold-blooded creatures. This means that the enzymes and bacteria that are present in them start breaking down the flesh at much lower temperatures than is the case in warm-blooded animals. For this reason, cold chain management is the most important consideration when it comes to handling seafood. At Rockpool, we use fishermen who follow a traditional Japanese 'stress minimizing catch methodology'. Briefly, the fish are line caught, immediately brain spiked (*ikijimi* killed) and ice slurried. This reduces the body temperature rapidly and brings on rigor mortis. As a result the fish is less damaged by stress, and the best flavour and texture are preserved. All our fish come in whole under ice and are dry filleted each day. The fillets are then kept in a cool room until needed. Thus we maintain total control of the cold chain process.

Like meat and poultry, fish is about seventy per cent water. The rest is made up of protein, fats, minerals and vitamins. The big difference is the lack of connective tissue. This can be a positive, and a negative. The positive is that fish is naturally tender — you don't have to break down the connective tissue and render it tender. The bad news is that it is very easy to overcook fish and have it dry or even falling apart. Overcooking is the single biggest problem to be aware of but, if you look after your fish and cook it perfectly, you will have a very good chance of cooking seafood better than the average restaurant; you certainly don't have the time pressures that many professional cooks have on them. Fish have varying degrees of fat, or oil content, and this will determine how you cook the fish. Generally speaking, the oily fish are known as round fish and the rest are fairly lean, which means they dry out very easily.

SELECTING SEAFOOD

When buying fish it is important to select the most vibrant, handsome-looking specimen you can. It is easier to tell if a fish is fresh by looking at a whole fish: the eyes should be clear and shiny and it will smell of the sea — a sweet fresh smell, not a fishy one. The gills should be bright red, not brown or grey, and the texture firm. Run your finger along the flesh from the back of the head to just past the fin (the shoulder of the fish); even if the fish is a soft-fleshed fish it will quickly spring back to shape. The scales should be shiny and tight, not loose and falling off. Shellfish should be either live, or look bright and vibrant if dead. Seafood such as oysters, mussels and clams (vongole) should be heavy and full of salt water. Squid and octopus should be vibrantly coloured and shiny. When buying, either take an esky with an ice brick to carry the seafood home in or make the trip quickly. Lastly, don't buy too far in advance; you don't want seafood kept in the refrigerator for more than two days.

FILLETING WHOLE FISH

I completely understand people's reluctance to fillet fish at home. It is messier than just bringing fillets home, and you have to get rid of the waste, which will smell the kitchen out if you accidentally leave a little scrap hidden away somewhere. So you do have to be diligent when cleaning! By all means purchase fillets and follow the recipes, or just be inspired by them, if that is what you are more comfortable with. But let's get back to the reasons why it is better to fillet your own fish (assuming that it has been well looked after before you get it). One, you can tell very easily whether the fish is fresh. Two, you can make sure you dry fillet it. By this I mean the opposite to wet filleting, which is what ninety-nine per cent of all fish that is filleted goes through. Those fish are rinsed in fresh water as they are being filleted, which makes the process quick and easy. But I hate standing at the fish market watching beautiful fish being sloshed through tubs of running water. Once a fish is dead it shouldn't see water again; the fresh water will only dilute the oils that give the fish its flavour, and you will end up compromising on flavour and texture. It is a great shame, but you can see fish fillets in bags with juice at the bottom heading into restaurants every day, all over the world. Wouldn't it be great if everyone looked after fish the way it should be?

To dry fillet you need a bit of time, a board and a damp cloth or some heavy paper towels that can be thrown away afterwards. First, scale the fish. Lay it on a board and draw the back of a large knife or scaling tool against the scales from tail to head. If you are serving the fish whole or it is a large fish that you want to serve with the skin on, it is essential that you remove all the scales. If you are going to skin the fish, then just remove the scales around the perimeter of the fish so your knife doesn't slip when you cut the fish. Scaling can be a messy job, so keep using your damp cloth or paper towels to wipe the board clean, removing the scales and sea slime as it gets in your way. Alternatively, you could also ask your fishmonger to scale the fish and wipe it (not wash it) for you. I remember, as a young kid, Dad would always scale the fish on the beach or in the river water and do the filleting at home.

To gut and fillet the fish, put it on the chopping board and cut the belly open. Remove the gut and discard. Make a cut behind the head and cut a line from the back of the head to the tail, then down the other side from the stomach to the tail. Depending on how big the fish is, slide your knife along the backbone all the way to the tail or, if large, cut to either side of the backbone and then work your knife over the backbone to release the fillet. Turn the fish over and repeat the process. Remember, use your damp cloth as needed; don't wash the fillet in water.

SEAFOOD IN ITS NATURAL STATE

Seafood has a delicate taste and texture, and there is some seafood that doesn't need cooking at all. The one that comes to mind first is the oyster. It is a great shame that up until the last fifteen years or so, oysters in Australia have been very badly treated: by that I mean always sold opened. However, it is now possible to get freshly shucked oysters in many good restaurants. It would be great if that occurred everywhere, but you never know, perhaps in time. There is a world of difference between an oyster that has been opened, washed and turned, placed between sheets of paper and sold, and one that is alive and has had the lid knocked off just prior to serving, with all of its brine water surrounding it. This is the oyster that needs nothing, save a squeeze of lemon, and the purists would even scoff at that. To my mind, a freshly shucked oyster, with thin rye bread spread with good-quality butter, is one of the most satisfying things you can eat. If you wish, you may make a little red wine vinegar and French shallot dressing or perhaps replace the red wine vinegar with a little champagne vinegar, but that is about where it ends (I do like oysters fried when they are quite large). Apart from that, just concentrate on getting the opening technique down pat. It really is quite easy, especially if you use a purpose-designed knife for the job. Fresh oysters make a sophisticated little canapé and are a nice way to start off a Sunday lunch party — opening oysters as your guests mill around the kitchen with a cool glass of white wine in hand. Three to four oysters per person is a good number; there is no need to go overboard.

HOW TO SHUCK AN OYSTER — Have ready an oyster knife and a tea towel. Fold a tea towel in one hand and, using the tea towel, hold the oyster firmly on a wooden board or clean work surface with the pointy end facing toward you. Take the oyster knife and gently wedge it into the middle of the two shells. Once you've got the oyster knife in, turn the knife on its side — the shell will lift and the muscle that holds the shell shut will snap. Slide the knife up and cut the muscle from the shell and your oyster is ready to serve. You can also cut the muscle on the underside and turn the oyster over for easier eating, if you wish, which can be a good idea if guests are standing up.

Raw shellfish makes beautiful ceviche. This is a South American dish, which relies on lime juice to 'cook' the seafood. Many shellfish are good this way: scallops, squid, lobster, scampi, prawns (shrimp) — the list could go on. All you need to do is put your shellfish, a single variety or a mixture, in a bowl, add sea salt and the juice of a couple of limes and allow to stand for a few minutes. Add diced red and green capsicums (peppers), as much fresh chilli as you like (I like it hot), fresh coriander (cilantro) leaves, diced tomatoes, slices of ripe avocado and some extra virgin olive oil. Give a really good grind of fresh pepper, spoon the ceviche into martini glasses (this looks really fabulous) and serve.

If you like raw fish, then the best way to serve it in a Mediterranean style is to keep it simple. I love to serve very fresh raw tuna, hiramasa kingfish, bonito or snapper, but use whatever fish you like, a single variety or in combination. You could serve a bit of squid or a superbly fresh scallop, or something of that nature. I cut slices of the fish and lay them out on a plate, drizzle them with a really good-quality extra virgin olive oil, something with a nice pepperiness to it, and then drop bits of preserved lemon salsa on top. Just as I'm about to serve it, I squeeze lemon juice over and add a little sea salt. Don't crush the flakes, just drop them on — they will add nice texture to a really simple dish.

We are lucky here in Australia to have such a great crab as the mud crab. It has a flavour and texture that really sets it apart from most crabs I have had in the world (although I haven't met a crab I didn't like). It is beautiful hot, stir-fried or steamed with any number of simple sauces, but it is at its best when part of a salad, or just served with a dressing. I mention it here because steaming crab preserves the flavour of the crab in its most natural form. If you make the effort to steam and pick your own mud crab, then serve it with a little aïoli or dressing; you will make a very simple dish seem like you care so much for your guests and you do. What could be more loving than taking a live mud crab, despatching it, steaming it and picking it for your friends? It will be the best simple starter they have ever tried.

A THOUGHT ON COOKING FISH

No matter how you decide to cook your fish you need to remember one thing: when you remove your fish from the heat source it continues to cook. If the fish is cooked perfectly in the pan or oven, then you will have sadly overcooked it by the time you start to eat it. Think residual heat: the hotter your cooking method the more the fish will cook on resting. There is a game you can play in your mind: the fish is cooking, and as it cooks the heat will penetrate from both sides and meet in the middle (even if cooking one side at a time). Now, as the 'doneness' of the fish is indicated by the heat meeting in the middle of the fish, the fish needs to be removed from the heat when it is three-quarters of the way cooked through on each side. Imagine: as the waiter picks up the fish the two sides are getting closer and closer, as the waiter puts it down they are starting to join, and as the customer plunges the fork into the fish they meet, with just enough heat for them to join. I get my staff to visualize the gentle embrace of the two sides at the moment of being perfectly cooked. The important thing is to really get a sense for what you think would be perfect. Tiger Woods imagines every ball before he plays it, and most times it goes where he wants. It's time for you to concentrate on perfect fish cookery. May the force be with you!

Sounds silly but it's not. If you are cooking oily fish like tuna or salmon, which you would want to cook rare, just imagine a nice warm strip of flesh running through the centre. It is quite good to think about what is happening to all the things you cook and, like Tiger, you will get it right most of the time. Having said that, there is another way to tell when a larger piece of fish is cooked — simply insert a digital thermometer into the fish and when it reads 48–50°C (118–122°F), the fish will be cooked.

Don't underestimate the power of sea salt, freshly ground pepper and lemon juice when cooking fish. These three things in concert make fresh seafood taste wonderful. You are lucky as the home cook, as you can present fish in its purest form. For many restaurants there is a need to embellish, as customers feel they need more done to seafood than they would do at home, when really, the only pressure should be to find the freshest seafood possible and cook it to the moment of perfection.

This chapter has around thirty seafood recipes that are the building blocks to hundreds of dishes. Just use good cooking technique from this chapter and build lots of different dishes using the pasta, salad, soup, vegetable accompaniments and sauce chapters. I have made various suggestions for each recipe, so use the index, but in reality there are many options; just remember to cook and eat well with the season.

STEAMING

Cooking seafood in the gentle moist heat of steam is a wonderful thing. It retains the fresh, sweet flavour of the sea and doesn't dry the fish out as easily as cooking over high heat does. Steaming relies on the natural flavour of the fish, so fresh is paramount. But don't think of the steamer as a place where you just put the fish and let the steam do its work. You can add lots of different flavours to the steaming water, or steam in a broth, or lay herbs and lemon slices under the fish or shellfish to help flavour it and keep it extra moist. It is also quite a good idea to steam large pieces of fish with the lid half or completely off, as this lowers the temperature and slows the rate of cooking to accommodate the larger size. There are some nice stainless steel steamers on the market, but I have always been fond of the bamboo ones you can buy in Chinatown. They are cheap and look good and you can bring them straight to the table if you like. Just make sure you have a saucepan the right size for the steamer, particularly if cooking with gas: if the steamer extends over the side of the pan it can catch fire. Always make sure you have enough water in the saucepan, as there is nothing worse than the pan boiling dry and the fish getting a smoky taste. If I had a dollar for every time that had happened in the old days at Rockpool I'd probably be retired by now. One very important point — don't forget that water is a good conductor. If you put your arm into an oven at 200°C (400°F) or above, you don't burn yourself immediately, as air is a bad conductor. However, if you lift the lid on a steamer and the steam goes up your arm you will get a nasty burn, even though the steam is only 100°C (212°F). That is what I mean by steam being a good conductor. So, take care and always allow the steam to dissipate into the air before you stick your nose in.

Steaming is a wonderful way to cook whole fish. We have all had steamed whole fish at Chinese restaurants, served with chilli, ginger and shallots or perhaps mushroom soy. So think along the same lines, but add Mediterranean flavours. Pour vinaigrettes or salsas (there are lots in the sauce section) over the fish when it comes out of the steamer and serve it with a group of interesting side salads. And, just as you would share courses when in Chinatown, you could also serve a tagine or some meat from the barbecue. You would be creating your own shared banquet, which is a lovely way to eat, and the way I eat most times I have guests. A last tip: score the whole fish down to the bone near the head and then put about four more cuts in it, at equal distances, just not so deep, along its length. This will do two things. Firstly, it will help the fish cook more evenly, as the fish is fatter at the head than at the tail, and secondly, it will allow you to easily see when it is cooked.

STEAMED BLUE EYE FILLETS ON A BED OF THYME WITH ANCHOVY BUTTER

This fish has got me into so much trouble. It is one of the classic examples of a fish that is known by a number of names depending on where you live (and doesn't everyone think they're right). Now, its correct name is blue eye trevalla (no relation to trevallies), but in most Australian states it has been known for some time as deep sea trevalla. It is also known as big eye, sea trevalla and, in my home state of New South Wales, as blue eye cod. When there was a push for all states in Australia to call the fish by the same name, it was decided that it should be blue eye trevalla. However, I keep getting letters saying this is not a cod, how dare you call it that and so on. Well, it is perfectly acceptable to market blue eye trevalla as blue eye cod in New South Wales, as it has been known thus for many years. Anyway, whatever you call this magnificent fish it is wonderful eating, as it is quite oily for a white-fleshed fish, which translates as very moist, and has a mild, sweet flavour and a beautiful firm texture. If you can't get blue eye, cod, turbot or even large snapper fillets would be suitable alternatives. So have fun steaming, barbecuing, pan-frying and roasting this fish.

This dish will fill the house with the heady smell of fresh herbs. They flavour the fish and make it delicious. It is also very simple to make; all that is needed is lots of herbs at the bottom of the steamer and the rest is left to the vapours.

INGREDIENTS

4 x 175 g (6 oz) blue eye fillets
10 fresh bay leaves
10 g (^{1}/4 oz/^{1}/2 bunch) thyme
2 limes, one thinly sliced, the other quartered
sea salt
4 x 1 cm (^{1}/2 inch) thick slices anchovy butter (page 358)
freshly ground pepper

METHOD

Fill a saucepan that is a suitable size for your steamer with water and bring to the boil. Check that the steamer has plenty of room for the four fillets to sit in one layer; you don't want to overcrowd the steamer or have the fish touching. Sprinkle the herbs over the bottom of the steamer and lay the lime slices over. Season the fillets with sea salt and put on top of the lime slices. Put the steamer on the saucepan and steam for 6–7 minutes. Just before the fish is cooked, place a slice of anchovy butter on top of each fillet, so that it will melt slightly. Remove the steamer from the heat.

With a fish lifter, carefully lift each fish fillet and place on a large white plate, squeeze over a lime quarter and give a good grind of fresh pepper. Serve immediately. Serves 4

ACCOMPANIMENTS

• Steamed greens and boiled pink eye potatoes are perfect with this dish, and are very healthy. You could also serve the fish with steamed asparagus and soft polenta, replacing the anchovy butter with herb butter.

• Boiled broccolini with lots of freshly squeezed lemon juice, potato purée and sauce Vierge spooned over the top of the fish would be great.

• Place some braised fennel on the plates, lay the steamed blue eye on top and add a dollop of aïoli; if you like it spicy, add harissa mayonnaise or tomato, almond and chilli salsa. These are just a few of the combinations possible.

THE FOOD I LOVE

STEAMED SNAPPER FILLETS WITH MOROCCAN FLAVOURS

Snapper is caught along most of the Australian coastline and is one of Australia's most popular eating fish. In restaurants, it is served whole, filleted and as cutlets: the small fish are called baby snappers or squires and would normally be served whole; the larger fish, which grow to weigh 4–5 kg (8 lb 8 oz–11 lb), would be filleted. I like to serve steaks from the larger fish. I love their mild flavour and medium to firm texture, but watch out: they have very little fat so will overcook easily. Snapper skin is quite delicious, particularly if slowly pan-fried skin side down and just turned over briefly to finish off. If you like to make fish stock (I don't), these fish are the very best at making an intense and clear stock. As with all large fish, if you catch or buy one, don't underestimate the reward of removing the cheeks and pan-frying them. They are quite exquisite.

This following dish is a sort of steamed tagine. It is fragrant and very full of flavour and is wonderful served with either couscous or rice. It is important to have a steamer large enough that it can hold a decent-sized bowl, which will contain both the fish and broth, or you can cook this dish in two bowls in two steamer baskets (or one large steamer with two trays); just juggle the steamer baskets or trays about halfway through cooking. If you wish, you could add some vegetables to the broth in advance and just cook them for 30–60 minutes, depending on what type they are. I like to just steam the fish and serve it with rice and Moroccan eggplant salad, which makes for a really easy, clean, flavoursome meal. I use large snapper steaks for this dish, which weigh about 200 g (7 oz) each. One reason for this is that it is easier to fit steaks in the steamer, rather than a long thin fillet, and the other reason is that they have a much flakier texture, which I like.

INGREDIENTS

4 x 200 g (7 oz) pieces snapper steak

125 ml (4 fl oz/$1/2$ cup) chermoula (page 372)

juice of 1 lemon

2 tablespoons honey

sea salt

1 preserved lemon, quartered, pith removed and rind finely sliced (page 380)

2 tablespoons chopped coriander (cilantro) leaves

METHOD

In a stainless steel bowl, mix the fish with the chermoula and leave to marinate for 1 hour. Transfer the fish to a shallow ceramic bowl for steaming (a large pasta bowl is often a good size for this job). Using the bowl containing any remaining chermoula, add the lemon juice, honey, some sea salt and 125 ml (4 fl oz/$1/2$ cup) water and mix. Pour the mixture over the fish and top with the preserved lemon rind. Place the bowl in the steamer or on the steamer tray and place over a wok or saucepan of boiling water. Cover tightly and steam for about 10–12 minutes. A flat fillet will only take 4–5 minutes. The timing will vary depending on the size of the fish pieces and the depth of the bowl the fish is sitting in. Remove the steamer from the heat.

Carefully remove each portion of fish with a fish lifter and place in white bowls. Spoon the sauce left in the bowl over the fish. Sprinkle with the coriander leaves and serve immediately. Serves 4

ACCOMPANIMENTS

• Couscous and broccolini with garlic and chilli would be great to serve with this dish, with a teaspoon of preserved lemon salsa dolloped on top of each fish just before serving. If you like it really hot, you may want to serve a little of any one of the harissas on the side.

• Saffron or plain rice pilaf is perfect with this dish, as are braised vegetables such as peas, Roman (flat) beans and fennel.

FOLLOWING PAGES steamed snapper fillets with moroccan flavours, left, and steamed mud crab, right

STEAMED MUD CRAB

This is my favourite dish in the world. It's really last supper material for me. I find these creatures to be the best tasting crab in the world; they have a wonderful sweet flavour, are very moist and have a firm texture. I love eating them at Chinese restaurants, either wok-fried with salt and pepper or steamed with black bean and chilli. They are, however, at their best when simply steamed and dressed with a good oil and lemon juice. You can steam the crab in Chinese bamboo steamer baskets; a 26 cm (10$^{1/2}$ inch) steamer fits one crab perfectly. I find this the easiest way to steam full stop. You can set the steamer over a wok filled with water or a saucepan of the same diameter. So if you want to treat your friends, do the following.

Buy live mud crabs, calculating between 800 g and 1 kg (1 lb 12 oz and 2 lb 4 oz) of crab per person for a main course — the recovery rate of meat to shell is fairly low, about twenty-five per cent.

Remove any wrapping (not the string) from your crab. Place your crabs in a freezer. This puts them to sleep, and is the most humane way of dealing with them. It may take 2$^{1/2}$ hours. When ready, cut off the string and put a plate with the first steamer basket on it near the sink. Wear an apron and gloves, if you wish. Take your first crab and turn it upside down in the sink — juice will come out and it is best to do this in a sink. Pull the 'v' shaped flap at the back up and carefully lift the whole top shell off. Remove the lungs by scraping them off with a spoon or knife or fingers, and under running water wash out the guts and wash the head. It is very important to remove all the lungs and clean the head thoroughly. Snap off the flap. Chop the crab in half by placing the base of a large chef's knife against the crab and pressing down on the knife with the palm of your hand, cutting firmly through the crab. When done, clean out any remaining internal organs. Use the same cutting action to cut each half in two, cutting between the claw and the legs.

With the back of a knife, meat mallet or a knife steel, crack the claws a couple of times from the nippers down to the elbow and what I call the forearm. Remove any excess cartilage from around the head. Put the crab and head in a steamer basket and repeat the process with the rest of the crabs. As you prepare each crab, add another basket to the pile of steamer baskets. This way, any juices are caught on the plate at the bottom, rather than on the bench or around the kitchen, which helps ensure a crab-smelling-free zone.

Put the stack of baskets containing the crabs over a saucepan of boiling water and steam for about 6–8 minutes, juggling the baskets from top to bottom to help them cook evenly. When done, the flesh will be white — check at the thickest part of the claw. Then, one at a time, place the crabs in a stainless steel bowl or other vessel for tossing. Drizzle over extra virgin olive oil and add the juice of 1 lemon, a good sprinkle of sea salt and a grind of fresh pepper. Add 1 small handful flat-leaf (Italian) parsley, finely shredded if you can be bothered. Toss and place the crab in a serving bowl, with the head back on top. Repeat with the other crabs and serve immediately. Each combatant will have a handsome-looking crab in front of them. They will also need a small finger bowl, a good strong napkin, possibly a bib (recommended for all those wearing white) and, of course, a large glass of riesling. Expect the conversation to dim somewhat for at least half an hour.

HOW TO PICK OUT CRAB MEAT — It is worth investing in some crab forks to make it easy for your guests to pick the meat easily from the crab shell. These are long metal utensils with a small two-pronged fork at one end and a small rounded spoon at the other end. These forks are great for picking into every part of the crab, especially the legs. As the hardest parts of the shell are already cracked, getting to the flesh should be easy. Crab legs are small and usually soft enough to crack in half with your hands. When picking out the flesh some parts will come away easily in large chunks and other pieces will require a bit more digging. Be careful to remove the cartilage inside the crab as you go.

FOLLOWING PAGES steamed mud crab, served with aïoli (page 352) 163

ROASTING

There is a fair bit of confusion when this term is used in relation to fish. Some people use the word baking, while lots of fish in restaurants are actually pan-fried and finished in the oven and called roasted or pan-roasted. In this section we will cook fish both ways: straight into the oven and started on top of the stove. Be careful when roasting fish, as they have a delicate, lean flesh — we don't want the oven's fierce dry heat to destroy the texture. For this reason make sure you preheat your oven; you will generally need a higher temperature the smaller the piece of fish is. The larger the fish the more likely it is that moisture will be added, such as wine, olive oil or tomatoes, or possibly all three. It is possible to cook fish on very low temperatures, at about 45–60°C (115–140°F), and get an incredible texture in the mouth. The fish will look for all intents and purposes as if it is raw, but the flesh has been set at the low temperature and it will cut like cooked fish. If you cook it submerged in olive oil the process is called confit. It is by this process that Sydney-based Tetsuya Wakuda, one of the world's great chefs, creates his signature dish Confit of ocean trout.

ROAST WHOLE SNAPPER WITH FENNEL AND OLIVES

There are two ways to cook this dish: you can use four small whole snappers or you can go all out and roast one big fish. The large fish is going to get the wow factor and you will get to do a little boning at the table — fancy. Cooking the fish on the bone is great, as the bones protect the fish during cooking and add to the flavour. It is also really easy, as you just chuck it in the oven and let the heat take its course.

INGREDIENTS

4 small whole snapper, each weighing 400–500 g (14 oz–1 lb 2 oz),
    or 1 large one weighing about 1.5–2 kg (3 lb 5 oz–4 lb 8 oz)

1 red onion, finely sliced

1 fennel bulb, finely sliced

2 tablespoons oregano, chopped

2 tablespoons thyme, chopped

60 ml (2 fl oz/1/4 cup) extra virgin olive oil

1 red capsicum (pepper), cut in half and finely sliced

1 green capsicum (pepper), cut in half and finely sliced

3 vine-ripened tomatoes, peeled, deseeded and quartered (page 66)

2 tablespoons salted baby capers, well rinsed and drained

6 anchovies

150 g (5 1/2 oz/1 cup) Ligurian olives

sea salt

250 ml (9 fl oz/1 cup) white wine

2 tablespoons chopped flat-leaf (Italian) parsley

freshly ground pepper

METHOD

Preheat the oven to 200°C (400°F/Gas 6). Take a roasting tin and check that it fits your fish; use two tins if necessary. Scatter the onion, fennel, oregano and thyme over the bottom of the tin and drizzle with half the extra virgin olive oil. Put the fish on top and cover with the capsicum, tomato, capers, anchovies and olives. Salt liberally and pour the rest of the oil and the wine over. Cook the smaller fish for 25 minutes, or until cooked, basting every 5 minutes, and the larger fish for 1 hour. Place the fish on individual plates or on a platter. Spoon the sauce and vegetables over and add the parsley and pepper. Serves 4

ACCOMPANIMENTS

• This dish is perfect with broccolini, garlic and chilli and roast potatoes. Any of the steamed, boiled or braised vegetables will work well, as will steamed potatoes tossed in salsa verde. Avocado salsa over the fish would be delicious.

SARDINES WITH TOMATO, OLIVES AND BASIL

The fish that we here in Australia call sardine is really a pilchard, closely related to the European anchovy. That is why we see cans of 'Australian anchovy' called auschovy, as it really isn't either sardine or anchovy. They are caught year round and until recently have been underrated in Australia. They are an oily fish, so must be really fresh, and they do have a strong taste, but are quite delicious even raw. Sardines go well with robust flavours such as these below, but are also yummy with a little preserved lemon salsa. Another nice thing to do with them is use them in escabeche. This is a Spanish dish where the fish is pan-fried rare, then doused in a combination of aromatic vegetables, herbs and red wine vinegar, the idea being that the vinegar cures the flesh to well done, which you then pull off the bone and eat cold with crusty bread.

This is a simple dish that uses three classic ingredients: tomatoes, olives and basil — natural, simple flavours that belong together. They go with just about anything, so whether you sauté veal, barbecue lamb, cook any fish or make pizza or pasta, they will be welcome additions.

INGREDIENTS

16 sardines
500 g (1 lb 2 oz) cherry tomatoes, quartered
40 g (1 1/2 oz/1/4 cup) Ligurian olives
extra virgin olive oil
sea salt
10 basil leaves
1 lemon, quartered
freshly ground pepper

METHOD

Preheat the oven to 200°C (400°F/Gas 6). Put the sardines side by side in a roasting tin that fits them snugly. Sprinkle the tomato and olives over the top, drizzle liberally with extra virgin olive oil and sprinkle with sea salt. Cook for 10–15 minutes, or until done. Remove the tin from the oven, tear the basil leaves over, squeeze lemon juice over and give a good grind of fresh pepper. Carefully place four sardines on each plate and spoon over the juices in the roasting tin. Serve immediately. Serves 4

ACCOMPANIMENTS

• This makes a great starter and is also good as a shared plate in the middle of the table, perhaps with a couple more seafood dishes, and some salads.

MUD CRAB AGAIN

Roasting is also a great way to cook mud crab. Prepare them in the sink as described for steamed mud crab (page 162), then toss with extra virgin olive oil and put in a large roasting tin or dish. Put in an oven preheated to 200–220°C (400–425°F/Gas 6–7) and cook for 10 minutes. Dress in the same way as for steamed mud crab, or try tossing in another vinaigrette of your choosing; lime juice and walnut oil is lovely. You can throw butter in during the roasting process — herb or anchovy butter is nice — or just serve with aïoli and some salad.

ESCABECHE IN MORE DETAIL

While I am talking about sardines I will provide a simple escabeche recipe. This dish works really well with any oily fish and is an absolute treat as part of a summer antipasto table. Season some whole sardines with sea salt and dust with flour. Heat a heavy-based saucepan and add some extra virgin olive oil. Add the fish and cook for 1 minute on each side, until you have a nice colour, then remove from the pan. Allow to cool, then pull the sardines open and remove the backbone and head: this is very easy, they should come out in a flash. Now lay the sardines in a nice shallow dish. Heat some extra virgin olive oil in a small pan and gently fry some sliced carrots, garlic and red onion, a small amount of chilli flakes, some black peppercorns and some white wine. Add a good dash of red wine vinegar and cook for 5 minutes. Sprinkle finely shredded flat-leaf (Italian) parsley over the fish and add the sauce to the fish while the sauce is still hot. Allow to cool and serve some hours later; this dish is great with a glass of aromatic white wine or a little glass of chilled dry sherry.

ROAST BLUE EYE WITH ROAST TOMATO SAUCE

The method for cooking this fish is not quite pan-roasting, as it is sealed then roasted. It is a very simple way to cook fish, so I have added it in as you could choose snapper, coral trout, barramundi, tuna, kingfish or just about any fish. Once the fish has cooked, you can serve it with many different sauces, salsas, vinaigrettes or butters and lots of different salads and vegetable garnishes. So this recipe is the template upon which you could build fifty recipes, the only given is that it is roasted.

INGREDIENTS

4 x 200 g (7 oz) blue eye fillets, skin scored
sea salt
extra virgin olive oil
500 ml (17 fl oz/2 cups) roast tomato sauce (page 378)
1 lemon, quartered
freshly ground pepper

METHOD

Preheat the oven to 200°C (400°F/Gas 6). Season the blue eye fillets with sea salt and brush with extra virgin olive oil.

Heat a heavy-based ovenproof frying pan to hot and add the fish presentation side down (that will be the skin side, unless you are serving them without the skin, in which case put the side that comes off the bone facing down). Sear for 1 minute, then carefully turn over. Put the frying pan in the oven and cook for about 8 minutes, or until a thin metal skewer slides easily into the flesh. Remove from the oven. Heat the roast tomato sauce in a small saucepan.

Divide the roast tomato sauce among four plates, carefully place a fillet onto the sauce on each plate, squeeze some fresh lemon juice over and give a good grind of fresh pepper. Serve immediately. Serves 4

ACCOMPANIMENTS

• Braised peas and parsnip purée on the side would be perfect.

• In place of the roast tomato sauce, try cream of corn, creamed spinach, braised Roman (flat) beans, braised peas, peperonata, braised Puy lentils, carrot purée — the list goes on. I like the zucchini, broccolini and cauliflower sauce from the pasta section under this fish, and while you're there, you could try the all'amatriciana sauce, and the artichokes and pancetta combination is great as well. I love this fish with pancetta: the flavours go so well together. Of course, a dollop of mayonnaise takes the fish to another level.

ROAST LOBSTER WITH HERB BUTTER

There are many crustaceans around the world known as lobster. The fact is that what Australians call lobster is really seawater crayfish. What Europeans and Americans call lobster has two claws and looks like a giant yabby. Australian ones have a different texture, which I'm fond of. The most common lobster in Australia is the rock lobster, and different types are available around the country. There is the green-black eastern rock lobster, what we call 'local crays', there is the southern rock lobster that comes from Tasmania and South Australia, the Western Australian rock lobster and the tropical rock lobster, as well. Confused? Well don't be, as many are available at different times of the year, and although they have slightly different textures and tastes, they can be substituted for each other in the recipe. Most rock lobsters have a sweet, rich flavour and firm texture, and they handle sauces and butters well. They are also brilliant just steamed or boiled and served with a little dressing or mayonnaise. Their shells make great soups and sauces, so don't throw these away, even if you freeze them for use later on. It's really worth the trouble of buying your rock lobster alive, as the enzymes in the flesh start to break the flesh down from the moment it dies. They are reasonably hearty and will live out of water for a couple of days, if kept damp and cold, however, they will be stressed and that is not good for the texture (or the creature). At Rockpool we have tanks that keep the shellfish alive until it is ordered, which is the ideal situation, but if you buy a live one straight from the market and get it home quickly you won't have any trouble successfully recreating these recipes.

This following recipe is very simple: just cut the rock lobster in half and roast. The butter will melt and soak into the flesh, giving it a wonderful flavour. There are two simple ways to despatch your lobster kindly, and if they die without stress the texture will be better. Method one: put the lobster in a sink filled with fresh water and put a chopping board over the top, as it will thrash about a bit. You are drowning the lobster. I have heard it is quite a good way to go, but that is just hearsay. Method two: put it in the freezer for an hour or two, which puts it to sleep, and is by far the easiest way to do it. Rock lobster is expensive, but it comes at a price that is well worth it, and if you just have it every now and again it is a wonderful treat. They tend to be in full season in summer, so that is usually when they are at their lowest price. You can also substitute the rock lobster with scampi, large prawns (shrimp), Balmain bugs, yabbies or marron, and follow the recipe as it stands.

INGREDIENTS

2 x 800 g–1 kg (1 lb 12 oz–2 lb 4 oz) live rock lobsters
sea salt
extra virgin olive oil
16 x 5 mm (¹/4 inch) thick slices herb butter (page 360)
juice of 1 lemon
3 tablespoons finely shredded flat-leaf (Italian) parsley
freshly ground pepper

METHOD

Preheat the oven to 200°C (400°F/Gas 6). Take the lobsters' lives with either of the methods described opposite. Put the first lobster on a chopping board, with its head facing you and the tail away, and carefully place a sharp knife between its eyes. Now, holding the tail, cut down towards you, right through the shell. Turn the lobster around and, holding the lobster by the head, cut through the tail; you should now have two halves. Pull out the digestion tract that runs down its length. Repeat with the second lobster. It is important when preparing lobster that you use a very sharp knife. Also, put the lobster in a position you are comfortable with and use firm, confident cuts.

Select a roasting tin or dish that can accommodate the four lobster halves. Season the lobster with sea salt and put in the tin. Drizzle over a little extra virgin olive oil and place four rounds of herb butter on each lobster half, from head to tail, so that all the meat is covered with butter.

Roast for about 12 minutes, being very careful not to overcook it. When it is perfectly cooked, you should be able to just move the flesh away from the shell near the head.

Place half a lobster on each of four large white plates. The butter should be melted and even slightly burnt in the bottom of the roasting tin. Add the lemon juice to the pan, 2 tablespoons extra virgin olive oil, the parsley, a little sea salt and a good grind of fresh pepper. Stir to mix. Spoon the dressing over the lobsters and serve immediately. Serves 4

ACCOMPANIMENTS

• Steamed greens, a green salad or English spinach with garlic would be perfect, along with either roast potatoes or pan-fried polenta.

• Like the roast blue eye and roast coral trout with herb crust (following page), the combinations are endless with rock lobster. The flesh is delicious with most of the sauces in this book and it goes well with the majority of the vegetable accompaniments. You can even chop it up and serve it in a broth of mussels and saffron, with aïoli and crusty bread alongside for a real treat.

ROAST CORAL TROUT WITH HERB CRUST

Coral trout is one of Australia's mighty warm water reef fish. It is not actually a trout, but a member of the rock cod family; however, its sleek appearance has earned it that name. It comes in a variety of vibrant colours depending on where it comes from on the reef. It has a delicate white flesh, with a fine but tight flake and is very sweet tasting. It has for a long time been one of the most sought-after reef fish for eating. It is beautiful for roasting, steaming and grilling on the barbecue.

The following is a technique that we use at Rockpool and at Qantas to protect the fish from the fierce heat of roasting and keep it moist. The crust also has loads of flavour and a nice crunch. You can add almost anything you like to the crust, just keep a nice balance of flavour. The crust goes with so many different fish — this method will give you one hundred and one different dishes. Make sure you have a roasting tin or dish that fits the fish neatly; if the surface area of the dish is too big, the water that helps cook and keep the fish moist will just evaporate.

INGREDIENTS

800 g (1 lb 12 oz) piece coral trout or snapper fillet, skinned (page 198)
1 lemon, quartered

FOR THE HERB CRUST
2 tablespoons extra virgin olive oil
1/2 brown onion, finely diced
2 garlic cloves, finely diced
80 g (2 3/4 oz/1 cup) fresh breadcrumbs (page 278)
2 tablespoons chopped fresh ginger
1 teaspoon coriander seeds, roasted and roughly pounded
3 tablespoons chopped coriander (cilantro) leaves
3 tablespoons chopped flat-leaf (Italian) parsley
3 tablespoons chopped chives
1 tablespoon grated lemon zest, making sure there is no bitter pith
sea salt and freshly ground pepper
90 g (3 1/4 oz) unsalted butter, softened

METHOD

Preheat the oven to 200°C (400°F/Gas 6). To make the herb crust, heat the extra virgin olive oil in a frying pan over medium heat. Add the onion and garlic and sweat for about 5 minutes, or until soft. Remove from the pan and put into a stainless steel bowl. Add the breadcrumbs, ginger, coriander seeds and leaves, the parsley, chives, lemon zest, sea salt and a good grind of fresh pepper. Mix thoroughly, then add the butter and mix again; it should start to come together.

On a chopping board, squash the mixture into a square that is just bigger than the fish fillet. Lay the fish presentation side down on the breadcrumb mixture and cut the fish and its coating into four pieces. Slide a fish lifter under the first piece, carefully turn the fish and its coating over and put in a roasting tin, crust side up. Repeat with the other portions. Pour 125 ml (4 fl oz/1/2 cup) water into the bottom of the roasting tin and cook for 10 minutes, or until a thin metal skewer slides easily into the fish. Remove the tin from the oven.

Carefully place one fish portion on each of four plates and squeeze some fresh lemon juice over the crust. Serve immediately. Serves 4

ACCOMPANIMENTS

• Steamed or boiled greens and potato gratin. I would also be tempted to serve some aïoli or herb mayonnaise on the side.

• You can serve any of the vegetables in this book in any combination you like with this dish. If they are wet like cream of corn, serve them on the side. As for sauces, the combinations are endless. Try spooning a little red capsicum sauce on the plate and topping with the coral trout. Equally as delicious would be roast garlic sauce or roast tomato sauce over the top. You could also just serve a spoonful of mayonnaise or salsa on the side.

GRILLING

This is a method of cooking not often used by Australians at home. At the restaurant we do use it, where we grill (broil) mainly fish and shellfish under a hot salamander (a commercial grill). Grilling (broiling) is similar to barbecuing except the heat comes from above. It is primarily a wonderful way to cook flat fish, which I think explains why it is more commonly used in the United States than here, where they have many delicious flat fish. Although we have flounder and sole, we would probably not count them among our most popular eating fish either at home or in a restaurant. We can, of course, all grill very successfully at home because every oven has an element where the heat comes from above, and half the time in my house it is used to make toast when a thick slice of sourdough bread won't fit in the toaster. I remember when I was young that we had an old stove that had a grill (broiler) drawer on top of the oven, and underneath the elements. It was an old electric range, and it really was fantastic to cook on. Mum would heat it up, pull the drawer out and cook steaks and lamb chops and cutlets on it. It was really the preferred method of cooking chops because it made the tails really crispy. The fat would melt away and drip through the slotted tray onto another tray below, giving you low-fat cooking, perfect for the mixed grill. This was, in a way, the prototype for the George Foreman grill, yummy low-fat cooking. I only wish I had realised it then and taken out the patent. You have the same basic set up now in all ovens, but it really is a pain leaving the door ajar as you are supposed to and I really liked the grill drawer — we would use it all the time and you could cook without bending. Anyway, Dad didn't really use this superb invention for cooking fish. He would usually pan-fry, deep-fry or barbecue our fish. Much later, when I started cooking in restaurants, I realized what a valuable method it was to cook and keep fresh fish moist. So, all you need is an oven with a grill, a tray for cooking and some fresh fish. I will explain the basic grilling method and a couple of variations, and you can cook and pair the seafood with simple light sauces and yummy vegetables and salads as you wish.

Preheat the grill (broiler) of your oven to high. You need to position the tray that you intend to cook your fish on about 5 cm (2 inches) below the heated grill bars, which will be red hot. This can be done by putting the tray on a rack or if the tray fits into the side racks of the oven it will be even simpler.

There are two options for cooking, either dry or wet. You can brush the fish with extra virgin olive oil or butter after seasoning it or cook the fish in a little water or court bouillon (after brushing with oil or butter and seasoning it). The advantage of this second method is that the liquid keeps the fish from drying out, and it will cook even quicker as the liquid simmers around the fish. Generally speaking, the thicker the fish the greater the need for extra moisture. Thicker fish can also be turned over halfway through the cooking time, but usually I select fish no thicker than 2 cm (3/4 inch) and then there is no need to turn them.

So, season, brush with oil or butter, pour a little water or court bouillon a third of the way up the fish — most of the time just a little water will do the trick — and cook until the fish is ready. Remove and serve with a simple sauce or just a squeeze of lemon juice, as this cooking method is very much about the pure taste of the fish. This is also a nice way to cook fish with the skin on, which will turn crisp and add great flavour to the dish.

Cooking lobster by this method is great; just split the lobster in half and place under the grill. Remove when almost cooked, place some herb butter over the top and put under the grill again until the butter melts into the flesh and the lobster is cooked.

BARBECUING

Barbecued fish is so healthy, but it is also a wonderful way of ensuring that the delicate, pure taste of fish is enhanced and not compromised. It certainly has become one of the most popular methods of cooking seafood at home, and why not, it really is incredibly easy and the smells of cooking stay outside. Are there any down sides to this wonderful way of cooking seafood? Well, if there are, it would probably be that fierce heat and delicate flesh can lead to overcooking! So, be careful, and don't leave your precious seafood alone for too long — have a glass of wine in hand, chat beside the barbecue, but be ready. Whole fish barbecue well, as do steaks from oily fish such as tuna, kingfish and salmon; white-fleshed fish like snapper, blue eye, jewfish and reef fish will barbecue well if the pieces are reasonably large; and all fish cutlets work well on the barbecue too. The great thing about the barbecue is that you impart a wonderful charred flavour to the seafood, so you need just a simple sauce as accompaniment, or just marinate the seafood. Really the only rules for barbecuing are selecting fish that will work well, seasoning it, getting the barbecue hot and being careful not to overcook. Then serve and enjoy. Sounds pretty straightforward and it is.

In the mid eighties I found a great site in Sydney's Bondi and opened it in 1986 as the Blue Water Grill. It had magnificent views going all the way down to Bronte. I decided to have an all out push for seafood. It was a large restaurant with a tiny kitchen so I decided that with a 1.5 metre (5 ft) barbecue chargrill I could cook a lot of seafood per hour, much more than on a stove of the same size. Having made the decision to go with the chargrill, I also deliberately decided to keep things fresh and simple. We flew our oysters up unopened from Tasmania and shucked them to order and then had about another twenty-five things on the menu that had no real divide between starter and main. It was the first of what was coined the 'grazing menus' and people loved it. Fish would be coming off the grill and all we had time for was to either put little butters or some salsa on the fish and out they went.

We would barbecue swordfish and top it with wonderful curry butter just before serving, so it would start to melt. Chargrilled tuna would be placed on an eggplant (aubergine) and red capsicum (pepper) salad and topped with a dollop of pesto. Kingfish would sit on a salad of avocado, tomato, chilli and lime, a sort of chunky ceviche. Blue eye would be barbecued and then served with a mint and chilli salsa, and so on. It was simple cooking, but it was bloody delicious. You can do this at home so easily, just look at the sauces, salads and vegetable sections for ideas.

GRILLED TUNA WITH PESTO

Tuna is the king of the sea, fabulous whether raw, cured, cooked or preserved. These fish never stop moving and searching for food. Our search for the best-quality tuna at the market is a daily occurrence at Rockpool. We love to serve it raw, as part of our 'six tastes from the sea', as well as on a sashimi plate, or cooked rare, studded with garlic and anchovies and served with a roast garlic sauce. It is so versatile, but it is almost at its best when slightly charred from the barbecue and topped with a simple salsa.

There are several types of tuna available at different times of the year, but the most common would be yellow fin, big eye and blue fin. Don't underestimate how good bonito or albacore tuna is either, raw or cooked really fresh. I don't know why they are sometimes thought of as lesser species.

Tuna is oily, has a medium-sweet flavour and should be quite moist when cooked rare to medium rare; it will dry out when overcooked. Its texture should be firm, but to the bite, and it will be extremely tender, especially when eaten raw. Tuna has, in fact, that wonderful texture that is so highly prized by the Japanese and eaters of raw fish around the world — firm and tender at the same time. Don't be caught in the trap of only enjoying raw tuna with wasabi and soy sauce. It lends itself to so many simple Mediterranean flavours. Try slicing really fresh tuna, arranging it on a plate and sprinkling it with sea salt, drizzling with extra virgin olive oil and, just as you take it from the kitchen, squeezing lemon juice over each plate. Nothing could be simpler or more delicious. As it relies on the quality of just a few ingredients, make sure they are perfect.

INGREDIENTS

4 x 200 g (7 oz) tuna steaks
sea salt
extra virgin olive oil
125 ml (4 fl oz/$1/2$ cup) pesto (page 366)
1–2 lemons, quartered
freshly ground pepper

METHOD

Preheat the barbecue to hot. Make sure the grill bars are clean. Season the tuna with sea salt and drizzle with extra virgin olive oil. Put the steaks on the grill at a 45-degree angle to the straight bars. Cook for 1 minute, then turn the tuna around (not over) 45 degrees in the opposite direction. Cook for 1 minute, turn over and cook for 1^1/2 minutes before removing from the grill.

Place one tuna steak on each of four large white plates and place a dollop of pesto on the middle of each steak. Squeeze lemon juice over each, drizzle with extra virgin olive oil, sprinkle with a little sea salt and give a good grind of pepper. Serve immediately. Serves 4

ACCOMPANIMENTS

• Place the tuna steak on a spoonful of peperonata, place a dollop of pesto on top and serve potato salad on the side.

• This is the classic barbecue recipe for fish steaks, so you can use any fish that barbecues well and serve it with many of the vegetable and sauce recipes. As with some of the other recipes in this book, look in the pasta and soup section for interesting combinations with barbecued fish. Lots of the salad recipes can also play a part in creating a dish. For instance, put the fish on the plate on top of some potato salad or a little Italian coleslaw, with roasted red capsicums (peppers) or boiled leeks on the side, then simply top with a little sauce, mayonnaise, salsa or dressing to create a fabulous summer dish.

FOLLOWING PAGES making pesto, left, and barbecued ocean trout fillet, served with curry butter (page 359), right 181

BARBECUED OCEAN TROUT FILLET WITH CURRY BUTTER

Ocean trout is a fish I like more than salmon. It has a higher oil content, and to my mind a better flavour. It is a slower-growing fish that requires more food, so it isn't as popular with the majority of growers as salmon is; however, those that are produced are of good quality. They are very good for eating raw and I do like the fish when it is barbecued. A whole fish weighing about 2–2.5 kg (4 lb 8 oz–5 lb 8 oz) is about right. At that size they make a great whole roasted, poached or barbecued fish that looks spectacular and feeds the entire family.

As with the tuna, you can put crisscross grill marks on the fish. Also, if the fish has its skin on, cook on the skin side for three-quarters of the total time, then turn over and finish cooking. This will produce a nice crisp skin.

INGREDIENTS

4 x 200 g (7 oz) ocean trout fillets
sea salt
extra virgin olive oil
four slices or spoonfuls of curry butter (page 359)
1 lime, quartered
freshly ground pepper

METHOD

Preheat the barbecue to hot. Make sure the grill bars are really well cleaned. Season the ocean trout fillets with sea salt and brush with extra virgin olive oil. Place the trout on the grill presentation side down and cook for 2 minutes, then turn over and cook for a further 2 minutes. After 1 minute, place a slice of curry butter on each fillet. Remove the fillets and rest in a warm place for 1–2 minutes. The butter will be soft and melting over the fish.

Place one fillet on each of four large white plates and squeeze lime juice over. Give a good grind of pepper and serve immediately. Serves 4

ACCOMPANIMENTS

• Creamed spinach and potato chips or potatoes grilled on the barbecue would taste great with the curry butter.

• As with salmon, you can choose your garnishes from the accompaniment section at will — they will all go well — and as for saucing, look far and wide through this book, as many of the pasta and soup recipes work nicely.

BARBECUED KINGFISH FILLET WITH SAUCE VIERGE

Kingfish is considered an oily, medium-flavoured fish, good both raw and cooked, and when it is not overcooked it is moist and has a nice firm texture. It is known as yellow tail in Australia and as hamachi in Japan and America. I have always enjoyed the wild-caught fish in Australia, but in the last couple of years there has been much interest in a new farmed species called hiramasa kingfish. It is available both here (from South Australia) and overseas. It is a large, handsome fish weighing about 2.5 kg (5 lb 8 oz). It tastes superb raw or cooked. I call it the new tuna due to its high oil content and wonderful texture; it is both soft and yet firm to the bite. At the fish markets it is slightly more expensive than its wild cousin, but worth a look. I like them both, and either work really well with this dish. The other great thing about kingfish is, if you're a fisherman, they are a really great catch, as pound to pound they fight like hell. The sauce is one of Roger Vergé's classics; serve it on any seafood you like, it perfectly complements the delicate nature of fish.

INGREDIENTS
4 x 200 g (7 oz) kingfish fillets, wild or farmed
sea salt
extra virgin olive oil
375 ml (13 fl oz/1^{1}/2 cups) sauce Vierge (page 365)
freshly ground pepper

METHOD
Preheat the barbecue to hot. Make sure the grill bars are clean. Liberally sprinkle the fillets with sea salt and brush with extra virgin olive oil. Put on the grill and cook for 2 minutes, then turn over and cook for a further 2 minutes. Remove and rest in a warm place for 3–4 minutes. The kingfish will present well if given the grill marks talked about in the previous recipes. Just follow the simple instructions for a lovely crisscross pattern. Place the fillets on white plates and spoon the sauce over. Add freshly ground pepper and serve. Serves 4

ACCOMPANIMENTS
• Put braised Roman (flat) beans and fried polenta on the plate side by side, put the fish on top and spoon the sauce over.

• Any of the combinations mentioned with tuna and salmon will also work well with the kingfish. Try putting the fish on a little Moroccan eggplant salad with a teaspoon of preserved lemon salsa on top. It would also be nice served on a bed of cherry tomato, pea and potato salad with herb mayonnaise on the side.

GRILLED SQUID WITH CHILLI AND HERB SALAD

Over the last decade squid has picked up in popularity in Australia. It has a mild flavour, and although it might be said to have a firm texture, I think it is the understanding of how to cook it properly that has helped raise its popularity. We have all had simple and delicious preparations like Chinese salt and pepper squid or Italian-style calamari with nothing but the juice of fresh lemon to sauce it, and in both cases the squid has been rendered tender by good, careful cooking. Squid can be eaten raw and has a lovely sweetness to it and a really pleasant crunchy texture. We serve it at Rockpool as either ceviche or mixed with a sauce of garam masala, lime and yoghurt — wonderful in the hands of a great sashimi chef. The two ways of cooking squid are either very quickly, to retain the soft texture, or very slowly, braising it so it goes from tender to tough and back to melting by the time it is done. The method we are employing here is the quick one, and with the charred flavour from the grill, this is just about as good as it gets. This dish is a wonderful starter, or great as part of an antipasto or mixed seafood barbecue. I find the more herbs the merrier; you can cook the squid and have the herbs finely chopped as part of a simple dressing, or you can, as I have done here, have them as a salad.

You can buy squid two ways, cleaned or uncleaned. It is really up to you, and it is far less messy if you buy it already cleaned. However, you will be rewarded if you go to the effort of buying really fresh squid and cleaning it at home. Fresh squid will look vibrant and have a real sheen to it, the colour in the markings on the body will almost glow and it will smell of the sea.

HOW TO CLEAN SQUID — First, pull out the head, taking the skin off in one go if possible. Cut the squid down the centre and open it out, scrape out all the internal organs along with the plastic-looking cartilage. (If you need the squid cooked in rings, leave the squid whole, remove the organs and cartilage and then cut into thin rings.) Remove the hard beak, or mouth, from the centre where the tentacles meet and cut the eyes off and discard. Don't underestimate how delicious the tentacles are barbecued or fried. Now, starting from the head end and using a sharp knife at a 45-degree angle, cut diagonal lines at about 5 mm (1/4 inch) intervals over the flesh, cutting halfway through the flesh and going all the way down to the end. Repeat the lines in the opposite direction to form a crisscross pattern. It will now be ready for this recipe.

INGREDIENTS

600 g (1 lb 5 oz) squid, cleaned and scored

60 ml (2 fl oz/¼ cup) extra virgin olive oil

4 red chillies, deseeded and finely chopped

2 garlic cloves, chopped

2 tablespoons chopped oregano

1 tablespoon chopped thyme

2 fresh bay leaves, very finely sliced

sea salt

1 large handful mint, roughly torn

1 large handful flat-leaf (Italian) parsley

1 large handful coriander (cilantro) leaves

juice of 1 lemon, plus extra wedges

freshly ground pepper

METHOD

Roughly cut the squid into 5 cm (2 inch) squares, then put in a bowl with the extra virgin olive oil, chilli, garlic, oregano, thyme and bay leaves. Season with sea salt and leave to marinate for 30 minutes.

Preheat the barbecue to hot. Make sure the grill bars are really well cleaned. Put the squid on the hot grill and cook for about 1 minute, turn over and cook for a further minute, then remove and put in a bowl. Add the mint, parsley and coriander to the bowl, drizzle with a little extra virgin olive oil, some sea salt and the lemon juice. Toss to mix.

Toss the squid salad and divide among four white plates. Give a good grind of fresh pepper and have lemon wedges on hand. Serve immediately. Serves 4

ACCOMPANIMENTS

• This is a perfect starter on its own or it could be part of a larger shared starter with some mussels, sardines and a couple of simple salads.

FOLLOWING PAGES grilled squid with chilli and herb salad, left, and barbecued sea scallops with herbs and garlic, right

BARBECUED SEA SCALLOPS WITH HERBS AND GARLIC

There are a number of scallops available in Australia, but for all intents and purposes, they fall into two types: the sea or saucer scallop, wild-caught from the warmer waters of Queensland; and the king or queen scallop, which grows in colder waters. These scallops are wild-caught or farmed. We get our scallops delivered live to Rockpool. This is a real treat, as you can't imagine the taste of a scallop shucked from the shell still alive and dropped into the mouth — it's like the most pure taste of the sea and a spoonful of sugar at the same time. The Queensland sea scallop is a fast-growing, sweet, elongated, textured scallop that works well in combination with meat like pork belly and birds such as duck. The cold water scallop has an intense flavour of the sea, with a very tight texture. It is wonderful and buttery, and to really appreciate how good they are, should be only lightly cooked until just warm in the centre. I should also say that that is the only way to eat sea scallops as well; these delicate shellfish will love the most gentle of treatments.

The very simple flavours in this dish work really well with any fish, and you can change the herbs as you like. Add chilli or finely sliced ginger; do whatever you like, just add flavour and enjoy. If having as a simple starter, serve three to four large scallops per person, if you want it as a main course, use six or seven.

HOW TO PREPARE SCALLOPS — Nearly all the scallops you buy will still have the crescent-shaped tendon that attaches them to the shell. You can see it easily, as it sits out from the scallop and looks like a piece of white sinew. Just peel it off or cut it off with a knife — if you don't remove it, it will toughen during cooking.

INGREDIENTS

    20 sea scallops, cleaned

    3 garlic cloves, finely chopped

    $1/2$ teaspoon chilli flakes

    $1/2$ teaspoon fennel seeds, roasted and crushed roughly (page 330)

    1 teaspoon chopped oregano

    1 rosemary sprig, leaves removed and bruised

    sea salt

    extra virgin olive oil

    juice of 1 lemon

    freshly ground pepper

METHOD

Put the scallops in a bowl and add the garlic, chilli flakes, fennel seeds, oregano, rosemary and some sea salt. Drizzle with extra virgin olive oil and leave to marinate for 30 minutes.

Heat the barbecue to hot. Make sure the grill bars are clean. Put the scallops on the grill and cook for about 1 minute, maybe even a little less if not large, then turn over and cook for a further minute. You want a nice caramelized crust on the scallops and a melting, just-warm interior. Remove the scallops from the barbecue and put in a bowl.

Squeeze the lemon juice over the scallops. Sprinkle with a little more sea salt and give a good grind of pepper, then gently toss. Place five sea scallops on each of four plates and serve immediately. Serves 4

ACCOMPANIMENTS

• This is a beautifully simple starter: plate the scallops and add a dollop of aïoli or herb mayonnaise, or you could serve a spoonful of red capsicum purée under the scallops. Harissa no. 3 would also be the perfect accompaniment to a plate of fresh scallops.

BARBECUED MARINATED KING PRAWNS WITH TARATOR

We are blessed with fantastic prawns (shrimp) in Australia. There are many different types and they range from cold and warm water species to farmed. I like to get really big specimens for this dish and cook them in the shell, cut in half like a lobster, but by all means remove the shell and just cook the flesh straight on the barbecue, particularly if you are having trouble finding really big prawns. The marinade will stick to the flesh and give the prawns an added burst of flavour. If marinating with the shell on, remind your guests and family to suck the shell, it's almost the best part. You can marinate the prawns and roast them in the oven or even cook them under the grill (broiler) — get into a bit of grilling; they will taste great. By the same token, don't just stick to prawns for this recipe: scampi, Balmain and sea bugs, large yabbies or marron and certainly rock lobster would be wonderful.

INGREDIENTS

20 large king prawns (shrimp), cut in half lengthways and deveined
extra virgin olive oil
freshly ground pepper
125 ml (4 fl oz/1/2 cup) tarator (page 368)
lemon wedges, to serve

FOR THE MARINADE
2 garlic cloves
2 tablespoons chopped fresh ginger
1 lemon grass stalk, peeled and chopped
2 tablespoons chopped coriander (cilantro) leaves
2 tablespoons chopped mint
1 teaspoon ground cumin
1 teaspoon ground coriander
1 teaspoon smoky sweet paprika
2 red chillies
zest of 1/2 lemon, plus juice of 1 lemon
1 teaspoon sea salt
125 ml (4 fl oz/1/2 cup) extra virgin olive oil

METHOD

To make the marinade, put all the marinade ingredients in a food processor and blend until smooth. If using a stick blender, be sure to use a tall, narrow container so the marinade doesn't fly everywhere while blending. Put the prawns in a bowl, add the marinade, cover and leave for 30–45 minutes.

Preheat the barbecue to hot. Make sure the grill bars are clean. Put the prawns cut side down on the grill and cook for 1 minute, then turn over and cook for a further minute — when done, the prawns should still be a little translucent at the thickest part. Remove from the barbecue.

Pile ten prawn halves on each of four plates, drizzle with extra virgin olive oil, give a good grind of pepper and spoon a dollop of tarator onto each plate. Add lemon wedges and serve immediately. Serves 4

ACCOMPANIMENTS

• A bowl of steamed mixed greens and barbecued potatoes would be good if serving the prawns (shrimp) as a main course. Otherwise, serve them on their own as a starter.

BARBECUED ROCK LOBSTER

Lobster is marvellous on the barbecue. Preheat the barbecue to medium–hot and cook the lobster cut side down for about 4–5 minutes, then turn over and cook for another 4–5 minutes. The flesh should be just pulling away from the shell when cooked.

You can marinate the lobster as in the previous recipe, and it is great with chermoula spread on the cut side and seared on the barbecue. A squeeze of lemon juice and you are ready to serve. Or, just barbecue it and serve with some aïoli and a couple of simple salads on the side. I guess I don't have to say it, but start with a live lobster: if you're going to go to all that expense and trouble, make it memorable. It really is worth treating yourself every now and again.

PAN-FRYING AND SAUTEING

Pan-frying and sautéing in fat are great ways to cook fish, particularly delicate white-fleshed fish that has very little fat, as they help to keep the fish moist. The most famous sauté would have to be à la meunière, which is the simplest way to cook fish in a pan, and also one of the best ways. The combination of lemon juice and nut brown butter is irresistible, and although most closely associated with sole, it goes well with many different fish. In Australia, whiting, small snapper fillets or bream work really well, and, of course, shellfish thrive in the pan with lemon and burnt butter.

Whenever I travel to Paris I always go to a little seafood restaurant called Café Le Dôme, around the corner from its famous sister Bistrot du Dôme on boulevard Montparnasse. It has a small menu of just six starters and six mains, and I often have some oysters or boiled scampi with aïoli, but I always have the same main course, which is solette meunière. These small soles, numbering two or three per serve, are cooked to the moment, with their wonderful gelatinous flesh that is so sweet, and sauced with lemon, parsley and nut brown butter. I find myself chewing the bones, it is so good. It is a very simple dish, but I go back there time and time again and I am never disappointed. That is what good cooking is all about, and you can easily cook beautiful meunière at home.

Once upon a time nearly all fish that was pan-fried would have been dredged first in flour. These days that isn't always the case, and it is easy to cook fish in a non-stick pan and still get an appealing colour on the crust. We always cook our fish in extra virgin olive oil or butter, or a combination of both. If using butter, clarify it first. This is simply done by removing the milk solids, as they are the bits that burn easily.

The process of pan-frying is very simple; you just select a pan — trying, as with all pan-frying, to use a pan that accommodates the fish without crowding them but is not so large that the oil burns the juices as they leave the fish and spread over the empty pan — then add oil and heat. Don't add too much fat; just enough to stop the fish from sticking. Regulate the temperature according to the size of the fish; the smaller the fish the hotter the temperature. Put the fish presentation side down first, which, unless you are serving it with the skin on, will usually be the side that is taken off the bone. Turn once only; you want a good crust to form and you don't want to break the fish. Don't overcook. Serve immediately.

WHITING MEUNIERE

We have a few different whiting here in Australia, each one a premium eating fish. In Sydney we would consider the sand whiting king; in Melbourne and Adelaide they would not consider eating anything bar the King George whiting. The truth is they are both wonderful fish and great in this dish — just choose whichever is freshest. Meunière is a classic butter and lemon pan-fry dish, and is fantastic with thin fillets that need quick cooking if they are to remain moist. Sole is probably the meunière of choice in the northern hemisphere but I really think the whiting is superior. If you have never tried cooking fish like this at home then you have a treat in store and it will definitely not be the last time you or your family enjoy à la meunière. The flour coating keeps the fish very moist and gives it a nice colour when cooked at high heat. You will need to make clarified butter for this dish, or you can just cook the fish in olive oil, or a combination of olive oil and butter, which in some cases burns a little at high heat — but I always think it tastes better when cooked in clarified butter.

HOW TO CLARIFY BUTTER — Melt butter in a saucepan and simmer it gently. It will split into the clear clarified butter and the milk solids, which crust up and drop out of the liquid. At this stage, just pour the liquid through a sieve, discard the solids and you have clarified butter; make a decent amount as it keeps for months in the refrigerator and is good for cooking all crumbed food. It is also the starting point for many a tasty Indian curry.

You will need about 150 g (5 1/2 oz) fish per person — two or maybe three fillets per person. You can skin the fish or leave it on; whiting skin is delicious.

INGREDIENTS

8 whiting or sole fillets, about 150 g ($5^1/2$ oz) per person
clarified butter
125 ml (4 fl oz/$^1/2$ cup) milk
125 g ($4^1/2$ oz/1 cup) plain (all-purpose) flour
sea salt
125 g ($4^1/2$ oz) unsalted butter, cut into small cubes
1 lemon, quartered
2 tablespoons chopped flat-leaf (Italian) parsley
freshly ground pepper

METHOD

You will need to cook the fish in two lots, so warm the oven and have a plate ready for the fish. Take a large frying pan and check that four fillets will fit in it at a time — a stainless steel or non-stick pan will be fine. Put the pan on the stove, pour in enough clarified butter to cover the base of the pan and heat it to hot. Meanwhile, dip the fish fillets in the milk, then in the flour and sprinkle with sea salt. When hot enough, add the fillets to the pan and cook for about 1 minute. Turn over and cook for a further minute. Transfer to the warm oven and repeat the process with the remaining fillets.

When you are about to plate the fish, add the cubed butter to the pan over high heat.

Place two fillets on each of four white plates, squeeze a little lemon juice over, sprinkle with the parsley and some sea salt and give a good grind of pepper. As the butter in the pan turns a nut brown colour, spoon it over the fish — the butter, parsley and lemon juice will mingle to create the meunière sauce. Serve immediately, yum. Serves 4

ACCOMPANIMENTS

• The classic accompaniment to this dish would be steamed or boiled potatoes and a green salad. Steamed or boiled green vegetables, the English spinach dishes or braised peas would also suit. The main thing is to keep it simple, as the fish and sauce are very delicate tasting.

PAN-SEARED OCEAN TROUT WITH CHERMOULA

One of the signature dishes at Rockpool in its first ten years was herb-and-spice crusted tuna. It all started with me making this dish with ocean trout in the weeks before the opening in 1989. We just spread chermoula on the fish, seared it until a blackened crust formed and served it on Moroccan eggplant salad. I thought I would never take the tuna off the menu, but it has given way, though the Moroccan influence has stayed with other fish, including a great lobster dish. I put this dish in because it is really easy and will taste good no matter which of the chermoula recipes you use. Don't forget that this fish likes to be served medium rare, so give it a rest and it will be warm in the middle and meltingly soft-textured, with a really good flavour kick. Also, remember when you are making the chermoula paste that if you like it hotter, or prefer the taste of a certain spice or herb, it is entirely up to you. The recipe is only a guideline; blend it to your taste. I like to serve this fish sitting on a finely sliced salad of raw fennel. To make the salad, shave fennel very finely with a Japanese mandolin, being careful not to cut your fingers, as the mandolin is very sharp. Otherwise, slice as thinly as you can with a knife. Squeeze lemon juice on the fennel and season with sea salt, then set aside to marinate for 30 minutes. Drizzle with extra virgin olive oil and give a good grind of fresh pepper. Put some on each plate and sit the ocean trout on top.

Find a nice heavy-based frying pan for this dish, large enough to hold the four fillets; cast iron will work well. It goes without saying that this dish is great when thrown onto a hot barbecue, so don't limit yourself to the pan.

HOW TO SKIN A FILLET OF FISH — Put the fillet skin side down on your chopping board. A fish filleting knife is best for this job but a chef's knife will also work. Hold onto the tail end, and with your knife slightly angled towards the board, cut the flesh free from the skin, cutting from the tail up to the head of the fillet.

INGREDIENTS

    4 x 200 g (7 oz) skinned ocean trout fillets
    125 ml (4 fl oz/1/2 cup) chermoula (page 372)
    extra virgin olive oil
    fennel salad, to serve (optional)
    1 lemon, quartered

METHOD

Put the fillets in a large glass dish and smear the chermoula over each fillet.

Heat a heavy-based frying pan to hot, add some extra virgin olive oil and the fillets, presentation side down first (the side that has been taken off the bone). Reduce the heat to medium and cook for 2 minutes, then carefully slide a fish slice under the fish and turn over (I say carefully because you don't want to disturb the crust that has formed). Now, don't panic, the crust should look blackened. Cook for a further 2 minutes, then remove the pan from the heat. Leave the fillets in the pan for a further minute.

To serve, place a pile of fennel salad, if you are serving it with the dish, in the middle of four white plates. Carefully place a fillet on the salad, squeeze lemon juice over and serve immediately. Serves 4

ACCOMPANIMENTS

• A great alternative is to put a spoonful of Moroccan eggplant salad on each of the plates, top with the fish, squeeze over some lemon juice and dollop with harissa mayonnaise.

• The spice crust will go surprisingly well with things like creamed spinach and braised peas, so just build little vegetable garnishes under the fish and top the fish with one of the simple sauces. Preserved lemon salsa would be a classic choice, as would any of the harissas.

PAN-FRIED BARRAMUNDI WITH HORSERADISH SAUCE

The large wild barramundi is one of Australia's greatest eating fish, as it barbecues, roasts and pan-fries beautifully. Australia now has a thriving barramundi aquaculture industry, and although these large salt-water-raised fish are very good, I prefer the large wild-caught fish for this dish. The flavour and texture will be better than that of their farmed brothers. This dish shows how the pan juices and burnt bits of butter left in the pan can be made into a great sauce. Make sure the pan fits the fillets without squashing them or having too much pan exposed while cooking.

INGREDIENTS

4 x 200 g (7 oz) barramundi fillets, or any white fish such as cod or snapper
sea salt
60 ml (2 fl oz/$1/4$ cup) extra virgin olive oil
30 g (1 oz) unsalted butter
finely shredded flat-leaf (Italian) parsley

FOR THE HORSERADISH SAUCE
100 g ($3^1/2$ oz) crème fraîche
60 g ($2^1/4$ oz) unsalted butter
freshly grated horseradish, to taste (I like at least 20 g/$3/4$ oz)
juice of 1 lemon
sea salt and freshly ground pepper

METHOD

Season the fish with sea salt. Heat a heavy-based frying pan until hot, add the extra virgin olive oil and butter and, when bubbling and just starting to colour, add the fish fillets presentation side down first. Reduce the heat to medium and gently cook the fish for 5 minutes. Turn the fish over and cook for a further 4 minutes. Remove the fish from the pan, put on a plate and keep warm.

To make the horseradish sauce, scrape the bottom of the pan with a wooden spoon. Turn the heat back up, add the crème fraîche and cook for 1 minute, then add the butter. Remove the pan from the heat. Stir until the butter has melted and incorporated into the sauce, then stir through the horseradish and lemon juice. Keep warm over low heat, add sea salt and a grind of pepper. Place a barramundi fillet on each of four white plates, spoon over the sauce and sprinkle with parsley. Serve immediately. Serves 4

ACCOMPANIMENTS

• This fish will go with just about any of the vegetables and sauces. The aim is to show how to pan-fry a fish; it is a blueprint that you can use with many fish.

PAN-FRIED SCALLOPS WITH SAGE AND BURNT BUTTER

These little jewels from the sea have the most delicious taste of, first, the wonderful fresh taste of the sea and, second, a long, nutty, buttery flavour, as well as a dense, melting, moist texture (if not overcooked). All this makes them one of my most loved seafoods. There are incredible scallops all over the world: I love the large Scottish ones that come live into the markets in London, as well as the incredible American scallops from the Boston coast, hand-caught by divers. Tasmanian scallops are true cold-water beauties and their flavour is second to none. They work well in this dish, as the pan-frying preserves their natural flavour and adds a nice caramelized taste to the outside, while the burnt butter adds to the already rich taste of the scallop. The interesting thing about these scallops is that if you eat them raw when very fresh, you will notice their incredible sweetness. If you poach them you will get an intense taste of the sea, and if you pan-fry them you get that sweetness back in the form of the caramelized exterior but with a slightly milder taste. Try them each way. I always serve this dish as a little starter, as it is too rich to eat as a main course, or I think so anyway. A small green salad is all that is needed. Like à la meunière, this treatment can be used for any pan-fried fish; the herbs, lemon and butter are a great combination.

INGREDIENTS

20 fresh scallops, cleaned (page 190)
sea salt
extra virgin olive oil
125 g (4^1/2 oz) unsalted butter, cut into small cubes
12 sage leaves
lemon wedges
freshly ground pepper

METHOD

Put the scallops in a bowl and season with sea salt and drizzle with extra virgin olive oil. Put a heavy-based frying pan on the stove and heat until hot. Add the scallops to the pan and sear them for 1 minute, then carefully turn over with a pair of tongs. Cook for a further minute, then remove, put on a plate and keep warm. Add the butter and sage leaves to the pan and start heating the butter.

While the butter is heating, divide the scallops among white plates, add a lemon wedge to each plate, sprinkle with a little sea salt and give a good grind of fresh pepper. The butter should be nut brown now and sizzling and the sage crisp. Use a spoon to pour the butter and sage over the scallops. Serves 4

DEEP-FRYING

Deep-fried fish is the way most kids are introduced to fish, either in batter or breaded. Fish is so delicate it will nearly always need a coating of some sort when it is deep-fried. I still love fish that is presented in this fashion — the trick is to make that coating as crisp and light as possible. I think at home it is often easier to use fine breadcrumbs that will be crisper and tastier than a batter.

Deep-frying is not bad for you if you follow a couple of rules: have the oil at the right temperature and have it constant. There are some really good little deep-fat fryers out there on the market that are cheap and easy to use, so I would suggest getting one. However, you can also use a saucepan of oil with a thermometer, which will allow you to reach the right temperature and keep it there. The temperature needs to be 180°C (350°F) for most average-sized pieces of fish or shellfish. (This book is about Mediterranean food, but while discussing deep-fat fryers, if you do get one, make sure you can fit a whole fish weighing about 1 kg (2 lb 4 oz) in it: it will be perfect for crispy fried fish with chilli sauce. Anyway, back to the Mediterranean.)

I said deep-frying is not bad for you because the right temperature will seal the food and stop the oil from soaking into the batter or crumbs; if the temperature is too low you will have greasy food, and if too high, the coating will burn before the fish is cooked. As fried fish usually has a crisp crust and moist flesh, you would normally serve it with just lemon and a simple aïoli or tartare sauce, which sounds a bit ordinary, but if you go to the effort of making your own tartare, you will raise the simple fish and chips to a place where your family and friends will be putting the order in before they come around. So, to cook, follow this simple procedure: have clean oil; get the temperature correct and constant; don't overcrowd the fryer, as it will make the temperature drop; have a plate with paper towels on it ready for the fish, which you need to shake well after removing from the fryer; and keep the cooked fish in a warm oven while you cook the rest of the fish, if cooking in batches. That's it. Vegetable oil is best for deep-frying, as it has a high burn temperature. When the oil is cool enough to handle, strain it if it is clean enough and it can be used again. Remember, and this is very important, keep the container the oil came in and refill it with the old oil when you have finished with it: the sink is not the place to dispose of old oil. We have to have good environmental practices at home.

CRUMBED KING PRAWNS

I love crumbed prawns (shrimp), but who doesn't? At most restaurants they are pretty ordinary, so here is a big chance to make some really yummy ones at home and put whatever you like with them. Just buy large fresh prawns and shell them, then cut them down the back and flatten them out a little. Set up your crumbing station and crumb and fry them as explained overleaf in the John Dory recipe. You can serve the prawns with just a squeeze of lemon juice or any of the mayonnaises in the sauce chapter, or a salsa, some harissa or barbecue sauce, and I also like them with yoghurt that has garlic, lemon juice and seasoning added to it — whichever option you choose, they will be delicious.

WHOLE FRIED SNAPPER

As I have spent many years both eating and cooking Asian-style whole fried fish dishes, I'm very aware of how delicious fish is when it is taken past what we would consider 'done' in Western cooking and becomes really crispy. So what I like to do is employ that theory of fish cooking but add a Mediterranean flavour to the sauce or dressing.

Put your oil in a saucepan or frying pan large enough to fit a whole snapper, or whatever fish you choose, and heat the oil to 180°C (350°F). Make sure the fish is well scaled, then cut score marks on both sides of the fish from the head to the tail about 2 cm (3/4 inch) apart, right to the bone. Fry the fish for about 10 minutes, or until it is very crispy. Remove and place the fish on paper towels to absorb any excess oil. You can now dress the fish with something like preserved lemon salsa or harissa mayonnaise, or make sauce Vierge — the sky is the limit. Serve with some salads, a tagine of chicken and perhaps a lamb or beef steak off the barbecue. That's real modern Australian entertaining.

CRUMBED JOHN DORY WITH BRAISED PEAS

John Dory is a fish of firm texture and sweet and delicate flavour, and has always been considered one of the kings of fish because of its ability to be completely free of bones and, of course, for that great flavour and firm texture. This dish is a wonderful marriage of fish and vegetables — you will use braised peas for lots of things when you see how good they taste and how easy they are to make, but with the crunch of the crumbs and the sweet flesh of the Dory they are superb. If you like, purée the peas in a blender and add a touch of butter for the most wicked sauce that goes wonderfully with the fish. It is very simple to deep-fry the fish, but you can easily pan-fry it in half butter and half olive oil, or in clarified butter. Make sure you give a little squeeze of fresh lemon juice when you serve it; it makes such a difference. John Dory comes in different sizes, as I guess all fish does, but the ones I use here are the smaller fillets that come between 70 and 100 g ($2^1/2$ and $3^1/2$ oz) each, which means we have two per person.

INGREDIENTS

8 John Dory fillets, each one weighing about 80 g ($2^3/4$ oz)
125 g ($4^1/2$ oz/1 cup) plain (all-purpose) flour
1 egg, beaten with 250 ml (9 fl oz/1 cup) milk for the egg wash
175 g (6 oz/2 cups) fresh breadcrumbs (page 278)
vegetable oil, for deep-frying
300 g ($10^1/2$ oz/2 cups) braised peas (page 314)
sea salt
freshly ground pepper
lemon wedges

METHOD

Set up a crumbing station with three bowls, left to right: bowl one, flour; bowl two, egg wash; bowl three, breadcrumbs. At the end, a clean plate to put your crumbed fish on. Start by coating the first fish fillet in flour, dusting off the excess. Dip in the egg wash, then place in the breadcrumbs and coat all over. Shake off the excess and place the fillet on the plate. Repeat with the rest of the fish, set them aside and clean your crumbing station.

Either heat a saucepan of oil large enough to take about three to four fillets at a time and check the temperature with a thermometer or turn on your deep-fat fryer. The temperature must be 180°C (350°F) and it must be maintained at that temperature during the entire process, so don't be tempted to overcrowd the fryer. You will need a plate large enough to hold the cooked fish and keep them warm — line it with paper towels to soak up any excess surface oil.

Put your first batch of fish in the pan or fryer and cook until golden brown, remove and place on the prepared plate and keep warm; repeat until all the fish fillets are cooked. Meanwhile, heat the braised peas in a saucepan.

Divide the peas among four large white plates, place two John Dory fillets on each plate, sprinkle with some sea salt and give a good grind of pepper. Put a lemon wedge on each plate and serve immediately. Serves 4

ACCOMPANIMENTS

• Along with the braised peas underneath the fish, pumpkin or parsnip purée on the side would be terrific.

• The Dory is nice served on any of the English spinach dishes, braised Roman (flat) beans or Brussels sprouts. Some of the soup purées would go well too. I like the thought of the zucchini, broccolini and cauliflower pasta sauce as a sauce for this dish. You could serve a little fresh tartare or aïoli on the side, or any of the salsas. I quite like the yoghurt and garlic sauce with it as well, and try making the pumpkin and pea risotto to serve underneath the fish.

FLATHEAD WITH BEER BATTER

Battered fish, yum! Battering the fish does two things: one, it protects the fish from the fierce heat, so that it gently steams inside the batter; and, two, it gives a great crunchy exterior. This is a really simple beer batter: leave it lumpy, as it seems to make the fish more crisp and more tender at the same time. If you whisk or incorporate it well, it makes it tougher. Flathead is a really sweet white-fleshed fish with a nice large flake; it is also easy to fillet and avoid the bones, which is one reason why many kids grow up on it. It was once considered cheap, but now has risen in value. It is a truly great fish, and one of my brother Robin's favourites. You can substitute any white-fleshed fish or shellfish; don't use oily fish though, as they are better suited to other uses. Cook the fish fairly quickly, as the faster they get to the table the better.

INGREDIENTS

4 x 200 g (7 oz) flathead fillets
vegetable oil, for deep-frying
seasoned flour
lemon wedges
sea salt

FOR THE BEER BATTER
plain (all-purpose) flour
350 ml (12 fl oz) beer, chilled

METHOD

To make the beer batter, add enough flour to the beer to give it the consistency of pouring cream. Mix it with a chopstick (it shouldn't be completely smooth), allow to stand for 10 minutes in the refrigerator, then add some ice cubes — the batter seems to turn crisp in the hot oil better if it is cold.

Heat the oil in a large frying pan or deep-fat fryer to 180°C (350°F). Dip the flathead fillets in the seasoned flour, then into the batter, shake off any excess and gently put into the oil. Don't try to cook all the fish at once, do it in two or three batches. Cook for about 5 minutes, or until the batter is golden brown, then remove the fish with a spider or slotted spoon and drain on paper towels. Keep warm while you cook the rest. When ready, place a fish fillet on each of four plates and serve with a lemon wedge and a sprinkle of sea salt. Serves 4

ACCOMPANIMENTS
• Go the whole hog: serve with home-made chips and fresh tartare sauce.

POACHING, STEWING AND BRAISING

Poaching is cooking in liquid at very low heat. It is a good method for cooking whole fish like salmon and ocean trout. Although poaching can be done in a liquid as simple as salted water, it is more than likely to be in a court bouillon, which is water flavoured with aromatic vegetables, herbs and wine. The most important thing to remember is that poaching must occur at low temperatures, so make sure you have a thermometer that will measure between 60 and 70°C (140 and 158°F). You must also cook the liquid first to make sure it is full of flavour before you add your fish or shellfish. The best thing about this method of cooking is that the fish will be delicate and moist when done; this is all achieved through strict temperature control. Poached fish or shellfish will nearly always be served with a separate sauce.

I include that little explanation so you will know how poaching differs from stewing and braising. As I prefer to cook and serve fish in its own sauce, and reserve simple side sauces for fish that have an appealing crust with flavour and texture, I much prefer roasting, barbecuing and frying whole fish to poaching. So there will not be a recipe for poached fish in this book, as I never cook it, or at least haven't for many years.

Braising and stewing are both variations on poaching in liquid where the poaching broth becomes part of the dish. Braising seafood is no different to braising meat (see page 284), except that the fish is already tender, so long cooking is not needed. What is needed is a careful consideration of temperature: don't boil the broth, or the delicate fish will fall apart. A stew is basically the same as a braise, but usually the seafood is cut into smaller pieces, so it is not uncommon for a stew to be fully covered by the liquid. Many fish stews feature combinations of different fish and shellfish, such as a traditional bouillabaisse, and we at Rockpool use lots of different aromatic broths to cook fish and shellfish in. So you can change the flavours of the stew, but still end up with a wonderful big party-size bowl of seafood to be served with lashings of toasted bread and aïoli or chilli mayonnaise. Make sure you concentrate on making a really flavourful broth, as this is the basis of the dish. No fish, cooking in just a few minutes, will be able to save a wishy-washy tasting broth.

JEWFISH WITH MUSSEL SAFFRON STEW

Jewfish are another of those Australian fish that suffer from a number of aliases. Its various names include mulloway, river kingfish, kingfish, school jewfish and, of course, jewfish, which is what I know it as. It is also mixed up with the Western Australian dhufish, which is related to pearl perch. It also suffers from being soft textured when it is young, so the juveniles are often called soapy jewfish. However, nothing could be further from the truth when it comes to the larger fish. I like them over 5 kg (11 lb); at that stage they have a medium to firm large flake to the fillets, a nice distinctive flavour and they cook up wonderfully moist. They are good to roast and stew and the cutlets are really good on the barbecue. This recipe uses the mussel and saffron soup from the soup chapter. I use half a quantity; however, you can go mad and use a full quantity of soup with a few different fish, some scallops, squid, prawns (shrimp) and even crab or lobster. That would make an incredible feast. This sounds like a crazy idea, but if you are cooking for a few, barbecue half the seafood, place on a platter and pour the rest of the stew over.

INGREDIENTS
4 x 200 g (7 oz) jewfish steaks, or use salmon or monkfish tail, cut into thirds
sea salt
extra virgin olive oil
1/2 quantity mussel and saffron soup, about 1.5 litres (52 fl oz/6 cups), mussels and butter reserved separately (pages 104–106)
3 tablespoons finely shredded flat-leaf (Italian) parsley
freshly ground pepper

METHOD
Season the fish with sea salt. In a heavy-based deep-sided frying pan, heat a small amount of extra virgin olive oil until hot (it will start to shimmer). Add the jewfish pieces and seal for 1 minute, then add the mussel and saffron soup broth, without the mussels and butter. When it starts to return to a simmer, increase the heat to just below boiling. Turn the fish over after 2 minutes, then add the mussels and cook for 2 minutes, by which time the fish should be cooked. Add the butter. Sprinkle the pan with the parsley and add a grind of fresh pepper. Either place on the table with a ladle and bowls for everyone, or put in four bowls. Serves 4

ACCOMPANIMENTS
• All this dish needs is lashings of aïoli, good crusty bread, a green salad and a glass of riesling. Rice or couscous could be used to soak up the lovely juices.

BLUE EYE FILLET STEWED WITH CLAMS

This dish has its roots in Spain. Bacon and clams (vongole) were made for each other — put them together in a pasta sauce and you will love it. I like the bite from the chilli, and the bacon and paprika team up to give this dish a nice smoky edge. For a real treat you could use chorizo instead of bacon, which would really give the Spanish influence a push along. You need a large saucepan that will hold all the ingredients comfortably and that has a lid; something like a casserole pot would work okay. Make sure you give the clams a quick rinse before use, as they can have sand on them. You usually don't have to soak them, as they are sold purged. Cod, turbot, scrod or snapper would all work well in this recipe if you can't get blue eye fillets.

INGREDIENTS

4 x 200 g (7 oz) blue eye fillets

sea salt

4 garlic cloves, roughly chopped

1 tablespoon chopped fresh ginger

1/2 teaspoon sea salt

1/2 tablespoon fennel seeds, roasted (page 330)

1/2 teaspoon smoky sweet paprika

1/2 teaspoon mild chilli flakes

extra virgin olive oil

1 red onion, finely sliced

2 rashers smoky bacon or pancetta, finely diced

250 ml (9 fl oz/1 cup) white wine

150 g (5 1/2 oz/1 cup) freshly shelled peas, about 250 g (9 oz) unshelled

250 ml (9 fl oz/1 cup) chicken stock (page 384)

600 g (1 lb 5 oz/3 cups) clams (vongole), quickly rinsed

60 g (2 1/4 oz) unsalted butter

freshly ground pepper

1 small handful flat-leaf (Italian) parsley, roughly chopped

METHOD

Season the fish with sea salt. Put the garlic, ginger, sea salt and fennel seeds in a mortar and pound with a pestle to form a rough paste. Add the paprika and chilli flakes and pound a little more; it doesn't have to be too fine. Heat a splash of extra virgin olive oil in a deep frying pan and when hot, add the fish fillets and sear on both sides to get a nice crust. Remove the fillets to a plate and add a bit more oil to the pan. Add the onion and bacon and a little more sea salt and cook for 5 minutes, or until the onion is just turning soft. Add the spice paste and cook for a further 2 minutes, then add the wine and cook out for 2 minutes. Add the peas, chicken stock and clams and bring to the boil. Return the fish and bring to a simmer. Cover and simmer gently for 8 minutes, or until the fish is cooked and the clams have opened. Discard any that don't open. Mix the butter in until just melted, but don't boil again. Give a good grind of fresh pepper, stir through the parsley and check the seasoning. Add more salt if necessary.

Divide the fish among four bowls, spoon the juices and clams over the fish and serve immediately with a couple of bowls for shells on the table. Serves 4

ACCOMPANIMENTS

• Steamed rice and spinach with garlic and lemon would keep the taste really simple, as there is plenty happening in the dish itself, and the rice will soak up all the juices.

• The number of side dishes is up to you. It would be nice to add some steamed potatoes, if you're not serving rice. The addition of aïoli or harissa mayonnaise would be pleasing.

FOLLOWING PAGES blue eye fillet stewed with clams, left, and tagine of bar cod, right 213

TAGINE OF BAR COD

Bar cod is one of my very favourite fish caught off the east coast of Australia. It has a great oil content, very firm flesh and the sweetest taste. I always have it on the Rockpool menu if it is available. Any large, white, broad flaked fish will do for this dish. You need a fish that can be cut into cubes and when the sauce is ready, braised very quickly. I use a tagine to cook this in at home, but any heavy-based saucepan with a lid will do. You can vary the vegetables and the chermoula to whatever mix you like. It is nice to get a balance between sweet, sour and hot. Strictly speaking, you would probably see nothing like this in Morocco — I doubt they cook fish like this (Morocco is usually the home of slow-braising meat and poultry) — but I find this dish truly delicious. Now, the important thing is to get the vegetables very soft before adding the fish.

INGREDIENTS

700 g (1 lb 9 oz) bar cod fillet

8 baby beets, skin on and washed

2 baby fennel bulbs, both ends trimmed and cut in half

8 baby carrots, skin on

8 little kipfler (fingerling) potatoes, skin on and washed

250 ml (9 fl oz/1 cup) chermoula (page 372)

juice of 1 lemon

2 tablespoons good-quality honey

1 teaspoon sea salt

40 g (1^{1}/4 oz/^{1}/4 cup) blanched almonds

55 g (2 oz/^{1}/4 cup) green olives

1 preserved lemon, quartered, pith removed and rind finely sliced (page 380)

METHOD

Cut the bar cod fillet into 3–4 cm (1^1/4–1^1/2 inch) cubes. Put a tagine or large saucepan on the stove that will fit all the vegetables and the fish when it is time to cook. Put the vegetables in and add 1 litre (35 fl oz/4 cups) water. Add the chermoula, lemon juice, honey, sea salt, almonds and olives. Bring to the boil, reduce to a gentle simmer and cook for about 1 hour, covered, or until the vegetables are well cooked. Remove the lid and add the fish and preserved lemon rind and stir through. With the lid off, gently simmer until cooked, stirring very gently from time to time. This should only take a few minutes. Remove the tagine from the heat.

Either divide among four bowls or serve the tagine or pan in the middle of the table. Serve immediately. Serves 4

ACCOMPANIMENTS

• Moroccan eggplant salad, almond couscous and a dollop of harissa on the side would make a beautiful Moroccan Sunday lunch.

• I love tagines with a raw fennel salad, a simple green salad and coucous; rice would also be good. Any combination of vegetables and salads will work: try this with braised beetroot, yam, peas and bean salad and perhaps a chicken tagine as well, some couscous or rice, a side dish of hot harissa and you have a Moroccan feast.

STEWED SNAPPER WITH CRAZY WATER

I love all of Marcella Hazan's cookbooks — as a matter of fact, I think if you read all of hers and all of Elizabeth David's you could stop there and be just about the finest Mediterranean cook possible. She has a recipe in one of her books called fish in crazy water. I liked the look of it and loved the taste of it and, even better, it is the simplest stew imaginable. You just boil up the ingredients in water, reduce it, simmer the fish briefly and there you have it. Marcella Hazan says that it is a Neapolitan creation and no one seems to know why it is called fish in crazy water. I have no idea either; however, I know this — it should be called simply delicious fish. You must use lovely ripe tomatoes here, so make this a summer dish, and I like to use small, thin whole snappers that are just under 1 kg (2 lb 4 oz) each in weight. Once filleted, you will end up with fillets weighing about 200 g (7 oz) each, with the skin on. Any white-fleshed fish works well. Simmer the ingredients well; it is this that turns the simple into the sublime. I love to make this sauce, braise squid in it quickly and serve it with aïoli — can you ever get enough garlic?

INGREDIENTS

4 x 200 g (7 oz) snapper fillets, skin on

7 vine-ripened tomatoes, peeled, deseeded and chopped (page 66)

3 large garlic cloves, thinly sliced

2 tablespoons finely chopped flat-leaf (Italian) parsley

2 small red chillies, deseeded and chopped

60 ml (2 fl oz/^{1}/4 cup) extra virgin olive oil

^{1}/2 teaspoon sea salt

METHOD

Use a heavy-based frying pan that will fit the fish fillets snugly. Put the tomato, garlic, parsley, chilli, extra virgin olive oil, sea salt and about 875 ml (30 fl oz/ 3^1/2 cups) water in the pan. Bring to the boil, reduce to a gentle simmer, cover and cook for 45 minutes. Remove the lid, increase the heat and cook until the volume has reduced by half. Add the fish skin side up and simmer gently for about 2 minutes. Carefully turn the fish over and cook for a further 5 minutes, by which time it should be done. Remove the pan from the heat. Gently place one fish fillet on each of four white plates, spoon the sauce over and serve immediately. Serves 4

ACCOMPANIMENTS

• Some favourite side dishes here are broccolini with garlic and chilli, either pan-fried or soft polenta and gnocchi. A dollop of aïoli also works wonders.

MEAT AND POULTRY

Meat has been a very important part of my life. One would imagine so, being the son of a butcher, and with three butcher brothers. Now, coming from a restaurant that is famous for its seafood, you may think that along the way I got sidetracked. Well, the truth is that I love meat, poultry and fish, and although Rockpool is famous for its fish, we have always done a number of meat and bird dishes to rival any restaurant in the world. I guess it helps to have a father who was both a fisherman and a butcher. I also have some pretty strong views on meat and poultry quality, how it should be aged and how it should be cooked. They will follow.

But let's talk about the good news. The good news is that it is easy to cook a great roast at home, quite often one that will be better than most restaurants' roasts, if indeed they have one on the menu. You can roast a large rib of beef, a whole rack of pork, a leg of lamb or large bird, and know that you are in complete control of a fantastic feast. I put roasts in the same group as pasta and risotto — in most cases yours will be better than the restaurant version. I have always roasted in the restaurant at low temperatures for large joints, cooking them whole, and taken the risk of either running out or having portions leftover. The simple reason is that this is by far the best way to cook the meat, as it gives it a flavour and texture that is totally different from individually cooked portions. The other reason is that no one else does it in Sydney like this. We roast large aged ribs of beef, full racks of milk-fed veal and boned large chickens, which we stuff and slow roast, carving five beautiful serves from each gorgeous chicken. We always season the large joint well in advance, cook at a very low temperature and seal the meat and caramelize the outside just before resting it for a considerable amount of time. All this means we can serve the tastiest slice of tender meat or bird imaginable.

In my view, the four most important elements to a great roast are: the quality of the raw product; the seasoning; the care taken in cooking (temperature); and the resting. We don't drown our meat or poultry in sauces, but serve them with a simple salsa and vegetable support.

COMPOSITION

Meat and poultry are mainly muscle, which, in turn, is made up of about seventy-five per cent water. This is why overcooking is easy and shrinkage from too high a heat a big problem. Protein makes up about the next twenty per cent. It coagulates during cooking, which gives us 'doneness'. It is also the reason for tough meat, when it is cooked too quickly. About five per cent is fat, which varies from cut to cut, but it is important, as fat keeps the meat and poultry juicy and tender (and let's not forget that fat is flavour, so a well-marbled piece of beef will taste stronger than other pieces, while the best part of a chicken can be its skin). Meat and poultry also contain a small amount of carbohydrate, which plays its part in the reaction that allows meat to brown on the outside, giving great flavour and a pleasing appearance. Meat, of course, has much larger muscle fibres than poultry and needs special consideration when carving — in particular, make sure you cut across the grain for a tender chew.

Meat comes as two main sorts: leaner cuts or those with a lot of connective tissue. Leaner cuts are known as primary cuts and include cuts such as fillet, sirloin, rib eye, rump, topside and round. In most cases, primary cuts are cooked with dry heat. Those with a lot of connective tissue, the harder working muscles, are often referred to as secondary cuts, and will generally be cooked with moist heat. They include cuts such as shank, brisket, chuck, short rib and silverside. The connective tissue starts to melt at around 53–55°C (127–131°F) and this allows us to braise and slow roast successfully. Once all those connective tissues have turned to gelatine the meat is melt-in-the-mouth tender.

It is generally acknowledged that the smaller the primary cut the higher the heat, and with secondary cuts the moist heat should be gentle, not fierce, so never boil, but gently simmer, and this way you will avoid ending up with tough meat.

BUYING MEAT AND POULTRY

You will get back what you put in. Good-quality meat usually has a vibrant bloom to it with fat that is quite white in colour, but there is no substitute for having a good butcher who has earned your trust. Veal should be pink to white, as should pork, which should also have creamy-white-looking fat. Chickens should be free-range and probably organic — there is a gulf of difference between a battery-raised chook and a really good one. It's the difference between ordinary and excellent.

Most meat that you buy in Australia has been wet-aged or cryovaced, which essentially means that the meat is packed in a bag with the air sucked out (vacuum-packed). This process allows the meat to be kept for a long time in the packaging and is a manageable system for both wholesaler and butcher. The problem with vacuum-packed meats is that the juice leaves the meat and lives in the packaging. The juice will seep back in after time, but when you open the bag, the meat will have a nasty odour that never leaves. The meat also loses more juice during cooking, and to me always has a slightly cardboard taste to it, kind of liverish. I guess that is because the meat dries out more.

The other, more traditional way to process meat is to hang and dry-age it for four weeks on the bone. This method produces the best-quality meat. Unfortunately, in Australia, it is almost impossible to buy such meat. This may be because the weight loss and the amount of time spent hanging is too much for the average consumer to support, price-wise. I'm lucky as my brother Robin hangs all my meat for me, and that is one of the reasons we end up with a superior piece of beef at the restaurant. During the hanging, the juice sets in the beef and the activity of the enzymes present in the meat increases the flavour and tenderness of it, a kind of controlled rotting I suppose. However, don't try to dry-age meat at home. The temperature control must be strict, the moisture level low, and an ionizer is needed to help rid the air of bacteria — all these things cannot be achieved at home. If you know a good butcher and he will hang some rib eye on the bone for you, then you have a true friend and one that will make your roast king.

RESTING

I cannot stress how important it is to rest meat and poultry properly. It always amazes me how many people say, 'what?' when I talk about resting. Though we read about it often, the message still doesn't seem to get through. So here it is: meat and poultry will taste better and be more tender if you rest them after cooking. It makes perfect sense.

When you apply heat to the surface of meat or poultry, the juice rushes away from the heat as it is driven out of the shrinking surface cells, and rushes to the middle and beyond if you keep cooking it. However, if you take the meat and put it in a warm place, the heat will subside through a process of reverse osmosis and the juice will move back to the outside and fill any cells that haven't been damaged completely. This allows us to have a crunchy, tasty crust and a melting interior. The meat or poultry will also relax and the final result will be a tastier, juicier, more tender meal. You can see this when you cut into a piece of meat straight off the heat. It will 'bleed' when you cut it, as all the juice is trapped in the middle. If you cut it after resting, it will be pink all the way through and release much less juice. As a rule, the larger the piece of meat, the longer it needs to rest.

Don't forget, as a piece of cooked meat rests, its internal temperature rises. This is due to the residual heat that keeps cooking the meat after it is removed from the heat source. The higher the heat during cooking the more it will continue to cook — conventional temperature cooking will raise the meat's core temperature by 6–8°C (11–14°F), which means your rare meat may turn medium and so on. Therefore, you need to always take your meat out of the oven before it reaches the desired final temperature. This is slightly complicated when we talk about slow roasting, as the cooking temperature is not far off the final temperature you want the meat to be at after resting. It will take a lot longer to cook, but won't need to rest as long. In this case, the temperature shift is likely to be around only 2°C (4°F). But we will discuss that in more detail when we get to the recipe for slow-roasted rib of beef (page 228).

CONTROLLED COOKING

To follow this method successfully two things are essential: an oven thermometer and a digital meat thermometer. The first is needed so that you can keep a check on your oven's true temperature, and the latter so that you can read the core temperature of large joints and birds and cook to your liking every time. Controlled cooking is a matter of knowing what core cooking temperature you need to give you rare, medium and well done meat after allowing for the residual cooking that will occur during resting. The amount of residual cooking will vary depending on the temperature at which you cooked the meat or poultry.

Remember, the higher the oven temperature, the more the temperature of the meat will rise during resting. Refer to the temperature chart below to see the different core temperatures and corresponding states of doneness for meat and poultry. When checking the temperature of a piece of meat with your meat thermometer, make sure you push the thermometer into the fleshy part of the joint and don't let it touch the bone if there is one, as it will give you a false reading and you will probably overcook the meat.

FINAL CORE TEMPERATURES OF MEAT AND POULTRY

Beef	55°C (131°F) rare, 62°C (144°F) medium, 70°C (158°F) well done
Lamb	55°C (131°F) rare, 62°C (144°F) medium, 70°C (158°F) well done
Veal	64°C (147°F) medium, 70°C (158°F) well done
Pork	74°C (165°F) well done
Chicken	70–75°C (158–167°F) well done

A word on these temperatures. They are international standards and are a very good guide to doneness. However, you need to check and take a few notes when you cook. For instance, I cook poultry and pork to temperatures quite a bit lower than those given above and I still get a result that would be considered well done. We bone whole chickens at Rockpool, roll them into a loose cylinder and cook them in a low oven until they reach a core temperature of 55–58°C (131–136°F), rest them and when we carve them they are completely cooked through. So what does that say? Well, it says that there are guidelines, but you can push them a little when you feel confident. Just do whatever feels good for you, and once you know the core temperature you like your meat and poultry cooked to, you will always be in control. In the end, however, nothing will serve you better than practice and taking the time to understand the theory behind this method of cooking.

SEASONING

I can't stress enough what salting your meat or poultry does to enhance flavour. Use good-quality sea salt and, if it is a large joint, season the night before. If small, season just before you cook. Seasoning properly is commonly the difference between the home and professional cook.

I stress season, season, season. Although I love marinades and herbs and spices with meat and poultry, particularly when barbecuing, I am not a big fan of peppering either before or after cooking. I think the aromatic and lifted flavour and aroma of pepper is lost and it can become bitter, so as a rule, I very rarely pepper when I season meat or poultry. I do, however, pepper madly when I serve it.

PLANNING AHEAD

I know how hard it is to be organized these days, especially when it comes to time, but you will get a much better result when cooking meat and poultry if you remember to remove them from the refrigerator and let them come to room temperature before you start cooking. This is especially true with smaller cuts that you intend to pan-fry or barbecue. The steak or chop will cook much more evenly and you can avoid the problem of having the main part cooked to your liking while another part is overcooked.

Each of the cooking methods for meat is represented in this chapter. I will go through them when appropriate to each dish. You may think as you read the book that I'm harping on about certain aspects that may seem the same for meat, poultry and fish cookery, but that is because I am — I don't want you to miss the point. I want you to take skills away from this book that can change the way you approach cooking or maybe enhance the things you do, if already skilled.

Again, like the seafood chapter, use this book the way it was written, not as two hundred recipes that are to be followed slavishly to create two hundred different dishes, but as a guide to many different dishes that can reflect your likes and loves for particular taste and texture and for all the beautiful ingredients that are available throughout the year. I have suggested accompaniments from the other chapters in this book, so use the index to help you locate them, but you can create hundreds of great combinations yourself, as you will cook with good technique and a strong understanding of what you are going to achieve through the many chapters in this book.

ROASTING

The term roast comes from the original spit-roasting that was done over open fires. Today, it is a term used for dry heat cooking usually done in an oven; this applies to both meat and poultry. This sort of dry heat cooking is usually called baking when talking about cakes and pastries and some vegetables. Of course, when I was a youngster, we always had the baked dinner, but the term seems to have generally changed to roast. Cooking uncovered is essential when roasting as covering would create steam, and you want to get that lovely browning effect. You will find that most ovens have little hot spots, and that the back of the oven is hottest, so make sure you rotate your dish during cooking to help ensure an even cooking, or place the largest or thickest part of the roast to the back.

SLOW-ROASTED RIB OF BEEF

I can't say enough about how fantastic this method of cooking meat is. We have had a long time to perfect it at Rockpool and you will need to do a little adjusting yourself, but the good news is that with a meat and an oven thermometer you will always be in control of the situation; it is foolproof. We slow cook at 75°C (167°F) in a combination oven that has a great deal of control — but you would certainly expect that at a cost of $40,000, and I will assume that you may not have spent quite that much. You are going to have to see how your oven performs. I have done functions at people's homes where the oven won't even start until around 100°C (212°F), and gas ovens tend to cut in and out at low temperatures and can be a bit flaky in terms of consistency. The most important thing to do is to check your oven temperature with an oven thermometer, a simple and inexpensive device. It doesn't matter if the lowest your oven can go is around 90°C (194°F) — this will just vary the cooking time — as you will be able to test the meat's core temperature with your meat thermometer, and thus remain in control. The one thing this recipe does demand is time. It will take up to three hours to cook a large 4-bone rib of beef that will feed six to eight people. The theory is quite simple. The meat's core temperature during cooking is not far off what we want the meat's core temperature to be after resting. This slow, gentle cooking allows the juices to set throughout the beef and not be sent rushing into the centre as the beef's outside cells are destroyed by high heat. The browning of the meat occurs after it is taken from the oven. In this way, you achieve the best of both worlds — a delicious crust and a melting interior. I like to serve this dish rare, although it may look very rare. The texture of the meat is set all the way through so it will be meltingly tender and very moist. To do this, we want to slowly take the meat's core cooking temperature to about 53°C (127°F) only, as it will rise to about 55°C (131°F) while resting. At this temperature, all the connective tissue will soften and the internal fat will be like jelly. If you want to take it a bit further than rare consult the temperature chart (page 226) for doneness and remember to calculate in the residual cooking, especially if you are having trouble keeping your oven low.

The catch with slow roasting is that it takes up oven space for a long time. If, like me, you only have one oven at home, don't despair! I often make a potato gratin beforehand in a lovely big casserole or roasting dish, slide it in the oven on the bottom rack with one hour to go to gently heat through. While I'm carving the meat I have Sam slide the gratin under the oven grill (broiler) with some butter and breadcrumbs on top for a nice glazed top. Sometimes I just boil potatoes, then sauté them with onions in a little duck fat. Yum. All you need then is a really good green salad.

When you have a bunch of people around, cook a full six-bone rib of beef and it will blow everyone away. The following method works no matter how big the piece of meat is.

INGREDIENTS

2- or 3-bone rib of beef (2–3 ribs will be enough for 4 people), preferably dry-aged for at least 3 weeks
sea salt
extra virgin olive oil
freshly ground pepper

METHOD

Preheat the oven to 75°C (167°F), or as low as it will go. Take the rib out of the refrigerator a couple of hours before you intend to cook it and season it well with sea salt. Let it come to room temperature. (Alternatively, you can do what we do at Rockpool and season it the night before.) Rub the rib with extra virgin olive oil and put in a large roasting tin. Put in the preheated oven and turn the dish every 30 minutes or so. About 1 1/2 hours into the roasting, slide the meat thermometer into the centre of the beef to check the core cooking temperature, remove the thermometer and continue to cook until the reading is 53°C (127°F). This will take up to 3 hours and beyond — it may take up to 4 hours in all. Remember that if your oven is a little hotter, you will need to take the meat out a degree or two earlier.

When the meat is done, remove it and put it on a chopping board. Carefully remove the bones from the beef and turn the oven down as low as it will go (you may need to pin the door slightly ajar), as you want to create a warm environment of around 60°C (140°F) in which to rest the meat. Put a frying pan that is large enough to hold the beef on the stove. Add a healthy splash of extra virgin olive oil and heat to just below smoking. Add the beef and sear, turning 3 cm (1^1/4 inch) at a time, until the entire rib has a lovely crust. Return it to the roasting tin and put in the oven for about 30 minutes to rest while you get the other parts of the meal together, or at least get your guests a drink. Alternatively, you can sear the beef as it is and serve on the bone.

On a chopping board, cut the rib into four beautiful rose-red round slices and place one each in the centre of four plates. Drizzle with extra virgin olive oil and season liberally with freshly ground pepper. Serve immediately. Serves 4

DON'T FORGET

You have a meat thermometer in your hand, so you can cook the meat at whatever temperature you like, but if you cook it on high heat — say at around 200°C (400°F) — you will have to take it out when its internal cooking temperature is 48–49°C (118–120°F), as the meat's core temperature will continue to rise a fair bit due to the residual cooking. The meat will also benefit from a much longer resting period, about 1 hour. You won't need to seal the beef, however, as the high heat will do that for you. Consult the temperature chart and cook your meat to whichever level of doneness you like.

ACCOMPANIMENTS

• This classic roast beef goes well with many things but I like to serve it with spinach purée, potato gratin and horseradish cream.

• Any steamed or boiled green vegetable will go well with roast beef, as will any of the English spinach dishes, the sautéed mushrooms and cream of corn. Roast potato, potato purée and pumpkin and parsnip purée are also good matches. As for sauce I like to keep it quite simple so that the flavour of the beef rules, but any of the butters at room temperature, sliced and placed in the middle of the beef would be delicious. So, too, would hollandaise and Béarnaise, served on the side, and some of the puréed soups in the soup chapter would make a good sauce, just don't add too much stock, as you want it thicker — just a bit thicker than pouring cream would be good. Flavours like Jerusalem artichoke, mushroom or fennel would work well. A bit of advice on red wine sauce: by all means serve it, but be careful to use just a tablespoon per portion, not a full ladle. I think it really overpowers and drowns the beef, especially when the flavour of the beef is supposed to be paramount.

SLOW-ROASTED RACK OF MILK-FED VEAL

It can be a problem to get good-quality milk-fed veal in Australia and the United States. In Europe, milk-fed veal is more widely available but sometimes the rearing arrangements may be a little questionable. The best option is to trust and work with your butcher, and they may be able to get good-quality veal racks that you can roast.

This recipe works on exactly the same principle as the previous one. The essential thing to do is to bring the veal to the correct core cooking temperature of around 60°C (140°F). It is higher than that of the beef as milk-fed veal is best served just below well done, rather than rare. The veal is cooked at a low temperature, which is sympathetic with the fact that veal is very lean and therefore dries out easily.

This recipe produces a succulent roast that goes well with a simple dressing. As with the beef, it is great to get a full rack and have a few friends over. It presents beautifully and is something that most people won't have seen. Make sure the butcher removes the chine bone from the ribs, otherwise carving will be difficult.

INGREDIENTS
> 3- or 4-bone rack of milk-fed veal, chine bone removed
> sea salt
> extra virgin olive oil
> freshly ground pepper

METHOD

Preheat the oven to 75°C (167°F). Remove the rack from the refrigerator a couple of hours before cooking and rub the rack with sea salt. (Alternatively, season it the night before.) Rub the rack with extra virgin olive oil and put in a large roasting tin. Put in the preheated oven and turn the dish every 30 minutes or so. After about 1 hour, check the core cooking temperature with a meat thermometer. Don't forget that veal is less dense than beef because of the muscle structure, so it will not take as long to cook. When the temperature of the veal reaches 58–60°C (136–140°F), depending on whether you like it closer to medium or well done, remove it from the oven. Don't remove the bone. Put a frying pan large enough to take the rack on the stove over high heat and pour a little extra virgin olive oil in. When the oil is nearly smoking, add the rack and hold it with tongs so that all of the flesh side gets a good browning.

Reduce the oven temperature to around 60°C (140°F), holding the door ajar if necessary, and return the veal to the oven. Rest the rack for about 30 minutes while you tend to other things.

Place the rack on a chopping board and carefully slide your knife under the flesh. Find the bone and gently work the meat off in one piece. You should have the meat sitting in front of you with the eye of the rack facing away and the tail towards you. Now cut the veal into thick boneless cutlets and place one in the centre of each plate. Alternatively, you can serve the veal on the bone. Drizzle with extra virgin olive oil and add a grind of fresh pepper. Serve immediately. Serves 4

ACCOMPANIMENTS

• Slow-cooked veal cries out for creamed spinach, pan-roasted potatoes and perhaps a little roast garlic sauce. I'm a big fan of not serving a sauce with good-quality veal, as the taste is subtle and refined. It goes nicely just with some vegetable accompaniments.

• As with all roasted meat and poultry, any steamed or boiled green vegetable is perfect, which you can dress with extra virgin olive oil or drizzle with melted butter. All the English spinach dishes, as well as braised peas, fennel and Roman (flat) beans would be good. You could try serving some peperonata under the veal as a sort of vegetable sauce for the plate. Roasted, puréed and gratinéed potatoes go well, as does the parsnip and pumpkin purée. The veal would also be nice with the peperonata and pan-fried polenta in combination, keeping with an Italian theme. The soup chapter has some potential sauces that would not overpower, and the butters, especially the herb butter, would be nice placed on the veal at room temperature just before serving.

FOLLOWING PAGES slow-roasted rack of milk-fed veal, served with creamed spinach (page 309), left, and rack of pork, right

ROAST RACK OF PORK

'The pig is our friend', I once heard New York chef Mario Batali say. He is, of course, completely right. I guess he could not think of a world without cured pork products and I agree entirely. But there is also that other part of my life that couldn't imagine pork not being in practically everything: my life cooking Asian food. So, although in the pursuit of eating a balanced diet I don't eat pork every day, I could imagine myself doing so happily and I don't think I could say that of any other meat. Pork has been the great workhorse of cuisine for a very long time. A lot of us consume pork in its many guises as a cured product but, unless you are eating Asian food, the pig doesn't star too often as the centrepiece in a roast. This roast will change that. Find good pork with a decent amount of fat. Yes, fat is flavour and you shouldn't shy away from it all the time. Have this dish occasionally but have it properly, with lots of crackling and a nice measure of creamy fat.

As you have a meat thermometer, you are going to be able to cook the pork perfectly. Most pork roasts usually end up dry, as fear of disease has often caused overcooking. You can rest assured that at 59°C (138°F) the parasite that is responsible for trichinosis is killed, so you can cook the pork to 75°C (167°F) without fear and still have pork that is moist and tender. If you have any trouble getting the crackling to work you can put some oil in a saucepan and heat to hot, almost smoking, then pour it over the pork when you remove it from the oven; the skin will bubble up. Make sure you buy good-quality young pork, as an older piece will be too large for one cutlet per person. Also, make sure the butcher removes the chine bone from the ribs, or carving will be difficult.

INGREDIENTS

4-bone rack of pork, skin on and chine bone removed
60 ml (2 fl oz/^{1}/4 cup) red wine vinegar
sea salt
500 ml (17 fl oz/2 cups) vegetable oil
freshly ground pepper

METHOD

Remove the pork from the refrigerator about 3 hours before cooking. Using a Stanley knife or one-sided razor blade, make cuts in the skin of the pork from the top to the bottom, running in the same direction as the bones, about 3 mm (^{1}/8 inch) apart. Cut through the skin but don't go too deep into the flesh. Using your fingers, rub the red wine vinegar into the pork skin. Next, using a massaging action, rub sea salt into the skin. Set the rack aside to dry.

Preheat the oven to 180°C (350°F). Put the pork on a wire rack in a roasting tin and put in the oven. Cook undisturbed for 30 minutes, then turn the heat down to 160°C (320°F) and cook for a further 30 minutes. At this stage, check the meat's core cooking temperature. It may need a little longer, so just keep checking the core temperature until it reaches about 71°C (160°F). When done, remove the pork from the oven. Turn the oven down, or leave the door ajar, so the temperature drops to around 60°C (140°F). Rest the meat in the oven for about 30 minutes. During this time the meat's core temperature should rise to around 75°C (167°F), but just be sure to check. Just before serving, heat the vegetable oil in a small saucepan until just smoking. Remove the roasting tin from the oven and, with a spoon, pour the hot oil gently over the pork skin to complete the crackling.

Place the wire rack on a chopping board and gently cut the meat away from the ribs, so you have the full loin sitting in front of you. Cut it into four thick cutlets and place the cutlets on serving plates. Sprinkle with sea salt and freshly ground pepper and serve immediately. Serves 4

ACCOMPANIMENTS

• This little piggy goes well with boiled green vegetables, pumpkin purée and I love to buy Italian mustard fruits and slice them on the side.

• The English spinach dishes, as well as the braised peas, Roman (flat) beans, fennel and green cabbage are perfect, as are potatoes, the gratins and the parsnip purée. I like to keep the saucing to a minimum but a little dollop of any of the salsas would be good, as would a simple Jerusalem artichoke or fennel sauce, both from the soup section.

ROAST LEG OF LAMB WITH ROAST GARLIC

I love lamb. Being Australian I have to say that we are lucky and have some of the best lamb in the world. It is particularly fantastic around springtime when it is possible to get milk-fed lamb, but this recipe is all about that lovely leg of lamb that will feed the family. The legs usually come anywhere from 2–3 kg (4 lb 8 oz–6 lb 8 oz). I leave the shank on, as it is good eating and gives you a handle for the quick-carve lamb that I like to do. Make sure your butcher removes the d-shaped hipbone from the leg, otherwise it's a bugger to carve. Again, the oven temperature is higher than it is for beef, but the principle of controlled cooking is still the same. I like to have the lamb come out pink, which is medium rare to medium, and well rested, so I want an internal temperature of about 60°C (140°F) after resting. Don't forget residual heat. To finish at this temperature, I need to allow for a lift of about 5°C (9°F), so I remove the meat from the oven when its core temperature is 55–56°C (131–133°F).

I love the roast garlic in this dish. It will mingle with the juices and fats from the roast, plus, as it is pre-blanched, it will take on a lovely mild flavour. I serve the whole cloves on the sliced lamb with a bit of drizzle from whatever is in the bottom of the roasting tin. Then, to eat, you simply pop each clove and spread it on the lamb or, as I like to do, on a slice of crusty bread and eat it with the lamb. I usually cook one whole head of garlic per person. Sounds excessive, but just wait till you start eating it and you'll be wishing there was more.

INGREDIENTS

2–3 kg (4 lb 8 oz–6 lb 8 oz) leg of lamb, shank on
sea salt
4 whole garlic bulbs
extra virgin olive oil
20 g ($3/4$ oz/1 small bunch) thyme
freshly ground pepper

METHOD

Preheat the oven to 180°C (350°F). Remove the lamb from the refrigerator 2 hours before cooking and season with sea salt. (Alternatively, season the night before.) Let the meat come to room temperature.

To prepare the garlic, break the bulbs into individual cloves, making sure to leave the skin on. Put the garlic cloves in a saucepan of cold water over high heat and bring to the boil. Remove the cloves and refresh under cold water, then drain well and pat dry. Rub the lamb leg with extra virgin olive oil and put in a large roasting tin. Add the garlic cloves with a little extra oil and season the cloves with sea salt. Find places for the garlic around the leg of lamb and split the thyme up and do the same thing. Cook for 20 minutes, then turn the lamb over and turn the oven down to 160°C (330°F). Keep turning the lamb every 20 minutes and push the garlic around in the juices and oil to keep it moist. After 1 hour, start checking the meat's core temperature, remembering that the final resting temperature should be 60°C (140°F) and that we need to factor in the residual heat, so 55–56°C (131–133°F) should be fine. Once that temperature has been reached, remove the tin from the oven and try to get the oven temperature down to 60°C (140°F) for resting, holding the door ajar if necessary. Once the oven has reached the right temperature, remove the thyme from the dish and return the lamb to the oven to rest for 30 minutes.

Place the lamb leg on a chopping board, positioning it on one of its sides. Holding the shank with a tea towel, take a sharp knife and, starting from the ball at the end of the bone, cut down the bone, removing one of the large muscles. Now turn the lamb around and remove the rest of the meat from the bone by cutting down each side of the bone and removing the large piece of muscle left. You should have two large pieces of meat on the board that you can now cut into slices. Place the piece from near the bone on the board and slice straight down, as if you were going down the length of the leg bone. This will give you semi-circular slices that will be across the grain, making the lamb more tender. You can cut the shank off now and fight over who gets to eat it.

Place three to five slices on each plate and top with roasted garlic. Spoon some of the fat and juices from the roasting tin over the lamb. Give a good grind of fresh pepper and serve immediately. Serves 4

ACCOMPANIMENTS

- Lamb loves peas, so braised peas would be my first choice, although one could just boil them. Pumpkin purée and a dollop of aïoli would go nicely when squeezing the roast garlic cloves out of their skin.

- Steamed and boiled greens, all the English spinach, pea and bean dishes, as well as the broccolini or pan-fried asparagus would be great here. Roasted or puréed baby carrots would taste great with the lamb and garlic. Potatoes of any kind would make a good starch accompaniment, and I fancy that soft polenta would be pretty good as well. The lamb would go really nicely with either the skordalia (a nice garlic double up) or a spoonful of the tomato, almond and chilli salsa. For that matter romesco, tarator and salsa verde would be yummy too. Try a spoonful of garlic yoghurt on top of the lamb — this isn't left of field for me because I've tried it on fish, meat and poultry, and always loved it.

SLOW-ROASTED SHOULDER OF LAMB

This dish is fantastic for a summer dinner. It really ends up as shredded lamb shoulder; you can cut the lamb with a spoon but I like to shred it off the bone and have a little spicy tomato relish and some fresh salad to serve with it. The shoulder is perfect for this recipe as it has so much connective tissue; you would be hard pressed to find a lamb dish with more flavour. You can use ground spices for this dish, as indeed you can for many others, but you will get a better result if you use whole spices and roast them and grind them yourself. At the very least, try to buy small jars of spice and replace them every six months. Fresh is best.

INGREDIENTS

2 lamb shoulders, on the bone, weighing about 1.25 kg (2 lb 12 oz) each
$^1/2$ teaspoon ground coriander
$^1/2$ teaspoon ground fennel
$^1/2$ teaspoon ground cinnamon
2 star anise, ground
$^1/4$ teaspoon ground cardamom
$^1/4$ teaspoon freshly ground white pepper
2 teaspoons sea salt
60 ml (2 fl oz/$^1/4$ cup) extra virgin olive oil, plus extra
lemon wedges
freshly ground pepper

METHOD

The night before, trim the excess fat from the edges of the shoulders. Mix the spices, sea salt and extra virgin olive oil together and rub over the lamb. Put the lamb in a container, loosely cover with plastic wrap, then refrigerate overnight.

Remove the lamb from the refrigerator 2 hours before cooking and preheat the oven to 130°C (265°F). Put the shoulders in a roasting tin large enough to fit both and drizzle with a little extra virgin olive oil. Add 125 ml (4 fl oz/$^1/2$ cup) water. Use two sheets of foil joined together to make a tent over the lamb, then cook for $2^1/2$–3 hours. Reduce the heat to 110°C (230°F) and cook for 4 hours more. When ready, the lamb will be very well done. Remove from the oven and allow to rest for 20 minutes, then shred the meat off the bone. Put on a platter or divide between plates and serve with lemon and freshly ground pepper. Serves 4

ACCOMPANIMENTS

• Sautéed Brussels sprouts, herbed pink eye potatoes and tomato and chilli relish would be perfect with the tender lamb.

ROAST CHICKEN

There are a thousand and one recipes for roast chicken. Here are four to choose from. Three of them cook the bird whole but at different cooking temperatures and positions or use flavourings, and the last one roasts the bird flattened out; that is, butterflied.

All chickens are not created equal, so do spend the money and you will really notice the difference. A properly roasted chicken is one of the most delicious dishes but the chook must taste like something — you need to use sea salt and a good-quality extra virgin olive oil and people will say, 'Why doesn't my chicken taste like that?'.

Now that you have a meat thermometer, roasting a chicken becomes a little easier. You want the internal temperature to be around 68–70°C (154–158°F) after resting, so if you are roasting at a high temperature, take the chicken out 5°C (9°F) earlier, and if slow cooking, about 2°C (4°F) earlier. Remember that if you want to get the best results, you must rest chicken just as you do meat. There is always a concern when roasting chicken that the breast will dry out while the leg takes longer to cook. I like the butterflied method of cooking as I think it minimizes that problem. The other way around it is to truss your chicken; it is a great skill to have and is easy to do. It helps to hold the bird in good form for the cooking process and protects the thinner parts of the breast.

HOW TO TRUSS A CHICKEN — Take a piece of kitchen string about 40 cm (16 inches) long. Put the chicken on a chopping board, breast side up, with the legs and the cavity facing you. Make a triangular loop in the middle of the string, place it around the bottom and take the string up to the legs on the inside. Loop each end over the drumsticks, cross the string in the centre and pull away from the bird. You will now have the legs in tight. Take the string on one side of the bird past the thigh and loop it around the wing. Turning the bird over, take the string to the other wing, loop it, and with the other loose end, make a knot and tie it just before the thigh. Trim away the excess string. Your bird is now secure and ready to roast.

INGREDIENTS

    2 kg (4 lb 8 oz) free-range chicken
    sea salt
    extra virgin olive oil
    freshly ground pepper

METHOD

Take the bird out of the refrigerator at least 2 hours before cooking. Cut the wing tips and neck off the bird and pull back the neck flap of skin. There you will see the wishbone. Using a sharp paring knife, cut along it and cut down into the spots where it joins the breastplate. Cut through it at these points, then move up to the top where the two ends meet. Cutting gently, carefully pull it out. You should find it comes out quite easily. It is important to remove the wishbone, as it makes it far easier to carve later on.

Truss the chicken and season inside and out with sea salt. (Alternatively, season the bird the night before.) Preheat the oven to 160°C (320°F). Rub the bird all over with extra virgin olive oil and put in a roasting tin large enough to fit it comfortably. Put the bird on its side in the tin and put in the oven. After about 20 minutes, turn the bird over onto its other side, then after a further 20 minutes, turn it on its back and leave it to roast for the last 20 minutes. At this stage, place a meat thermometer in the thigh of the chicken, avoiding the bone. You want the final core temperature to be 68–70°C (154–158°F), so take the bird out a little before that to allow for the residual heat. Remove the bird from the tin and place it in a bowl with the breast side down and the legs in the air. Skim and discard the fat from the juices left in the roasting tin, and pour the juices over the bird. Cover with foil and rest for 20 minutes.

Put the bird on a chopping board and cut off the legs. Cut the legs in half by sliding your knife through the middle of the drumstick and thigh. Remove the breasts with the wings attached. Cut in half on the diagonal. The thicker half of the breast should have the wing attached but will not be quite as long as the other half. To plate, take four large plates and put half a leg on each plate, then half a breast. There should be some juice in the bowl you rested the bird in; add to it a little extra virgin olive oil and lots of freshly ground pepper, stir and pour some over each serving of chicken. Serve immediately. Serves 4

ACCOMPANIMENTS

• Boiled or pan-fried beans with burnt butter and almonds, potato and celeriac gratin and bread sauce would make this a classic roast chook.

• All the green vegetables — steamed, boiled or braised — go well with roast chicken. As do steamed and boiled potatoes. The steamed potatoes could be flavoured with some pesto or salsa verde. Herb mayonnaise would be a classic sauce to serve on the side.

SLOW-ROASTED CHICKEN

This version uses lower temperatures than the first recipe to cook the chook. The bird spends its whole time on its back, then, after resting, is jointed and put back in the roasting tin and placed under the grill (broiler) to brown. The meat will be succulent and delicious. With your trusty meat thermometer this will be child's play.

INGREDIENTS

2 kg (4 lb 8 oz) free-range chicken
sea salt
20 g ($3/4$ oz/1 small bunch) thyme
a few flat-leaf (Italian) parsley sprigs
extra virgin olive oil
freshly ground pepper

METHOD

Take the bird out of the refrigerator 2 hours before cooking and season the outside with sea salt. (Alternatively, season the night before.)

Preheat the oven to 75°C (167°F). Remove the wing tips, neck and wishbone as discussed in the previous recipe. Fill the cavity of the bird with the herbs and sprinkle the cavity with sea salt. Truss the bird (page 242) and rub it with extra virgin olive oil. Put it in a snug-fitting roasting tin on its back, pop it in the oven and cook until the chicken's core cooking temperature is about 65°C (149°F) — this might take about 2$1/2$–3 hours. Transfer the chicken to a bowl and rest, covered with foil, for 20 minutes. When the bird is cool enough to handle, cut it up into eight pieces as in the previous recipe. Put the pieces skin side up and side by side in the roasting tin and brush with extra virgin olive oil. Turn the grill (broiler) on and add the roasting tin, not so close to the grill bars that the skin burns, but close enough that the chicken can cook for about 5–8 minutes, browning the skin and thoroughly reheating the chicken.

Take four large plates and place two pieces of chicken on each, making sure there is a breast and a leg on each one, unless you have difficult people in the house. Season with freshly ground pepper and drizzle a little extra virgin olive oil over the chicken. Serve immediately. Serves 4

ACCOMPANIMENTS

• This dish goes well with all the things that the first roast chicken goes with, but steamed sugar snap peas with extra virgin olive oil drizzled over, soft polenta and anchovy butter would be a nice combination with this silky chicken.

ROAST CHICKEN WITH LEMON AND PARSLEY SALAD

This is a delicious dish that utilizes some of the ingredients that go so well with roast chicken. You have the choice to either pour the dressing and salad over the chicken on individual plates, or mix it all together and serve it on a large plate in the middle of the table for people to help themselves to. This is the way I would normally do it, with a big plate of roast potatoes and some salads alongside — what a mouth-watering lunch. The cooking method is the same as that used in the first roast chicken recipe, but by all means slow roast it, then crisp the skin under the grill (broiler) and toss it through the salad. This is what cooking is all about: learning the skills to move from one method to the next. It's about mixing and matching and keeping it fun.

HOW TO SEGMENT A CITRUS — Trim 1 cm ($1/2$ inch) from both ends, then sit the lemon on one flat end. With a small sharp knife, cut the skin away, from top to bottom, removing all the skin and pith. Working over a small bowl, cut between the membranes, letting the segments fall into the bowl. Squeeze the membrane to release any remaining juice. You will now have a bowl with segments floating in lemon juice.

INGREDIENTS

2 kg (4 lb 8 oz) free-range chicken

sea salt

1 lemon

a few flat-leaf (Italian) parsley sprigs

extra virgin olive oil

FOR THE SALAD

2 lemons, segmented

4 large anchovies, julienned

50 g (1 3/4 oz/1/2 cup) Ligurian olives

1 teaspoon salted baby capers, well rinsed and drained

35 g (1 1/4 oz/1/4 bunch) flat-leaf (Italian) parsley, small leaves picked,
  washed and dried

1 large handful mint, small leaf tips only picked, washed and dried

sea salt and freshly ground pepper

60 ml (2 fl oz/1/4 cup) extra virgin olive oil

METHOD

Take the chicken out of the refrigerator 2 hours before cooking. Season the chicken inside and out with sea salt. Cut the lemon in half, squeeze a little juice into the cavity of the bird, then put the lemon halves with the parsley sprigs into the chicken cavity. Truss the chicken (page 242), rub all over with extra virgin olive oil, then put in the oven and follow the method as described in the first roast chicken recipe (page 242–243), until you have the bird resting in a bowl.

To make the salad, combine the lemon segments, anchovies, olives, capers, parsley and mint and season with sea salt and freshly ground pepper. Add the extra virgin olive oil. Remove the lemon halves from the chicken and squeeze any remaining juice on the salad, then add the juices that have accumulated in the bottom of the bowl in which the chicken is resting.

Carve the chicken into eight equal pieces as described previously (page 243). Place two pieces on each of four large white plates, mix the salad well and place on top of the chicken. Serve immediately. Serves 4

ACCOMPANIMENTS

• You can mix and match here, as with the other roast chicken dishes, but steamed herbed pink eye potatoes and boiled green beans would make a simple, complete meal with the roast chicken and lemon and parsley salad.

FOLLOWING PAGES roast chicken with lemon and parsley salad, left, and butterflied chicken with ricotta and garlic stuffing, served with herb mayonnaise (page 351), right

BUTTERFLIED CHICKEN WITH RICOTTA AND GARLIC STUFFING

This is a great way to cook chicken. The stuffing is under the skin, which helps to protect and moisten the breast, and as the bird is cut down the backbone and flattened out, it cooks quickly. Butterflying also seems to be the best way to solve that age-old problem with chicken: that is, the breasts cooking and drying out before the legs are cooked. Putting the stuffing under the skin is not difficult – you just need to loosen the skin first. To do this, simply work your hand up slowly between the chicken skin and the breast, being careful not to tear the skin, then move your fingers down into the thighs and drumsticks; you will be surprised at how easy it is. I always cut this chicken up and serve it with the bones, but you can debone it, if you like.

INGREDIENTS

2 kg (4 lb 8 oz) free-range chicken
extra virgin olive oil
sea salt
freshly ground pepper

FOR THE STUFFING
4 garlic cloves, finely chopped
sea salt
1/2 red onion, finely chopped
125 g (4 1/2 oz) unsalted butter, chopped and brought to room temperature
2 tablespoons finely chopped flat-leaf (Italian) parsley
2 tablespoons finely chopped chives
125 g (4 1/2 oz/1/2 cup) ricotta
juice of 1 lemon
freshly ground pepper

METHOD

To make the stuffing, put the garlic and a little sea salt in a mortar and pound with the pestle until a paste forms. Add the onion and crush slightly, then the butter and mix through, and next the herbs and ricotta. Finally, add the lemon juice and seasoning — you will need both sea salt and freshly ground pepper.

Take the chicken out of the refrigerator 2 hours before cooking and bring to room temperature. Prepare the chicken by cutting down the backbone and pushing down gently on the breastplate. It should start to flatten out. Push it right down and you will have the chicken butterflied in front of you. Remove the wishbone, then gently loosen the skin from the flesh as explained in the introduction opposite. Next — and this is the best part — take some stuffing in your hand and put it under the skin of the legs. Take a little more and continue until the pocket is full and even. Repeat the process with the skin on top of the chicken breasts. Smooth the skin out and you should have a very handsome bird sitting in front of you, all puffed up and shiny.

Preheat the oven to 160°C (320°F). Rub the skin with extra virgin olive oil and season all over with sea salt. Put the chicken in a roasting tin and cook for 40–50 minutes, then remove the tin from the oven, cover with foil and rest for 30 minutes. Place the chicken on a chopping board, cut down the middle, then remove the legs. Cut the legs into thighs and drumsticks, and cut each breast into two. Put the chicken pieces on plates and spoon over the juices and oil from the roasting tin. Add a healthy grind of pepper and serve. Serves 4

ACCOMPANIMENTS

• Braised Roman (flat) beans, potato purée and herb mayonnaise would go really nicely with the chicken and its stuffing.

• The potential stuffing mixes are many. Always add plenty of fresh herbs and have fun with spices as well. Here are two more combinations. Pound the ingredients together, then stuff under the skin as described above.

No. 1: Combine 125 g (4 1/2 oz) unsalted butter, at room temperature, 3 garlic cloves, 2 peeled, sliced and pounded lemon grass stalks, 1/4 teaspoon ground cumin, 1/2 teaspoon ground chilli, 1/4 teaspoon ground coriander, 1/2 teaspoon ground fennel, 3 tablespoons chopped coriander (cilantro) leaves, 3 tablespoons chopped mint, the juice of 1 lime, 1 teaspoon sea salt and some freshly ground pepper.

No. 2: Combine 125 g (4 1/2 oz) unsalted butter, at room temperature, 4 wild green chillies, 2 tablespoons finely chopped fresh ginger, 3 garlic cloves, 1 tablespoon garam masala, 3 tablespoons chopped flat-leaf (Italian) parsley, 3 tablespoons chopped mint, the juice of 1 lemon, 1 teaspoon sea salt and some freshly ground pepper.

ROAST DUCK

I call this dish roast duck, but it is actually twice-cooked. There are a few ways you can go about this. In the old days, I may have roasted it twice, however, as I love Chinese multiple cooking, I now either steam or poach the duck first. This does two things: it allows me to render some of the fat from the duck; and, when the duck is cooked, it makes it possible to cut it into portions, which is great when entertaining. By the time you want to pop the duck in the oven, you are ready, your duck is ready and there is no mess — you have already cleaned up.

INGREDIENTS

2 x 2 kg (4 lb 8 oz) Peking ducks
sea salt
1 teaspoon extra virgin olive oil

METHOD

Put a duck on the chopping board and remove the fat deposits in the cavity. Cut the neck off and remove the first two wing joints, then season inside and out with sea salt. Repeat the process with the second duck. If you have two stacking bamboo steamers or one large one you can cook both ducks at once, otherwise cook them one at a time. Steam the ducks over boiling water for 45 minutes, making sure not to boil the saucepan dry. If using two steamers, halfway through the steaming place the top one on the bottom.

When the ducks are cool enough to handle, put one on a board and remove the legs. Cut the backbone out and cut the two breasts down the middle, leaving the breastplate in place. Repeat with the other duck. You now have four breast pieces and four legs. Preheat the oven to 220°C (425°F). Rub the duck pieces with the extra virgin olive oil and season with sea salt. Put in a roasting tin skin side down and cook for 15 minutes, then turn over. Pour out any excess liquid and cook for a further 15–20 minutes. The duck should be cooked and the skin crisp; remove from the oven when done.

You can either cut the legs in half and remove the breast from the breastbone and carve it into slices, or you can serve as is, and let your guests eat off the bone. That is my preferred method, as it cuts down on the mess. Serves 4

ACCOMPANIMENTS

• Braised cabbage, roast carrots and a dash of roast garlic dressing would be perfect with this dish. Boiled, braised and steamed greens, the English spinach recipes and all of the purées also go well. As a little sauce on the side, you could try either the tomato jam or any of the harissas, all would be very nice.

BARBECUING

I guess I wouldn't be much of an Australian chef if I didn't include a section on barbecuing. This form of cooking certainly suits our lifestyle and it does create a very social experience. Friends come over and we all gather around the barbie, beer and wine in hand. What a way to enjoy a great Australian summer.

Barbecuing, along with spit-roasting, was the original dry heat cooking method, with a simple grid placed over the flame of the fire. These days there is an endless array of wood, charcoal and gas burners for the avid cook to choose from. The thing they all have in common is that the heat comes from underneath the grill bars. The meat is seared on one side, and the other side is not cooked until the meat is turned over. Although it is possible to barbecue large pieces of meat and birds, the barbecue is really the place for smaller cuts of meat; generally, steaks or chops cut from large primary cuts. These cuts figure largely, as barbecuing is mostly quick, high heat cooking and the secondary cuts would burn before they got a chance to cook through. That is not to say that it can't be done. Texas barbecue usually includes beef brisket, and it is cooked for a minimum of eight hours. Go figure!

It is important to generally only turn your meat or bird once. I say generally because, if you had a larger piece of meat or were cooking a whole chicken, you may end up turning it several times to stop it from burning as it cooks. But let's talk about turning only once. You can, if you like, turn the meat or bird 90 degrees on the same side halfway through cooking that particular side, to give it crisscross grill marks. You would have seen this in restaurants and magazines — it only adds to presentation, so don't worry about it too much. The reason I want to turn the meat only once is to get a really good crust on each side. This is what barbecuing is all about — the added complexity of flavour gained from charring the outside of the meat while retaining a melting interior.

Getting a handle on your barbecue and judging the temperature needed for different sized cuts of steak is at the very heart of the art form, so take note of changes to the food from varying heats and you will really become the barbie master. Don't forget, as a basic rule, the thinner the cut of meat, the hotter the temperature it can be cooked at. This means, don't put your thicker pieces of meat on the hottest part of the grill. Each barbecue will have hot and cool spots that you can move meat to if you need to react to the drama of the flame. Big rule — rest the meat and you will get a tastier and more tender result.

You can test your steak for doneness by using a meat thermometer, but remember that as you are cooking with high heat and the cut of meat is smaller and thinner than the cut used for roasting, the residual heat will have a greater impact, making it more difficult to calculate... actually, quite difficult. However, you can also check by touch. This is what most professional chefs with plenty of experience do. The theory is, that a rare steak will be soft to the touch and will spring back when pressed. As it cooks, the steak will become firmer and firmer to the touch. With experience, this is a great way to judge doneness. You can also judge it by watching the juices moving up through the steak as the second side cooks. (You will have missed rare and probably medium rare by that stage.) If the juices come to the surface as red droplets your steak will now be medium rare, probably heading to medium after resting, and if the juices are pink to clear you have a well-done steak.

As a basic rule it is important to oil well whatever you are cooking, then shake off any excess oil. That should be enough to stop it from sticking but without risking flare up from too much oil. This is why most of the marinades are fairly dry. You can also put together dry spice rubs that are most agreeable. Having a nice clean grill is essential to achieving a good crust and nice clear grill marks on the meat. The good news is that that can be achieved by simply heating the barbecue to hot, then giving the grill bars a good scrub with a hard wire brush. You can also give them a good rub with lots of rolled up newspaper, remembering first to read the newspaper.

It is best to use a fairly simple method to check the heat of the barbecue: hold your hand 10 cm (4 inches) from the grill bars and you should be able to hold it there for about 2–3 seconds if it is hot, about 4–5 seconds if it is medium-hot and about 8 seconds if it is medium. Most of your cooking will be done at hot to medium-hot, unless you're cooking a large joint or a whole butterflied chicken.

BARBECUED BEEF SIRLOIN WITH PARSLEY AND LEMON

This is a really simple way to enjoy steak. As cooking on a barbecue is a quick and hot experience it is important to get the steaks to room temperature before you start cooking. You will find that the meat cooks a lot more evenly. It is often hard to judge cooking time, as it depends so much on the heat of the barbecue, but as a starting point, steaks of this size on a hot barbecue will take about 5 minutes for rare, another 1 1/2–2 minutes for medium rare, another 1 1/2 minutes again for medium and 2 minutes on top of that for well done.

INGREDIENTS

4 x 250 g (9 oz) aged beef sirloin steaks
sea salt
extra virgin olive oil
3 tablespoons chopped flat-leaf (Italian) parsley
freshly ground pepper
1 lemon, quartered

METHOD

Remove the steaks from the refrigerator 2 hours before you intend to start cooking and season liberally with sea salt. Preheat the barbecue to hot. This could take up to 1 hour if using natural fuel or 15 minutes for a gas barbecue. Make sure the grill bars are clean. Splash the steaks with a little extra virgin olive oil and shake off any excess. Put the steaks on the grill at a 45-degree angle to the grill bars. When halfway through cooking that side, turn the steaks 45 degrees in the opposite direction. When done, turn them over and cook the other side. You should have nice grill marks. Put the steaks on a plate, cover with foil and keep near the barbecue so they keep warm. Rest for 10 minutes.

Sprinkle the parsley over the steaks, drizzle with more oil and season with sea salt and freshly ground pepper. Squeeze lemon juice over. Place the steaks presentation side up on plates and mix together all the juices at the bottom of the resting plate. Pour these juices over the steaks and serve. Serves 4

ACCOMPANIMENTS

• This needs nothing more than chips or roast potatoes and a green salad. This and the next recipe are both perfect for some fried onion rings. Another thing I love with this dish is creamed spinach and macaroni and cheese. It sounds rich and, well, it is, but it is also completely divine. If just serving the steak with a green salad try a little aïoli or herb mayonnaise on the side; if you like it hot some harissa or harissa mayonnaise would be good.

OPPOSITE PAGE barbecued beef sirloin with parsley and lemon, served with fried onion rings (page 338)

AGED BEEF RIBS BARBECUED WITH ANCHOVY BUTTER

I love slow-roasted beef ribs, but they are equally good when charred on the outside and melting in the middle. Beef rib has a large amount of connective tissue and fat, which is why it has so much flavour, and is also why I like to eat it more medium rare than rare — all the tough bits will have turned to jelly. The anchovy butter is a classic with any kind of barbecued meat or poultry, so try it on lamb or chicken, as well. It is really delicious. You can make the butter the night before cooking and roll it in foil into a log shape. The next day cut neat circles to put on the beef. That is how it would be done in a restaurant, but I also like to make it in a mortar and pestle just before cooking the steak and have it at room temperature. I just put a spoonful on top when the steak is served. You can also add some fresh herbs to the butter: parsley, chives and sage are nice. Just crush them up at the beginning with the anchovies. I am also fond of a little garlic.

INGREDIENTS

4 x 250 g (9 oz) aged beef ribs
sea salt
extra virgin olive oil
4 slices or spoonfuls of anchovy butter (page 358)
freshly ground pepper

METHOD

Remove the steaks from the refrigerator 2 hours before cooking and season with sea salt. Drizzle the steaks with extra virgin olive oil and shake off any excess. Grill as described in the previous recipe and rest on a plate in a warm place. You may want to add 1 minute on the time I suggested for rare and then rest well; that should give you a perfect medium-rare rib steak.

Place one steak on each of four white plates. Pour the juices that collected on the resting plate over the steaks and add a slice or spoonful of the anchovy butter. Add a grind of fresh pepper and serve immediately. Serves 4

ACCOMPANIMENTS

• A more complex butter might have anchovies, parsley, sage, garlic, a little fresh chilli, lemon juice and a little grated lemon zest. Instead of the butter you could use Béarnaise, hollandaise or aïoli. The roast garlic sauce or just a splash of home-made barbecue sauce would be perfect.

• Any of the green vegetables partnered with the potato recipes or pan-fried polenta would go nicely — try barbecued zucchini salad with potato purée.

BARBECUED BEEF FILLET WITH SALSA VERDE

As a rule I'm not a big fan of beef fillet — sure, it's tender, but don't we have teeth? Of the harder-working muscles, it does the least amount of work and has the least amount of flavour. However, there are two reasons I include this recipe. One is I acknowledge that a lot of people do like beef fillet, so this one is for you. The other reason is that I offer two different ways you can cook it, so I hope the second way, which is whole, starts you thinking more about the possibilities. Beef fillet is small in dimension so even if cooking it whole you don't really need a different heat on the barbecue. If I was to do the same with beef rib, which I urge you to try at some stage, then that would require a little variation of the barbecue temperature because of its size. The good thing about barbecuing a whole piece of meat is that your meat thermometer can come into play in a more accurate way.

BEEF FILLET NO. 1
INGREDIENTS
4 x 175 g (6 oz) portions prime fillet of beef
sea salt
extra virgin olive oil
250 ml (9 fl oz/1 cup) salsa verde (page 367)
freshly ground pepper

METHOD
Remove the meat from the refrigerator 1 hour before cooking and season with sea salt. Preheat the barbecue to hot. Make sure the grill bars are clean. Brush the fillets with extra virgin olive oil, shake off any excess oil and place on the barbecue. If you would like crisscross grill marks on the presentation side, proceed as described for beef sirloin on page 257. Halfway through cooking, turn the fillets over and cook to the required doneness. (Fillet is a lean cut with no connective tissue, so cooking time will be about a minute less than that for the sirloin.) Remove the fillets to a plate, cover with foil and rest in a warm place for 15 minutes.

Place the beef fillets on four large white plates, add a dollop of salsa verde on the side, sprinkle with sea salt and finish with freshly ground pepper. Serve immediately. Serves 4

BEEF FILLET NO. 2
INGREDIENTS
750–800 g (1 lb 10 oz–1 lb 12 oz) piece prime fillet of beef
sea salt
extra virgin olive oil
250 ml (9 fl oz/1 cup) salsa verde (page 367)
freshly ground pepper

METHOD
Remove the meat from the refrigerator 2 hours before cooking and season
with sea salt. Preheat the barbecue to hot. Make sure the grill bars are clean.
Brush the entire fillet with extra virgin olive oil and shake off any excess oil. Put
on the barbecue and cook for about 2 minutes on its side, then roll the fillet
onto the next quarter and cook for a further 2 minutes. Continue for about
8–10 minutes until the whole fillet has a crust. Put a meat thermometer into the
centre of the fillet — when the internal temperature is 50°C (122°F) remove,
put on a plate and cover with foil. Rest in a warm place for 15 minutes.

Put the fillet on a chopping board and either carve it into four portions or slice
it into eight or twelve slices. Divide the meat among four large white plates
and drizzle the salsa verde on top. Season with freshly ground pepper. Serves 4

ACCOMPANIMENTS
• Peperonata and barbecued polenta would carry on the Italian theme nicely.

• Most of the vegetable section would be perfect with this steak. Any of the
sauces suggested for barbecued beef ribs would be delicious, as would any
of the salsas. And, although gremolata is most often associated with braised
food, it is quite nice to sprinkle a little over the steak with a bit of extra virgin
olive oil. The aromas really bring the steak to life.

• Try marinating the fillet for more flavour in either of these two marinades.
Blend to a paste and rub on the meat. Leave for 1 hour to marinate.
No. 1: Combine 1 large handful flat-leaf (Italian) parsley, 1 small handful
mint, 1 large handful coriander (cilantro) leaves, 1 tablespoon sea salt,
1 tablespoon chilli flakes, 60 ml (2 fl oz/1/4 cup) each of balsamic vinegar and
extra virgin olive oil.
No. 2: Combine 1 teaspoon ground cumin, 1 teaspoon ground coriander,
1 teaspoon chilli flakes, 1 teaspoon ground paprika, 2 crushed garlic cloves,
1 large handful mint, the juice of 1 lemon and half the zest, 1 tablespoon sea
salt and 60 ml (2 fl oz/1/4 cup) extra virgin olive oil.

OREGANO AND THYME MARINATED LAMB CHOPS

Barbecued lamb is one of my favourite things and chops are so easy to cook and eat. Both lamb chops and cutlets are made for the barbecue. They are young and tender and are thin cuts, so they cook fast — just what the doctor ordered for the barbie. They also have a sweet, long and distinct flavour, which means they are great to marinate. You can add lots of flavour to complement them, without overpowering their superb natural flavour. Being quite thin, it is much harder to put a crisscross grill mark on them, but not impossible. As they are marinated and covered in quite a lot of herbs I tend not to bother. I like to cook lamb chops about medium rare; with resting they will be nice and pink inside. Usually I would allow two to three chops per person; however, you know your guests and there is no shame in four, particularly if the chops are from young lambs. There are a couple of ways to make the marinade. I usually use a mortar and pestle as it is a lot of fun, having a good old pound on some beautiful ingredients, and it is really much easier to clean up. But I also use a stick blender, blender or even a food processor, so it is really whatever you're comfortable with.

INGREDIENTS

8–12 good-quality lamb chops
2 garlic cloves, finely chopped
1 teaspoon sea salt
2 tablespoons chopped oregano
1 tablespoon chopped thyme
3 tablespoons chopped flat-leaf (Italian) parsley
$1/2$ teaspoon chilli flakes
60 ml (2 fl oz/$1/4$ cup) extra virgin olive oil, plus extra
freshly ground pepper
lemon wedges

METHOD

Remove the chops from the refrigerator 1 hour before cooking. To make the marinade, put the garlic and salt in a mortar and pound to a paste with the pestle. Add the herbs and continue pounding for about 2 minutes. Add the chilli flakes and the extra virgin olive oil and stir until completely incorporated.

Mix the chops with the marinade on a plate and leave for 1 hour to infuse. Preheat the barbecue and make sure the grill bars are clean. When hot, put the chops on the hottest part. Cook for $1^1/2$ minutes on one side, then turn over and cook for a further minute. Remove and transfer to a plate. Cover with foil and rest in a warm place.

Place two to three lamb chops on each of four large white plates. Mix a little extra virgin olive oil with the juices on the resting plate. Pour over the chops, give a really good grind of fresh pepper and serve a lemon wedge on the side for family and guests to squeeze over. Serves 4

ACCOMPANIMENTS

• Boiled peas, beans and sugar snap peas mixed together with extra virgin olive oil and lemon juice would be great here, with a sweet purée like pumpkin or carrot, and if you wanted to sauce it, just a little aïoli.

• Serve with spinach and garlic, barbecued potatoes and mint and cucumber salsa. Or, try harissa mayonnaise, pan-fried spicy eggplant and tabbouleh salad.

LAMB CUTLETS WITH LEMON GRASS AND GINGER

Growing up, the lamb cutlet was the star of the 'meat and three veg' plate that was so famous in the fifties and sixties. A lot has changed since then, but there is nothing I like more than a barbecued lamb cutlet.

INGREDIENTS

12 good-quality lamb cutlets
2 garlic cloves, chopped
2 lemon grass stems, peeled and sliced into fine rounds
3 cm (1^1/4 inch) piece fresh ginger, chopped
1 teaspoon sea salt
3 tablespoons chopped coriander (cilantro) leaves
3 tablespoons chopped mint
60 ml (2 fl oz/^{1}/4 cup) extra virgin olive oil, plus extra
freshly ground pepper
lemon wedges

METHOD

Remove the cutlets from the refrigerator 1 hour before cooking. To make the marinade, put the garlic, lemon grass, ginger and sea salt in a mortar and pound into a rough paste with the pestle. Add the herbs and pound for a further minute, then stir in the extra virgin olive oil and mix together well.

Mix the chops with the marinade and leave for at least 1 hour to infuse. Preheat the barbecue and make sure the grill bars are clean. When hot, put the cutlets on the hottest part. Cook for about 2 minutes on each side for medium rare. Put on a plate and cover with foil. Rest in a warm place for 10 minutes.

Place three lamb cutlets on each of four plates. Mix a little oil with the juices on the resting plate and pour over the cutlets. Give a good grind of fresh pepper, place a lemon wedge on each plate and serve immediately. Serves 4

ACCOMPANIMENTS

• Barbecued asparagus, potato and mushroom salad would be great with some curry butter just melted over the marinated lamb cutlets.

• Any of the barbecued salads with some pan-roasted or barbecued potatoes would be good. You can use any mayonnaise or any of the butters except the prawn butter. A spoonful of the all'amatriciana sauce from the pasta section on the plate, topped with the cutlets, would be nice. The other thing that is really yummy is a spoonful of braised Puy lentils, topped with the cutlets and served with a green salad.

BARBECUED BUTTERFLIED LAMB LEG

Butterflying is a really nice way of cooking leg of lamb on the barbecue. If you don't want to butterfly the meat yourself, ask your butcher to do it for you. It takes a lot of the work out of the dish, but it won't be as much fun, will it? Another good option is to get your butcher to cut the leg, on the saw, into leg steaks. This will give you steaks with all the muscle groups around a centre bone. If you choose to do this, then just marinate the steaks in any of the marinades mentioned in this chapter and you will be pleased. I marinate the lamb in nothing more than extra virgin olive oil and balsamic vinegar. It is even better if you remember to do it the night before. The lamb forms a crust that is truly delicious and the centre is beautiful and pink.

HOW TO BUTTERFLY A LEG OF LAMB — Lay the lamb leg on a chopping board, the outside of the leg facing down. Have the shank end pointing toward your left hand. If you look at it you will see that the natural seam between all the muscle structures is quite evident. You just need to cut along the line with a sharp boning knife, following the bone. Now lay the meat out and carefully cut around the bone to remove it. The leg will be laid out in front of you and you will see the two largest muscles at either end of the meat. Keep the knife parallel to the board and slice, from the centre out, into the largest one, the topside. Cut it three-quarters of the way through and open it up. Repeat the process with the other muscle, the round, and you will have a butterflied leg of lamb that is roughly the same thickness throughout. Divide the leg in half along the centre giving you two roughly equal pieces.

INGREDIENTS

2.5–3 kg (5 lb 8 oz–6 lb 8 oz) leg of lamb, shank removed and butterflied
1 tablespoon sea salt
125 ml (4 fl oz/1/2 cup) balsamic vinegar, plus extra
60 ml (2 fl oz/1/4 cup) extra virgin olive oil, plus extra
freshly ground pepper

METHOD

Remove the lamb from the refrigerator 2 hours before cooking. Place the butterflied leg of lamb in a dish or bowl large enough to hold both pieces. Rub with the sea salt and then rub all over with the balsamic vinegar and extra virgin olive oil. Marinate overnight or as close to that as you can.

Preheat the barbecue to hot. Make sure the grill bars are clean. Add the lamb pieces, skin side down, and cook for about 5–6 minutes. The outside will start to burn; turn over carefully and cook for a further 4–5 minutes. Remove the lamb from the heat, put on a plate and cover with foil. Rest in a warm place for 15 minutes.

Put the lamb on a chopping board and cut into 5 mm (1/4 inch) thick slices. Divide the lamb among four large white plates or put on one large platter for the middle of the table. Drizzle a little extra vinegar and extra virgin olive oil into the resting plate to mingle with the resting juices, add a really good grind of pepper and pour over the lamb. Serve immediately. Serves 4

ACCOMPANIMENTS

• This dish is perfect with pan-roasted potatoes and spinach with garlic and lemon. You could follow the instructions, but instead of pan-frying the potatoes, just boil and cook them on the solid top area of the barbecue. I think sauce Vierge would be perfect in summer, or perhaps a little garlic-flavoured yoghurt.

• You can serve this with just about anything in the vegetable accompaniment chapter and it will work a treat. I like making a sauce out of the spicy tomato soup recipe and bringing a Middle Eastern feel to a shared table. The meat is also wonderful with the curry, herb or marchand de vin butter melted over it. Try it with the tomato jam and relishes, and any of the salsas are perfect as well.

BARBECUED CHICKEN WITH TOMATO, ALMOND AND CHILLI SALSA

When it comes to chicken, I really do prefer the dark meat — with lots more connective tissue and fat, it stays moister and tastes better. The whole leg is boned down the side and the meat with the skin attached is beaten out a little to regulate the cooking time. By all means, if you don't want the skin and don't want to bother boning the leg out, then just buy skinless thigh fillets.

HOW TO BONE CHICKEN LEGS — Put the leg on a chopping board, skin side down. With a sharp boning or paring knife, cut down the length of the leg along the bone. Now work the knife along the bone so you loosen and finally remove the entire bone. You will now have the leg laid out in front of you. Repeat with the other leg. Put each leg between a folded piece of baking paper and give it a good bash with a rolling pin or meat mallet. An empty wine bottle works well too.

INGREDIENTS

8 pieces free-range chicken legs
3 garlic cloves
sea salt
2 long red chillies, split and deseeded
80 ml (2^1/2 fl oz/^{1}/3 cup) extra virgin olive oil
freshly ground pepper
250 ml (9 fl oz/1 cup) tomato, almond and chilli salsa (page 362)
lemon wedges

METHOD

About 1 hour before cooking, bone and flatten the chicken legs as described above. Put the garlic and some sea salt in a mortar and pound with the pestle. Add the chilli and continue to pound, then stir through the extra virgin olive oil. Rub the chicken legs and thighs with the marinade, cover and set aside to let the flavours infuse.

Preheat the barbecue to hot and make sure the grill bars are clean. Put the chicken on the grill and cook for about 3 minutes. Turn over and cook for a further 3 minutes. Remove to a plate, cover with foil and rest in a warm place for 10 minutes.

Place two chicken pieces on each of four plates. Pour the juices from the resting plate over and season with freshly ground pepper. Place a spoonful of salsa and a lemon wedge next to the chicken. Serve immediately. Serves 4

ACCOMPANIMENTS

• Barbecued asparagus and a dollop of soft polenta would be perfect with the spicy salsa.

• This dish, like the barbecued chicken breast (following page), can consist of just the legs marinated and cooked, then served with whatever vegetable combination you like, with any salsa, mayonnaise, butter or just a dollop of preserved lemon salsa on the side. Whip up a couple of salads and you have a great meal. Simply by using the different chapters to build your own meal you have an example of how this one simple dish can become a hundred and one ways with chicken leg, Mediterranean style.

• Duck can be cooked in exactly the same way: that is, marinated and served with the salsa. The way we do it is to poach the duck first in salted water and then barbecue it to impart that lovely smoky flavour. Simply remove the fat deposits in the duck's cavity and cut the neck off and the first two joints of the wing. Find a saucepan large enough to cook the duck, or two or three pans, or however many you need for your number of ducks, and fill the pan or pans with water and bring to the boil. When the water is boiling, add sea salt and add the duck breast side down. Keep the water simmering and cook for 25 minutes, then turn the duck over and cook for a further 5 minutes. Remove the pan or pans from the heat and allow the duck to cool in the poaching liquid. When cool, remove and pat dry with paper towels. Apply the marinade and leave to infuse. Cut each duck into two legs and two breasts and proceed with the barbecuing. Make sure you place the duck skin side down first on the grill and watch the fire flare up with the fat from the duck.

• Try these three marinades for chicken and lamb. Purée the first marinade in a blender or pound in a mortar; the second can be just mixed in a bowl. Leave for 1 hour for the flavours to develop.

No. 1: Combine 2 tablespoons ground cumin, 1 tablespoon chilli flakes, 1 teaspoon ground cinnamon, 1 roasted and ground star anise, 2 tablespoons mild curry powder, 1 large handful coriander (cilantro) leaves and 60 ml (2 fl oz/ 1/4 cup) extra virgin olive oil.

No. 2: Combine 60 ml (2 fl oz/1/4 cup) soy sauce, 2 tablespoons honey, 2 deseeded and finely chopped long red chillies, 2 finely chopped garlic cloves, 1 tablespoon finely chopped fresh ginger, 3 tablespoons chopped coriander (cilantro) leaves, 1 teaspoon sesame oil, 2 tablespoons peanut oil and the juice of 1 lime.

No. 3: You can marinate any meat or poultry in chermoula (page 372). Marinate for 1 hour and then barbecue, rest and plate up. Squeeze the juice of 1 lemon over the top and serve. You'll get a little blackening on the outside but that adds to the complexity of taste. This really is a wonderful preparation.

BARBECUED CHICKEN BREAST WITH ZUCCHINI SAUCE

You can have these chicken breasts with the skin off or on, whatever fits your lifestyle. I come from the 'fat is flavour, don't overindulge and she'll be right' school of chicken eating. If you leave the skin on, you can also leave the wing bone on. It makes for a nice presentation and a little bit of a chew at the end. This sauce really started out as a soup, but the flavour is so lovely it ended up being a sauce for a number of different meats and poultry.

INGREDIENTS

4 free-range chicken breasts
sea salt
extra virgin olive oil
juice of 1 lemon
freshly ground pepper
1 tablespoon chopped flat-leaf (Italian) parsley
1 tablespoon chopped chervil

FOR THE ZUCCHINI SAUCE
6 large zucchini (courgettes)
80 ml (2^1/2 fl oz/^{1}/3 cup) extra virgin olive oil
sea salt
3 garlic cloves, roughly chopped
50 g (1^3/4 oz) unsalted butter
freshly ground pepper

METHOD

Remove the chicken from the refrigerator 1 hour before cooking and season liberally with sea salt.

To make the zucchini sauce, cut the zucchini into 1 cm ($1/2$ inch) thick rounds. Put the extra virgin olive oil in a saucepan and heat. Add the zucchini, along with a good dose of sea salt, and cook over medium heat for about 8 minutes, or until the zucchini softens. Stir occasionally so the zucchini doesn't stick to the bottom. Add the garlic and cook for a further 2 minutes, then add 750 ml (26 fl oz/3 cups) water and simmer gently for 15 minutes, or until the zucchini is very soft and the water has reduced by at least half. Remove from the heat and purée in a blender. Push the sauce through a sieve if you want a silkier texture. Return the purée to the pan and whisk in the butter. Check the seasoning and give a good grind of fresh pepper.

Preheat the barbecue to hot. Make sure the grill bars are clean. Brush the chicken with extra virgin olive oil and shake off any excess. Put skin side down on the grill at a 45-degree angle to the bars. Halfway through cooking on the first side, carefully lift and turn the chicken 45 degrees in the other direction, creating a crisscross pattern. When ready, turn the chicken over and finish cooking. The chicken will take about 12–15 minutes all up, depending on the size. Remove from the grill, put on a plate and cover with foil. Leave to rest for 10 minutes in a warm place.

Spoon the zucchini sauce onto four large white plates and place the chicken breasts gently on top. Drizzle a little extra oil over the juices in the resting plate and add the lemon juice and a grind of fresh pepper. Add the herbs, mix and spoon the dressing over the chicken. Serve immediately. Serves 4

ACCOMPANIMENTS

• Cream of corn on the side and steamed herbed pink eye potatoes are good with zucchini and chicken.

• Try a dollop of soft polenta with the chicken and serve it on braised peas instead of zucchini sauce. This dish would also go really well with a number of puréed soups from the soup chapter. Or, simply serve the barbecued chicken breast with any of the mayonnaises, salsas or tomato relishes, plus a couple of salads for a simple Sunday lunch full of flavour.

PAN-FRYING AND SAUTEING

To sauté is to cook usually small pieces of food in a small amount of fat. As a matter of fact, the French verb sauter means 'to jump', as the pieces of food are tossed in a pan. Perhaps it is the French version of stir-frying, but that is another story. Pan-frying normally means food cooked in a moderate amount of fat. As you add more fat you move towards shallow-frying and then into deep-frying. The most important thing to remember when you sauté or pan-fry is to preheat your pan; the food must start cooking as soon as it hits the pan, otherwise it will stick and stew in its own juices. The other important thing is to not overcrowd the pan, as it lowers the temperature too quickly and the food will once again stew. There is a flip side to this: if the pan is too big, the fat will generally burn. So a very important thing to get right is the pan size. Large enough to comfortably fit what you're cooking, but not so large as to have lots of exposed area once the food is in the pan.

Don't forget that pan-frying follows the same principles that all cooking does: the smaller the piece of meat, the higher the heat; the larger, the lower. This is just common sense cookery.

Particularly large cuts of meat or poultry can be started off in the pan and then finished off in the oven. This is usually done to stop food from burning and drying out, and is one of the most popular restaurant cooking methods. However, at Rockpool, we cook large pieces of meat or bird at low temperatures in the pan very successfully. I love chicken cooked slowly in olive oil; we cook it for about 1 3/4 hours, turning it about every 3 minutes. It is like a rotisserie but in a pan; it is a lot of fun and the texture of the chicken is melting and the skin is really well caramelized — all cooked on top of the stove. I say fun because it just goes to prove that there are a hundred ways to skin a cat when it comes to cooking.

One of the great things about pan-frying is that the juices of what you've just cooked get left behind, so there is always a little start for a simple sauce. The juices that come from the meat start to evaporate and a solid crust is left at the bottom of the pan. At this point, you can deglaze and take the flavours back that would otherwise be lost to the kitchen sink (great shame that). Things to add to the pan to deglaze with and make a sauce out of can be wine, vinegar, stock, cream, crème fraîche and butter, in combination or all together, or you could simply deglaze with a little lemon juice and a dash of extra virgin olive oil for a simple but delicious flavour.

PAN-FRIED RUMP STEAK WITH PEPPER

This is another classic dish that is easy to cook and delivers lots of wonderful flavour from the pan. Rump is another cut of meat I love: a good old working muscle with lots of flavour and a winner in the pan or on the barbecue. When I was a youngster, my Dad would bring home a whole rump whenever there was a bit of a get together on Sundays. He used to trim it and cut it into 5 cm (2 inch) steaks. He would barbecue them, really char them on the outside, and let the meat rest so it was very tender in the middle. I used to love chewing on the burnt fat on the top of the steaks. I guess I have always been addicted to flavour.

INGREDIENTS

4 x 200 g (7 oz) rump steaks
sea salt
25 g (1 oz/$\frac{1}{4}$ cup) mixed white and black peppercorns
60 ml (2 fl oz/$\frac{1}{4}$ cup) extra virgin olive oil
40 g (1$\frac{1}{2}$ oz) unsalted butter
60 ml (2 fl oz/$\frac{1}{4}$ cup) brandy
500 ml (17 fl oz/2 cups) pure (whipping) cream
1 lemon, cut in half

METHOD

Remove the steaks from the refrigerator 1 hour before cooking and season liberally with sea salt. Put the peppercorns in a mortar and roughly crush with the pestle. Transfer to a flat plate. One at a time, press the steaks firmly on both sides into the peppercorns. You will probably cook the steaks two at a time, so put half the extra virgin olive oil and half the butter into a heavy-based saucepan. When hot, add the steaks and cook for 2 minutes. Turn over, cook for a further 2 minutes, then remove and set aside on a plate in a warm place to rest. Repeat with the remaining steaks.

Once all the steaks are resting, add the brandy to the pan. As it flames and reduces, scrape the bottom of the pan with a wooden spoon. When the flames have gone, add the cream and cook until reduced by half. Squeeze the lemon juice over, check the seasoning and add a little more sea salt if necessary. Put the steaks on plates, pour some sauce over and serve immediately. Serves 4

ACCOMPANIMENTS

• Sautéed mushrooms and roast potatoes would be great. A simple pan sauce instead of the pepper sauce, or any of the mayonnaises, butters and salsas would work, and don't forget that it is nice to sprinkle steak with gremolata.

PAN-FRIED SKIRT STEAK WITH HORSERADISH CREAM

Skirt steak is not a cut of meat that you see often, but it is one worth seeking out. I have eaten it at home, and in restaurants in America often, but for some reason I don't see it in Australian restaurants much at all. It is a working muscle and has elongated fibre. It is also very lean, so it needs to be cooked rare and sliced into thin strips, cutting the muscle against the grain. When that is done it has the most superb flavour and the most wonderful gelatinous texture. It is perfect for pan-frying and barbecuing and goes well with a simple red wine or pepper sauce. So ask your butcher — you will be really pleased with the result.

It is easy to make a simple red wine sauce to go with this steak. As you have the lovely flavours already lurking on the bottom of the pan, it is nice to deglaze them rather than throw them out. When you remove the steaks you should add a few finely diced French shallots and cook for 1 minute, deglaze with red wine and cook quickly, reducing until the liquid becomes syrupy. You then have a choice: season and pour the sauce over your steak or you can go the whole hog and whisk in a little butter — this gives it another degree of silkiness and really improves the flavour, and as you have a balanced diet this little bit won't hurt. The other important thing is to use a good-quality red wine and you will get a good-quality sauce; don't cook with wine you wouldn't drink.

INGREDIENTS

4 x 175 g (6 oz) skirt steaks
sea salt
extra virgin olive oil
freshly ground pepper
250 ml (9 fl oz/1 cup) horseradish cream (page 353)

METHOD

Remove the steaks from the refrigerator 1 hour before cooking and season liberally with sea salt. Warm the oven so you can rest the meat there. Put a heavy-based frying pan on the heat and when hot, brush the steaks with extra virgin olive oil and put the first two in the pan. Cook for 2 minutes, then turn over and cook again until you get a nice crust, but still rare inside. It should take 6 minutes all up, or a little longer, depending on the thickness. Put on a plate and rest in the oven, and repeat with the remaining two steaks.

Put a steak on the chopping board and, with a sharp knife, slice the steak across the grain, cutting each slice about 5 mm (1/4 inch) thick. Place on a large white plate and repeat with the other steaks. Drizzle some extra oil onto the resting plate to mingle with the juices and season with a little sea salt and lots of freshly ground pepper. Mix and pour some over each steak. Put a dollop of horseradish cream on the side. Serve immediately. Serves 4

ACCOMPANIMENTS

• The vegetable combinations are endless — boiled or steamed greens, one type or a mixture, are nice here, with potato or pumpkin purée alongside. I also personally love pan-fried meat with chips, home-made of course.

• Any of the simple sauces go well, and you can deglaze the pan with a little wine and add one of the butters, whisking all the time. Season, add a few drops of lemon juice and you have a wonderful pan-ready sauce.

VEAL CUTLET CRUMBED WITH PARMESAN

I love crumbed food. One of my fondest childhood memories is of Mum's crumbed lamb cutlets, served with home-made mint sauce. There were always mounds of the stuff growing around the garden tap. These days, Sam makes us crumbed veal cutlets when we want a real down-home-on-the-range kind of meal. This is, of course, a much more sophisticated dish than my childhood favourite. I usually serve it with lemon and plenty of salad, or when I really feel like going all out, I make the pumpkin and pea risotto, lay the cutlet right on a big spoonful of it and then really go to town.

This dish isn't dusted in flour, dipped in egg wash and then crumbed. It is dipped in whole beaten egg and then dipped in crumbs that consist of about one-third grated Parmesan. This makes for a different texture and taste from your average crumbed dish. You can do the veal two ways: with the bone on or off. I like it on as it makes a bit of a statement on the plate. Whichever way you do it, you will have to beat the meat out a little, gently, as the crust will burn by the time the meat cooks if you don't. If you do want to leave it thick, you could finish the cutlets in the oven and not pan-fry them from start to finish, or crumb them in the traditional way in just breadcrumbs.

It is easiest to cook one or two cutlets at a time and I usually cook them in a non-stick pan, resting them in the oven on paper towels while I cook the rest. As they are thin the cooking takes no time at all, which is what you want when you're eating with friends and family.

HOW TO MAKE BREADCRUMBS — You can purchase packet crumbs, if you need to save time, but you will get a much better result if you buy good-quality bread (preferably sourdough) and use the leftovers to make your own breadcrumbs. To make fresh breadcrumbs, cut a crusty loaf of sourdough bread into squares. Put in the processor and process to a crumb consistency; this can vary from fine to coarse depending on the recipe. Freeze for later use, if you wish, but remember to defrost the crumbs before using. A thoroughly more agreeable crumb for your best veal. You can also add fresh herbs to the crumbs if you like. I don't, as I like to keep the veal flavour central, and the Parmesan is enough.

To make toasted breadcrumbs, follow the instructions for fresh crumbs. Put 80 g (2¾ oz/1 cup) fresh breadcrumbs in a roasting tin, drizzle with 2 tablespoons olive oil, season and toast at 200°C (400°F/ Gas 6) for 20 minutes, or until golden. This can also be done in a pan.

INGREDIENTS

4 large veal cutlets

2 eggs, beaten lightly with a fork

175 g (6 oz/2 cups) fresh breadcrumbs

100 g (3^1/2 oz/1 cup) grated Parmesan

sea salt

90 g (2^3/4 oz) unsalted butter

80 ml (2^1/2 fl oz/^{1}/3 cup) extra virgin olive oil, plus extra

2 lemons, cut in half through the 'equator'

freshly ground pepper

METHOD

Remove the veal from the refrigerator at least 1 hour before cooking and trim the bone of excess meat. Put each cutlet between sheets of wax paper and, using a meat mallet or rolling pin, gently beat each cutlet until it is about 1 cm (^{1}/2 inch) thick. Using something open like pasta bowls, put the egg in one and the crumbs and Parmesan mixed together in the other. Season the crumb and Parmesan mixture with sea salt. Preheat the oven to low and put four plates in to warm. Place on top of the plates a tray lined with paper towels.

Decide how many cutlets you want to cook at once and, working quickly but without stress, put the non-stick or heavy-based frying pan on the stove over high heat. Add 1 tablespoon each of butter and extra virgin olive oil for each cutlet you are cooking per batch. When the butter starts to bubble, dip the cutlet in the beaten egg and shake off any excess. Dip both sides of the cutlet firmly into the breadcrumbs and shake off any excess. Add the cutlet to the pan and cook quickly. It should brown in about 1–1^1/2 minutes. Turn over and cook for the same time on the other side. Remove from the pan and place on the lined tray in the warm oven to rest. Repeat with the remaining cutlets. Between each cooking stint there should be little oil left in the pan, but it is a good idea to wipe the pan out with a bit of paper towel to prevent any crumbs left behind from burning, and add new butter and oil. While the last cutlet is resting, add a little more oil to the pan, add the lemon halves cut side down and cook for 1 minute to caramelize.

Place a cutlet on each of four large white plates and place a lemon half next to it. Add a grind of fresh pepper and a sprinkle of sea salt. Serve immediately. Serves 4

ACCOMPANIMENTS

• I love this dish with Italian-style coleslaw and either potato purée or chips.

SAUTE OF CHICKEN WITH RED WINE VINEGAR

This is a beautiful and simple way of cooking chicken. The skin gets caramelized, the flesh cooks gently and the residue in the pan makes a lovely sauce or glaze. This is one of the first things I learned to make when I first started to cook from cookbooks. It is inspired by my very first cookbook, *Cuisine Gourmande* by Michel Guerard. I bought it in 1978 and it really taught me how to cook. If you love cooking, you could do a lot worse than have it in your library. These sorts of dishes can be as simple as sautéed chicken with lemon and a little extra virgin olive oil, or have cream, crème fraîche or butter finishing the sauce, or a combination of all of the above. I like to deglaze with good-quality red wine vinegar and just finish with a little butter and some fresh herbs; I find it a little fresher and lighter. You can, of course, add any single or combination vegetable to the sauce as well. Cucumber, leek, celery, tomatoes, mushrooms, olives — the options are endless. They help make a great Sunday lunch with a few salads, some bread and, yes, friends and wine.

Generally speaking, you need a good heavy-based saucepan to sauté well. Copper is great, but a cast iron one is good as well. I like to cook no more than a 1.6 kg (3 lb 8 oz) chicken cut up. At a pinch you will get four serves from it, but it is just as easy to get a couple of slightly smaller chooks and cook them in two pans. Then there is always a little left over for the hungry guest. If you overcrowd your pan, the moisture that is created will not be able to escape and you will end up stewing the chicken. On the other hand, if the pan is filled too sparsely your residues will burn, so a nice fit is paramount. You can cook duck in the same way; either poach (page 269) or steam it first (page 252), then follow the recipe below.

INGREDIENTS

1.6 kg (3 lb 8 oz) free-range chicken

sea salt

2 tablespoons extra virgin olive oil

100 g (3^1/2 oz) unsalted butter

8 unpeeled garlic cloves

100 ml (3^1/2 fl oz) good-quality red wine vinegar

1 vine-ripened tomato, peeled, deseeded and diced (page 66)

3 tablespoons chopped flat-leaf (Italian) parsley

freshly ground pepper

METHOD

Remove the chicken from the refrigerator 1–2 hours before cooking. Put the chicken on a chopping board and remove the wing tips. Remove both legs and cut them in half. Remove the backbone, cut down the breastplate, then cut each breast in half. Season the chicken pieces with sea salt.

Heat the extra virgin olive oil and half the butter in a heavy-based saucepan until hot. Add the chicken pieces skin side down and cook for 5 minutes, or until the skin is nice and brown. Turn the chicken pieces over and add the garlic. Cover and reduce the heat to low. After about 20 minutes, remove the breasts and keep in a warm place. Cook the legs for another 5 minutes, then add them to the breasts. Keeping the heat on low, add the vinegar to the pan and scrape with a wooden spoon, then add the remaining butter and whisk it until it melts and forms a sauce. Don't let the sauce boil or it will split. Check the seasoning, add the tomato and parsley and freshly ground pepper to finish.

Divide the chicken among four large white plates and spoon the sauce over. Serve immediately. Serves 4

ACCOMPANIMENTS

• Like barbecued chicken, this is a classic way to cook chicken, rendering it full of flavour and keeping it moist, so any of the vegetable combinations that you like will work well. You can also, as with meat, make a simple pan sauce by deglazing with wine and adding the butter of your choice. The prawn butter is quite beautiful with it, and plays on the French Burgundian dish of Bresse chicken and freshwater crayfish, which are like Australian yabbies. Any of the salsas work well, as do the sauces containing garlic, or just sauté your chicken and serve it very simply with vegetables such as pan-roasted potatoes or steamed pink eyes, then all you need is a green salad. One hundred and one recipes with pan-fried chicken?

BRAISING AND STEWING

Braising is the cooks' alchemy. It is the art of rendering tough cuts of meat into melting flavours of comfort — it is where the finished dish outweighs the sum of its parts. It is in this type of cooking that time is the most important player, and the reward for patience is gold. It may seem complex, but nothing could be further from the truth; just follow a couple of golden rules and the most delicious of meals will be yours.

Braising means to cook in small amounts of liquid, usually after an initial browning of the main ingredient, so it is a combination of dry and moist cooking. Braises are generally served with the cooking liquid, which forms the sauce. Braises and stews can be cooked either on the stove over low heat or in a low oven, in a large saucepan or ovenproof dish with a tight-fitting lid. As I said, the most important thing to remember is time. A good braise cannot be rushed. Quick cooking will just toughen the meat. A stew is basically the same as a braise, but usually the ingredients are cut into smaller pieces, so it is not uncommon for a stew to be fully covered by the liquid.

IMPORTANT RULES

1. Always season the meat or poultry well.
2. Choose a saucepan that fits the braise snugly.
3. Brown the meat or poultry evenly, but don't burn it.
4. Don't let the braise boil. Simmer it very gently and this is how you will achieve great taste and texture.

THE BASIC STEPS OF BRAISING OR STEWING

1. Trim the meat if required, and dust in seasoned flour if required.
2. Brown the meat or poultry on all sides in a small amount of fat.
3. Remove the meat or poultry from the pan and add the aromatic vegetables to soften.
4. Return the meat or poultry to the pan, add the required amount of liquid and herbs, if using, and bring back to a gentle simmer. Never let it boil.
5. Cook until meltingly tender.

So, on the back of the basic step list, I'll go through a dish we used to make at Stephanie Alexander's restaurant way back in 1982. I have made it many times since, and if you are an oxtail fanatic like me I'm sure you'll love it.

Take some sliced oxtails and dust with flour. Using a frying pan large enough to hold all the oxtail at once, heat a little oil. Brown the meat carefully on all sides (you may need to do this in two batches). When all the meat has been browned, return it to the pan. Pour some brandy over and flame; when the flames die out, transfer the oxtail to a saucepan. Add a little bit more oil to the frying pan and add some chopped onion and carrot and brown thoroughly. Pour over some good-quality red wine and boil fiercely to evaporate the alcohol. Add the vegetables and liquid to the oxtail, along with a bouquet garni, a few whole garlic cloves and some strips of orange zest. Pour enough chicken stock in to cover the meat, bring to a simmer and push a buttered wax paper circle down on the meat. Cover the saucepan with a lid and cook very slowly for 2 1/2 hours. When the oxtail is nearly falling off the bone, remove from the heat and allow to cool, then refrigerate overnight. The next day, there should be a crust of fat on the top of the pan; remove and discard it. Sprinkle over black olives and slowly reheat. To serve, place the oxtail in bowls and season the sauce with freshly ground pepper and sprinkle with freshly chopped herbs, if you like, then pour over the oxtail. This dish is wonderful served with potato or parsnip purée.

BEEF BRAISED WITH GUINNESS

This is a classic braise. Hours of slow cooking render the shin's tough connective tissue into flavourful melting gelatine. Shin and beef cheek are my two favourite cuts of beef for braising. Sorry, I do apologize, I should add oxtail to that, as I do love it as well. What do all these cuts have in common? Lots of connective tissue and a sprinkling of fat. What does that mean? Taste and texture. Is there any other reason to cook?

INGREDIENTS

1 kg (2 lb 4 oz) beef shin, cut into 2 cm (^{3}/4 inch) cubes
sea salt
80 ml (2^1/2 fl oz/^{1}/3 cup) extra virgin olive oil, plus extra
2 fresh bay leaves
1 medium brown onion, chopped into 2 cm (^{3}/4 inch) cubes
1 medium carrot, peeled and cut into 2 cm (^{3}/4 inch) lengths
1 medium leek, white part only, cut into 2 cm (^{3}/4 inch) lengths
2 garlic cloves, finely chopped
2 thyme sprigs
250 ml (9 fl oz/1 cup) Guinness
freshly ground pepper
2 tablespoons chopped flat-leaf (Italian) parsley

METHOD

Remove the beef shin from the refrigerator 1 hour before cooking and season with sea salt. Put the extra virgin olive oil and bay leaves in a heavy-based saucepan with a tight-fitting lid over high heat. When hot, add half the beef and brown all over. Remove and repeat with the remaining beef. Add a little more oil to the pan, if need be, then add the onion and cook for 10 minutes over gentle heat. Return the beef to the pan, add the carrot, leek, garlic, thyme, Guinness and 250 ml (9 fl oz/1 cup) water. Bring to the boil, then reduce to a gentle simmer and cover. Cook for about 1^1/2 hours. Remove the lid and continue cooking for a further 20–30 minutes, or until the beef is very tender. Remove the pan from the heat.

Remove the bay leaves and thyme and season with lots of freshly ground pepper. Divide among four deep bowls and sprinkle with the parsley. Serves 4

ACCOMPANIMENTS

• This dish is perfect with steamed rice or potato purée, with roast carrots on the side. It can also be served with any green vegetable combination. Soft or pan-fried polenta works well, and some gremolata will add a little life.

BRAISED LAMB SHOULDER WITH GREMOLATA

This simple braise is ageless. The meat is browned, aromatic vegetables added, the wine reduced and stock added, and then the whole thing is simmered gently for two hours. Shoulder is the best lamb cut for this dish, as it gives melt-in-the-mouth tenderness and great flavour.

INGREDIENTS

800 g (1 lb 12 oz) lamb shoulder, cut into 3 cm (1^{1}/4 inch) cubes

2 tablespoons plain (all-purpose) flour

80 ml (2^{1}/2 fl oz/^{1}/3 cup) extra virgin olive oil

30 g (1 oz) unsalted butter

2 garlic cloves, finely chopped

1 small leek, finely chopped

sea salt

250 ml (9 fl oz/1 cup) red or dry white wine

1.25 litres (44 fl oz/5 cups) chicken stock

1 tablespoon tomato paste (purée)

400 g (14 oz) can whole tomatoes, chopped

2 rosemary sprigs

2 thyme sprigs

1 fresh bay leaf

8 baby onions, peeled

8 baby carrots, peeled

gremolata (page 369)

freshly ground pepper

METHOD

Dust the lamb shoulder cubes with the flour. Heat the oil and butter in a large heavy-based saucepan and cook the lamb in batches until browned all over; be careful not to burn the flour. Remove the lamb from the pan. Add the garlic, leek and sea salt and cook for 5 minutes over medium heat until soft. Return the lamb to the pan, add the wine and simmer gently, stirring occasionally, for about 5 minutes, until it reduces and slightly thickens. Add the stock and bring to a simmer. Add the tomato paste, tomato and herbs and continue to simmer very gently for 1 hour. Add the onions and carrots and cook for a further hour, stirring occasionally, until the lamb is very tender. Remove from the heat and discard the herbs. Divide among bowls, making sure each dish gets two baby carrots and two onions. Sprinkle with the gremolata and add pepper. Serves 4

ACCOMPANIMENTS

• This would be yummy with parsnip purée and steamed greens.

CINNAMON-SCENTED LAMB

I love the sweet-sour nature of this dish. It combines dried fruit and spices with meat, which is typical of Middle Eastern cooking. It is important to braise this dish with a firm-fitting lid as it doesn't have a lot of stock in it and would easily simmer dry if left uncovered. We have used this recipe on Qantas for quite some time; its flavours just get better with age, which makes it a perfect airline dish. This is also one of those braises that works well as a shared meal; just add a fish dish and a couple of vegetables or salads and you have a lovely Saturday night or Sunday lunch banquet with which to impress friends. The addition of extra chopped coriander (cilantro) leaves and mint at the end as a garnish would be welcome. This dish is fantastic with duck; just steam (page 252) or poach (page 269) the duck first, then cut it into small pieces and proceed with the recipe.

INGREDIENTS

600 g (1 lb 5 oz) lamb shoulder
2 small eggplants (aubergines)
sea salt
150 ml (5 fl oz) extra virgin olive oil
1 tablespoon raisins
1 tablespoon red wine vinegar
1/2 brown onion, sliced
2 garlic cloves, finely chopped
2 vine-ripened tomatoes, peeled, deseeded and chopped (page 66)
125 ml (4 fl oz/1/2 cup) chicken stock
1 teaspoon ground coriander
1 teaspoon ground cumin
1 teaspoon ground turmeric
1 teaspoon ground cinnamon
juice of 1/2 lemon
1 teaspoon chopped mint
freshly ground pepper

METHOD

Trim the lamb, then cut into 4 cm (1^1/2 inch) dice. Cut the eggplants into 2 cm (^{3}/4 inch) thick slices, then cut the slices into quarters. Sprinkle with sea salt and let stand for 30 minutes. Rinse the eggplant quickly under cold water and dry thoroughly with paper towels. Heat 60 ml (2 fl oz/^{1}/4 cup) of the extra virgin olive oil in a heavy-based frying pan and fry half the eggplant until golden brown on all sides. Drain on paper towels. Repeat with the remaining eggplant. Put aside.

Combine the raisins and vinegar in a bowl, then set aside. Heat the remaining oil in a heavy-based saucepan that has a tight-fitting lid and lightly brown the lamb in batches. Remove the lamb from the pan. Add the onion to the pan and sweat over very low heat for about 10 minutes, or until soft. Add the garlic and some sea salt and cook, stirring, for 1 minute, then add the tomato, raisin mixture, browned lamb, stock and spices. Bring to a very gentle simmer, cover and cook for about 1^1/2 hours, or until the lamb is very tender. Stir through the prepared eggplant, lemon juice, mint and freshly ground pepper and remove the pan from the heat.

Divide between four large pasta bowls and serve immediately. Serves 4

ACCOMPANIMENTS

• Serve with steamed jasmine rice or pumpkin purée and creamed spinach.

• A bowl of steamed greens or a simple salad served on the side would be nice, with couscous served alongside or in the bowl along with the braise.

FOLLOWING PAGES cinnamon-scented lamb, left, and persian-style lamb stew, right

PERSIAN-STYLE LAMB STEW

I became interested in Persian cooking some years ago — I guess it was a natural follow on from my love of all things Moroccan. This braise is really a *khoresht*, the Persian word for sauce. Originally, Persian cooks saw the khoresht as a sauce that flavoured plain white rice. In reality it is much more than that. There are many combinations of fruit and meat, fowl and fish that make these stews irresistible. They usually contain dried or fresh fruits, lots of herbs and spices, and are almost always soured with the addition of lemon juice, powdered dry limes, verjuice, tamarind or pomegranates. Cooked gently, they look after themselves, and with a bowl of rice are quite magical.

INGREDIENTS

700 g (1 lb 9 oz) lamb shoulder

80 ml (2^1/2 fl oz/^{1}/3 cup) extra virgin olive oil, plus extra

2 brown onions, cut into 1 cm (^{1}/2 inch) dice

1 teaspoon ground cinnamon

1 teaspoon ground cumin

4 cardamom pods, split, seeds removed and crushed

2 teaspoons sea salt

375 ml (13 fl oz/1^1/2 cups) chicken stock

110 g (3^3/4 oz/^{1}/2 cup) pitted prunes

1 teaspoon caster (superfine) sugar

juice of 2 limes

^{1}/4 teaspoon saffron threads, dissolved in 1 tablespoon boiling water

1 large handful mint, roughly chopped

roasted almonds or pistachios (page 30), to garnish (optional)

FOR THE PUMPKIN

400 g (14 oz) butternut pumpkin, peeled and cut into 3.5 cm (1^1/2 inch) dice

sea salt

1 tablespoon extra virgin olive oil

METHOD

To make the lamb stew, cut the lamb into 4 cm (1^1/2 inch) dice. Heat the extra virgin olive oil in a heavy-based saucepan. Add the lamb in batches, stir over medium to high heat until browned, then remove from the pan. Add extra oil to the pan if need be, then add the onion and stir until lightly browned. Add the spices and sea salt and stir for 1 minute, or until fragrant. Add the stock. Return the lamb to the pan and simmer over low heat, covered, for 1 hour, stirring occasionally. Add the prunes, sugar, lime juice and saffron water. Cover and simmer for a further 30 minutes, or until the lamb is very tender.

Meanwhile, for the pumpkin, preheat the oven to 200°C (400°F/Gas 6). Combine the pumpkin pieces with some sea salt and the extra virgin olive oil. Put in a roasting tin and bake for about 20 minutes, or until just tender and lightly browned all over.

Add the pumpkin and the mint to the stew. Carefully stir through to mix.

Serve the stew in a large bowl, with a bowl of rice in the middle of the table. Garnish the dish with roasted almonds or pistachios if you like. Serves 4

ACCOMPANIMENTS

• Saffron rice pilaf is a must with this dish. The lamb also goes really well with pan-fried spicy eggplant.

• Any of the rices, with steamed or boiled green vegetables, would be nice with the lamb. I quite like this dish served on soft polenta with a Moroccan eggplant salad or tabbouleh on the side.

SPICED PORK BRAISED WITH PRUNES AND APRICOTS

This dish is a marriage made in heaven — the rich flavour of the pork in perfect harmony with the cutting sweetness of the prunes. Thank God there are classics; life is richer for it. The spices also have a wonderful affinity with the pork and the fruit.

INGREDIENTS

1 kg (2 lb 4 oz) pork shoulder
1 teaspoon ground coriander
1 teaspoon ground fennel
1 teaspoon ground cumin
1 teaspoon ground cinnamon
2 teaspoons sea salt, plus extra
80 ml (2^1/2 fl oz/^{1}/3 cup) extra virgin olive oil
1 brown onion, cut into 2 cm (^{3}/4 inch) dice
125 ml (4 fl oz/^{1}/2 cup) port
250 ml (9 fl oz/1 cup) red wine
8 pitted prunes
8 dried apricots
grated zest of 1 orange
2 fresh or dried bay leaves
500 ml (17 fl oz/2 cups) veal stock (page 384)
freshly ground pepper

METHOD

About 1 hour before cooking, cut the pork into 2 cm (^{3}/4 inch) dice. Mix the spices and sea salt together. Rub them over the pork pieces, cover and leave to marinate. In a large heavy-based saucepan with a tight-fitting lid, heat the extra virgin olive oil. When hot, add half the pork, fry until evenly browned, taking care not to burn the spices, then remove and repeat with the next batch. Set aside. Add the onion to the pan and a little more sea salt and cook for 5 minutes over medium heat until softened. Add the port and reduce by half. Add the red wine and boil for 5 minutes to burn off the alcohol. Return the pork to the pan, add the prunes, apricots, orange zest, bay leaves and stock and bring to the boil. Reduce the heat to a gentle simmer, cover and cook for 1^1/2 hours. Remove the lid and cook for a further 20–30 minutes, or until the pork is tender. Remove the pan from the heat. Remove the bay leaves. Divide among four bowls, add a good grind of pepper and serve. Serves 4

ACCOMPANIMENTS

• I love this with polenta, rice or couscous to soak up the lovely braising juices.

OPOSITE PAGE spiced pork braised with prunes and apricots, served with pan-fried polenta (page 344)

SPANISH-STYLE CHICKEN CASSEROLE

This dish is incredibly simple, and lots of garlic and paprika give it a real Spanish feel. If you wish, you could remove the skin from the chicken, but it doesn't produce quite as good a flavour. You can also use chicken breast if you like, and cut the cooking time down to about half an hour. Remember the breast is leaner, so it won't be as moist.

INGREDIENTS

6 free-range chicken legs

80 ml ($2^1/2$ fl oz/$^1/3$ cup) extra virgin olive oil

1 brown onion, roughly chopped

2 garlic cloves, crushed

3 teaspoons smoky sweet paprika

sea salt

1 red capsicum (pepper), sliced

250 ml (9 fl oz/1 cup) dry sherry

400 g (14 oz) can peeled tomatoes, roughly chopped

2 tablespoons tomato paste (purée)

125 g ($4^1/2$ oz/$^3/4$ cup) green olives, pitted and halved

1 large handful flat-leaf (Italian) parsley

1 lemon

freshly ground pepper

METHOD

Put the chicken legs on a chopping board and separate the thighs from the drumsticks. Heat the extra virgin olive oil in a large, deep saucepan with a tight-fitting lid and add the chicken in batches. Cook over medium heat for 4 minutes, or until browned, then remove. Add the onion, garlic, 2 teaspoons of the paprika, some sea salt and the capsicum. Cook for 5–8 minutes, or until soft.

Add the sherry and cook for 2 minutes, or until slightly reduced and the alcohol is burnt off. Add the tomato and tomato paste, stir well and cook for 2 minutes. Return the chicken to the pan and add 250 ml (9 fl oz/1 cup) water. Gently simmer, covered, for 1 hour, then uncover and cook for 15 minutes. Add the olives and parsley, cook for a further minute, then remove from the heat. Sprinkle the chicken with the remaining paprika, squeeze lemon juice over and give a good grind of pepper. Divide among four bowls and serve. Serves 4

ACCOMPANIMENTS

• Like all the other braised dishes, steamed rice, couscous or polenta would be a perfect accompaniment to this dish, with cauliflower, pine nut and raisin gratin on the side. I also wouldn't mind this with potato or parsnip purée.

CHICKEN TAGINE

We make tagines at home all the time, as they are so easy to make and taste so delicious. Once you see how easy it is to make chermoula, you will cook with it all the time. The best thing is that you can vary it at will. In Thailand, they don't have a word for curries. It is called *gang*, meaning a paste. It can be as simple as garlic, French shallots and white pepper pounded together, or as complex as a *gang panang* — there are literally thousands of them. Think of chermoula in the same manner. It really can be a paste of whatever you like, as complex or simple as you want, and you can change the flavour by varying the ingredients you cook with. Vary the amount of garlic, the amount of herbs or spices; it's really up to you. Once the chermoula is made, the rest of the dish relies on a simple slow braise. Chicken, lamb, duck and fish work beautifully in tagines. The beans in this dish are cooked for the entire time, so don't expect them to be bright green, but do expect them to taste fantastic. I cook all these dishes in one of the many tagines I have at home, but you can also use a large wide stockpot or heavy-based saucepan with a tight-fitting lid.

INGREDIENTS

2 kg (4 lb 8 oz) free-range chicken

250 ml (9 fl oz/1 cup) chermoula (page 372)

1 red onion, cut into 6 pieces

2 carrots, cut into 4 cm (1 1/2 inch) long pieces

1 medium yam, peeled and cut into 4 cm (1 1/2 inch) long pieces

30 green beans

12 whole almonds, skin removed

sea salt

extra virgin olive oil

2 tablespoons honey

juice of 1 lemon

8 fresh dates, pitted

1 small handful black olives, pitted

1/4 preserved lemon, pith removed and rind finely chopped (page 380)

2 tablespoons chopped coriander (cilantro) leaves

2 tablespoons chopped flat-leaf (Italian) parsley

METHOD

Put the chicken on a chopping board and remove the wing tips. Remove the legs and cut the thighs and drumsticks in half. Remove the backbone to leave the breasts and wings on the double ribcage. Cut down the centre to separate the two breasts and cut each half into three pieces.

Combine the chicken pieces with the chermoula, onion, carrot, yam, beans, almonds and a little sea salt in a bowl. Leave to marinate for about 1 hour. In a tagine or a large saucepan with a tight-fitting lid, heat a little extra virgin olive oil. Add the chicken, vegetables and any marinade to the pan and settle the pieces down reasonably flat. Half cover with water, then add the honey and lemon juice and cover with the lid. Reduce the heat to a very gentle simmer. After about 30 minutes, remove the lid and turn the ingredients over carefully. Remove the chicken and add the dates and olives. Cover the pan again and cook for a further 30 minutes; by this stage everything should be tender. Return the chicken to the pan for the last 5 minutes of cooking. Remove the tagine or pan from the heat.

You can serve the dish in the tagine or pan you have cooked it in, spoon it onto a large platter or divide among plates. Just before serving sprinkle with the chopped preserved lemon rind and the fresh herbs. Serves 4

ACCOMPANIMENTS

• Almond couscous and a side salad of tabbouleh couldn't be easier to prepare.

• Steamed rice or rice pilaf, Moroccan eggplant salad, spicy pan-fried eggplant and steamed potatoes would all work well.

ACCOMPANIMENTS

Vegetables have been a part of my life for as long as I can remember. My father loved his garden. We would spend time out in it whenever he wasn't at work or fishing, his other great love. Being a boy from the country, he couldn't imagine life without it. It was all very practical really, mint around the tap and lots of other herbs down the side of the house. Passionfruit vines grew on the back fence, choko on the side, and in the little plot at the back of the house were seasonal vegetables ranging from zucchini (courgette), tomato and squash in the summer to all sorts of root vegetables in autumn and early spring. I still remember summer watermelons lying on the ground, growing by the day. These are memories that evoke the season and the great taste of fresh fruit and vegetables eaten the day they're picked. These days the variety and choice of vegetables available both in Australia and in many countries around the world is staggering. When I was growing up in the sixties, asparagus, artichoke, celeriac, fennel and so on were very rarely seen in the grocery shop, and even less often cooked by the average Australian. In those days we were just starting to develop into our multicultural Australia and people from the Mediterranean were the predominant new Australians. They brought with them eggplant (aubergine), a love of garlic, okra and red capsicums (peppers) and many other foods that at the time would have been considered exotic. How things have changed. We live in a country that offers everything that is available in Europe and Asia. The garden of Australia is a place of riches and if we eat in season its vegetables will offer great value and fabulous taste. I don't need to get into lecture mode, as I know everyone is aware of how important vegetables are in a balanced diet. If we look after the balance, then we don't need to go on fad diets. Balance is a great life philosophy, not just in food but in all things.

This chapter supports the meat and poultry and seafood chapters. There are a number of ways in which these recipes can be served. They can be individually plated with the meat, poultry or seafood dish that you have cooked, to enable you to put complete plates of food on the table for each of your guests and family. You can serve them as side dishes that accompany the main plate of food, which is really a family style of serving and the way I serve food at home most of the time. Or you can cook up a few of these dishes and have a vegetarian feast.

This chapter is intended as one long group of vegetable recipes, however, to my way of thinking — that is, as a chef — it is broken into two sections. The first section looks at what I always think of as the vegetable side of the plate — green leaves, pods, seeds, mushrooms, vegetable fruits, stalks, shoots and the onion and cabbage family. The second section looks at the starch side — squash family, roots, tubers and grains. These two components would go with a protein — meat, poultry or seafood. That is how chefs see the food that comes to your table — as a number of components that marry well together and make you feel that you have eaten a stunning dish, but are actually three separate recipes, perhaps pulled together by a separate sauce recipe, perhaps not. My imaginary line starts in this chapter at roast baby carrots. So I guess I could have done it in two separate chapters, but they do all belong together as vegetables.

All of these dishes are tried and true. They are classic complements to the food in the previous chapters and, like them, they form a group of recipes that will give you a really good grounding in quality cooking and the skills to take your cooking to wherever you like. Not to mention, enabling you to cook really delicious food at home.

When selecting vegetables remember that they are mostly composed of water. If something looks withered and dry, it probably is. Older vegetables generally dehydrate quickly, so it pays to shop with a close eye. Don't be afraid to rummage around to get the freshest ingredients. Very importantly, go to the market, fruit shop or supermarket ready to change what you're having for dinner if something other than what is on your shopping list looks fresh and wonderful.

BOILING AND STEAMING VEGETABLES

Boiling and steaming are both very pure ways of cooking vegetables. Most green and root vegetables can be cooked successfully by either method. Steaming is so easy; all you need is a saucepan of boiling water and a bamboo or other steamer basket. Make sure you don't boil the pan dry and don't burn yourself with the steam; other than that, you are away. You may find that when steaming you lose a little colour from green vegetables, though you will lose less of the nutrients. Steaming will also take a little longer than boiling, maybe up to a third longer. That being said I do, in the most part, prefer boiled vegetables over steamed. There is an argument that says that salt is added to water only to increase the boiling temperature and that it has no effect on the taste. I have always disagreed with that. I find salted vegetables taste better, no matter what the scientists say.

When boiling I will generally boil the vegetable, drain well and toss with extra virgin olive oil, sea salt and freshly ground pepper. It is then that you experience the true flavour of the vegetable. So when you pick fresh, in season vegetables for this process you will get real flavour.

Things to remember when boiling vegetables are: have fiercely boiling water; add to it a considerable amount of sea salt (it should taste like the sea); and don't cover green vegetables, as it can make them lose their colour.

Cook vegetables to your liking by checking them as they are cooking: remove a pea or bean and have a munch. When you like what you taste, quickly remove them from the saucepan by draining them into a colander or fishing them out with a steel-mesh strainer such as a spider; whichever option you follow make sure you're ready and move quickly.

MY FAVOURITE VEGETABLES TO BOIL ARE

• **asparagus** — they take about 3–5 minutes, depending on their thickness.

• **broccoli** — they take about 5 minutes, and their flavour will really increase if you cook them for the full amount of time.

• **Brussels sprouts** — they will take about 8 minutes to cook, but I quite often just cut them in half and they take no time at all.

• **corn** — this vegetable needs about 6–8 minutes to cook. You can take the corn off the cob and serve, or roll the cob in a little butter and olive oil. They are one of my favourite things and the vegetable that my daughter Josephine loves the most.

• **green beans** — they will take about 7–8 minutes. Don't forget that you want to cook beans for long enough in order to convert the starch to sugar and thus get really sweet beans.

• **peas** — they will take about 3 minutes if young.

• **snow peas (mangetout)** — they will take about 2 minutes.

• **sugar snap peas** — they will take about 2–3 minutes.

I like to boil root vegetables such as yams, parsnips, carrots, celeriac and squash like pumpkin in just enough water that the water is almost completely reduced by the time the vegetables are cooked. To do this, I don't completely cover the vegetables with water, but have the water level at about three-quarters of the height of the vegetables. I add some butter and sea salt and boil; the exposed parts will cook in the steam. Then I season, drizzle with extra virgin olive oil and serve. Quite often the vegetables will be breaking up when ready, but don't worry, as they are almost self-saucing and incredibly delicious. Follow this method when making purées, as the little bit of water leftover at the end is full of flavour and can be incorporated into the purée.

ASPARAGUS

To prepare asparagus for cooking all you have to do is snap the dry fibrous ends off. They will break where the stem starts to have moist suppleness. Many recipes call for you to peel asparagus, but most young shoots have very tender skin, and the skin offers a nice textural contrast to the creamy flesh.

Asparagus is one of many vegetables that can be cooked in a variety of ways and its flavours change a little depending on which method you use. You can boil or steam for a very pure taste of asparagus. You can pan-fry them, which will intensify their flavour, or you can barbecue them, which will intensify the flavour as well as give them a gentle hint of smokiness. This is probably my favourite way to prepare asparagus; you can cook them and flavour them, or cook them with many other vegetables to make a great warm salad on a hot summer's day. These next three recipes are classic examples of how a vegetable can be cooked with exactly the same ingredients and yet taste different because of the cooking method.

The three recipes are very simple. You could use red wine or balsamic vinegar (or any vinegar really), lime juice or walnut oil to flavour the asparagus after removing it from the heat, and mix it with any number or combinations of flavours. These dishes are just to start you thinking about how versatile vegetables are. Try these same recipe concepts with beans, snow peas (mangetout), red capsicums (peppers), broccoli, artichokes and more.

STEAMED ASPARAGUS
INGREDIENTS
350 g (12 oz/2 bunches) asparagus
extra virgin olive oil
sea salt and freshly ground pepper
1 lemon, quartered

METHOD
Break the tough ends off the asparagus. Set up a saucepan of boiling water and place a steamer basket on top. Put the asparagus in the basket, cover and steam for about 4—5 minutes, depending on their size. Remove when cooked and toss in extra virgin olive oil, sea salt, freshly ground pepper and enough fresh lemon juice to balance the flavour. Serves 4

PAN-FRIED ASPARAGUS

INGREDIENTS

350 g (12 oz/2 bunches) asparagus
extra virgin olive oil
sea salt
1 lemon, quartered
freshly ground pepper

METHOD

Break the tough ends off the asparagus. Mix the asparagus, extra virgin olive oil and some sea salt in a bowl. Put a heavy-based sauté pan on the stove and heat to medium. Add the asparagus and cook for about 4 minutes, shaking the pan and turning the asparagus from time to time. Squeeze the lemon juice over and give a good grind of pepper. Remove from the pan and place on a plate. Serves 4

BARBECUED ASPARAGUS

INGREDIENTS

350 g (12 oz/2 bunches) asparagus
extra virgin olive oil
sea salt
1 lemon, quartered
freshly ground pepper

METHOD

Break the tough ends off the asparagus. Mix the asparagus, extra virgin olive oil and some sea salt in a bowl. Heat the barbecue to hot and make sure the grill bars are clean. Put the asparagus on the grill bars. Turn the asparagus from time to time to ensure a nice crust forms and they get some good grill marks on them. Cook for about 4 minutes, then remove and put on a plate. Drizzle with more extra virgin olive oil, sprinkle with sea salt, squeeze the lemon juice over and give a good grind of fresh pepper. Serves 4

SPINACH

The spinach that I use for all the spinach recipes in this book is flat-leaf English spinach. Now, that is what it is called in Australia because many years ago in a century now gone we called silverbeet (Swiss chard), spinach. So when the real spinach turned up we had an issue on our hands, hence silverbeet is known as silverbeet or spinach, and the real spinach as English spinach. Sorry about that!

I've included three favourite spinach dishes here. The first, spinach purée, produces the most fantastic concentrated spinach flavour, and we love it at Rockpool with roast beef. There are two major things that can go wrong: one is to undercook the spinach, making it impossible to get a smooth finish, and the other is to overcook it, turning it grey. You also need to resist the temptation to squeeze lemon juice over the dish, as it will discolour it. With all these recipes, always make sure you give spinach a good wash before use, as it comes with lots of dirt and mud.

The second dish, creamed spinach, is one of my all-time favourite vegetable dishes. It turns up on menus in the UK, USA and France and is a perfect partner for macaroni cheese with a steak and a good glass of wine. I should know; I've eaten it on several occasions. The last dish is the classic Italian side dish, which I have every time I go into an Italian restaurant. Of course, no one makes it seem easier to do than my good friend Armando Percuoco from Buon Ricordo in Sydney but the good news is that gorgeous food like this was designed to be made and eaten in the home — with a roast or barbecue it is superb. The three mistakes that can be made here are: overcooking the spinach; burning the garlic; and not using fresh lemon juice. Avoid these things and it is child's play.

SPINACH PUREE
INGREDIENTS
2 kg (4 lb 8 oz/4 bunches) English spinach, stems removed, washed
150 g (5 1/2 oz) unsalted butter, cut into small dice and softened
2 1/2 teaspoons sea salt
freshly ground pepper

METHOD
Steam the spinach in a steamer basket set over a saucepan of boiling water for 8 minutes until wilted. Squeeze out any excess water and chop the spinach. Use a stick blender to purée the spinach with the butter, sea salt and some freshly ground pepper for 5 minutes, or until smooth and creamy. Serves 4

CREAMED SPINACH

INGREDIENTS

1 kg (2 lb 4 oz/2 bunches) English spinach, stems removed, washed

50 g ($1^3/4$ oz) unsalted butter

1 brown onion, finely diced

1 garlic clove, finely diced

$1^1/2$ teaspoons sea salt and freshly ground pepper

250 ml (9 fl oz/1 cup) pure (whipping) cream

$1/2$ teaspoon freshly squeezed lemon juice

METHOD

Add the spinach in batches to a hot frying pan and stir constantly for about 2 minutes, or until the spinach is just wilted. As each batch wilts, remove the spinach from the pan and squeeze out the excess water.

Melt the butter in a pan. Add the onion and garlic and cook over low heat for about 8 minutes, or until the onion is soft. Add the spinach, sea salt and freshly ground pepper and cook for 1 minute. Add the cream, bring to a simmer and cook for about 2 minutes. Stir in the lemon juice.

In a food processor or blender, or with a stick blender, process the mixture until finely chopped and well combined. Check the seasoning, then serve. Serves 4

SPINACH WITH GARLIC AND LEMON

INGREDIENTS

1.5 kg (3 lb 5 oz/3 bunches) English spinach, stems removed, washed

60 ml (2 fl oz/$1/4$ cup) extra virgin olive oil

3 garlic cloves, sliced

sea salt

pinch of chilli flakes or 1 small fresh red chilli, chopped

1 lemon, quartered

freshly ground pepper

METHOD

Heat the extra virgin olive oil in a sauté pan and add the garlic. Cook over medium heat until the garlic is light brown. Add the spinach in about three batches, pushing it around with a pair of tongs. Turn the heat up to high and add some sea salt and the chilli and continue to stir. The spinach should become glossy and wilted as it is coated with the oil. Squeeze lemon juice over and give a good grind of fresh pepper. Serve immediately. Serves 4

BOILED GREEN BEANS WITH BURNT BUTTER AND ALMONDS

These beans are simply boiled and then dressed with burnt butter. Make sure you cook the beans properly — by that I mean for the right amount of time. There is a tendency in restaurants these days to undercook beans. They still taste starchy, and although crunchy, the flavour is just not that of a beautiful sweet bean. If you don't want to add butter to the vegetables for health or other reasons, by all means just drizzle over a little extra virgin olive oil instead. The beans that I'm using here are quite a bit larger than the wonderful haricot vert that the Europeans have, however, you can get 'beanettes' or baby beans for a part of the year. If you are cooking with those just boil for 3–4 minutes.

INGREDIENTS

400 g (14 oz) green beans, ends trimmed
$1^1/2$–2 tablespoons sea salt, plus extra
1 tablespoon chopped chervil
1 tablespoon chopped tarragon
1 lemon, quartered
80 g ($2^3/4$ oz) unsalted butter
1 garlic clove, thinly sliced
30 g (1 oz/$^1/4$ cup) slivered almonds, roasted (page 30)
freshly ground pepper

METHOD

Bring a large saucepan of water to the boil. Add the sea salt to make it taste like the sea. Add the beans and cook uncovered for 7—8 minutes, stirring from time to time. When cooked, drain the beans into a colander. Transfer to a bowl and sprinkle with the herbs and lemon juice, to taste. Set a small frying pan over high heat and add the butter. Just as it starts to foam, add the garlic and a little sea salt. As it turns nut brown, remove the pan from the heat, stir through the almonds and spoon the sauce over the beans. Add some sea salt, give a good grind of fresh pepper and serve. Serves 4

SAUTEED BRUSSELS SPROUTS WITH BACON

You hear people say, 'Brussels sprouts — yuck'. Nothing could be further from the truth. They are delicious, with a wonderful mustard taste to them. I love to throw them into tagines or just sauté them in extra virgin olive oil, butter, garlic and ginger, and let them caramelize and develop a yummy crisp crust.

Here they pair perfectly with bacon, but don't underestimate how good they taste boiled, dressed simply with butter or extra virgin olive oil and seasoned liberally.

INGREDIENTS
300 g ($10^1/2$ oz) Brussels sprouts
$1^1/2$–2 tablespoons sea salt, plus extra
100 g ($3^1/2$ oz) piece smoky bacon, diced
1 tablespoon extra virgin olive oil
40 g ($1^1/2$ oz) unsalted butter
1 tablespoon thyme
freshly ground pepper

METHOD
Remove any torn or discoloured leaves from the sprouts. Trim the bases and cut out and discard the cores. Bring a large saucepan of water to the boil. Add the sea salt to make it taste like the sea. Plunge the sprouts into the boiling salted water and blanch for about 3—5 minutes, or until the leaves just begin to open. Drain, rinse under cold water, then blot dry and cut into quarters.

Cook the bacon in a saucepan over medium heat for 5 minutes until rendered but not yet crisp. Add the extra virgin olive oil and butter and when the butter starts to bubble, add the sprouts, thyme and seasoning. Reduce the heat to medium—low and cook until golden brown. Add some freshly ground pepper and serve immediately. Serves 4

BRAISED PEAS

These peas are great but remember to use frozen before you use out-of-season old woody ones. This dish is bloody delicious with just about anything, and I quite often add half a teaspoon of chilli flakes to it. Make sure you cook the peas for quite a while; they need to be melting and sweet and definitely not a bright green colour.

INGREDIENTS

300 g (10^1/2 oz/2 cups) freshly shelled peas, about 700 g (1 lb 9 oz) unshelled
2 tablespoons extra virgin olive oil, plus extra
30 g (1 oz) unsalted butter, diced
8 anchovies, chopped
sea salt
freshly ground pepper
juice of ^{1}/2 lemon

METHOD

Heat the extra virgin olive oil and butter together in a frying pan. Add the anchovies with a pinch of sea salt and allow the anchovies to melt in. Add the peas, toss well to coat, then add 400 ml (14 fl oz) water and leave until the liquid is reduced and the peas are soft. This will take at least 20 minutes. Finish with a grind of pepper, a splash of oil and the lemon juice. Serves 4

BRAISED ROMAN BEANS

These beans have a wonderful full flavour and sweet taste when properly cooked. Whatever you do don't undercook them; they are marvellous with just olive oil, garlic and one hour of long, slow braising. Normal green beans can be cooked in the same way with great success, just reduce the cooking time, but not by too much now. If you're used to eating undercooked starchy green beans don't get scared when these emerge a dark green colour. They are not meant to be a vibrant bright green colour; however, they will be the sweetest beans you have ever tasted.

INGREDIENTS

400 g (14 oz) Roman (flat) or butterbeans (lima beans), washed, topped and tailed

80 ml (2^1/2 fl oz/^{1}/3 cup) extra virgin olive oil

1 garlic clove, finely chopped

1 red onion, cut into 5 mm (^{1}/4 inch) dice

sea salt

2 x 400 g (14 oz) cans good-quality Italian chopped tomatoes, with their juices

3 tablespoons dill leaves, stems removed

1 teaspoon lemon juice

freshly ground pepper

METHOD

Cut the beans in half on the diagonal. Heat half the extra virgin olive oil in a heavy-based saucepan. Add the garlic, onion and some sea salt, and stir over low to medium heat for about 10 minutes, or until the onion is soft. Add the tomatoes and their juices and stir to heat through. Add the beans and half the dill. Simmer over very low heat, covered, for about 20 minutes, stirring often.

Remove the lid, simmer for a further 35 minutes, or until the beans are soft and tender and the sauce has reduced. The beans should be very soft and will have lost their colour slightly. Add the remaining dill, the lemon juice, the remaining oil and some freshly ground pepper. Check the seasoning. Serves 4

BRAISED FENNEL

Fennel is one of the most delicious and versatile vegetables in the kitchen. It is gorgeous when eaten raw; makes the best purée for fish and poultry; loves to be in pasta or the main player in a soup; and is a wonderful vegetable to braise, as it is here. It also roasts and grills well. It needs only to be cut into slices and barbecued, then drizzled with extra virgin olive oil and balsamic vinegar. To roast fennel, cut the bulbs into portion sizes, either halve or quarter down the length of the bulb, then coat with extra virgin olive oil and sea salt, put in a hot oven and cook for 25–35 minutes, turning once. Remove from the oven and drizzle with balsamic vinegar, more oil and fresh herbs (if you like), then season. This is truly delicious when served with barbecued fish.

INGREDIENTS

2 small fennel bulbs, cut in half and 1 cm (^{1}/2 inch) trimmed off the tops
2 tablespoons extra virgin olive oil
30 g (1 oz) unsalted butter
^{1}/2 small brown onion, thinly sliced
1 carrot, peeled, cut in half and thinly sliced
4 garlic cloves
sea salt
freshly ground pepper
3 tablespoons chopped flat-leaf (Italian) parsley

METHOD

Choose a heavy-based saucepan large enough to fit the fennel. Add the extra virgin olive oil and heat over high heat until fairly hot. Add the fennel, cut side down, and cook for a couple of minutes until it caramelizes, then turn over and cook for a further 2 minutes. Remove the fennel and put on a plate.

Add the butter and reduce the heat. Add the onion, carrot, whole garlic cloves and some sea salt. Cook, stirring, for about 5 minutes to soften the vegetables. Return the fennel to the saucepan and add enough water to come halfway up the side of the vegetables. Bring to the boil, then reduce the heat to a gentle simmer. Cover and cook slowly for about 45 minutes, or until the fennel is tender. Give a good grind of pepper and sprinkle with the parsley. Remove the pan from the heat and spoon the fennel and juices into a serving bowl. Serves 4

SAUTEED MUSHROOMS

There are a number of different mushrooms available in Australia. The wild mushrooms don't have the flavour of their cousins in the northern hemisphere, but in their own way they are satisfying when in season, particularly the saffron milk cap (pine mushroom). To me, in terms of both taste and texture, that is Australia's best wild harvested mushroom. I can remember when I was about ten or perhaps eleven, my family lived for a couple of years on a property of fifty acres. We used to pick field mushrooms and I can still remember the taste. The pan would run black with colour and the flavour was meaty and the texture fine. Today these field mushrooms are cultivated and available everywhere. They don't really have the taste that I remember but if cooked and really concentrated they are pretty good. Don't forget that mushrooms are eighty per cent water, so they shrink down heaps.

INGREDIENTS

800 g (1 lb 12 oz) field mushrooms
60 ml (2 fl oz/$1/4$ cup) extra virgin olive oil
40 g ($1^{1}/2$ oz) unsalted butter
1 teaspoon thyme
3 garlic cloves, minced
sea salt
lemon juice, to taste
freshly ground pepper
3 tablespoons finely shredded flat-leaf (Italian) parsley

METHOD

Clean and slice the mushrooms into 2.5 mm ($1/16$ inch) thick slices. Add the extra virgin olive oil and butter to a heavy-based frying pan large enough to hold the mushrooms. Raise the heat to high and when the butter starts to foam, add the sliced mushrooms and thyme and toss to coat. Lower the heat to medium and cook for 10 minutes. Add the garlic and some sea salt and raise the heat again; the mushrooms should start to caramelize. Cook for a further 10 minutes. Remove the pan from the heat, add lemon juice to taste, give a good grind of pepper and sprinkle the parsley over. Mix well, then spoon into a serving dish. Serves 4

BRAISED RED CABBAGE

Cabbage is one of those vegetables that tastes great raw or cooked. I love cabbage just shredded and dressed with extra virgin olive oil and red wine vinegar. When cooking cabbage, it can be either very quickly prepared or braised and simmered until the whole dish is full of flavour and meltingly tender. This recipe uses red cabbage and is slow-braised. You can also replace the red cabbage with green and carry on with the recipe; however, I would usually use red wine vinegar, not cider, in that case. You can use vegetable or chicken stock or even water if you find that easier; the flavour will not suffer much by the time the dish is done. Don't hesitate to fry off some smoked bacon with the onion and garlic. It is a match made in heaven — cabbage loves pork.

INGREDIENTS

$1/2$ small red cabbage, outer leaves removed

2 tablespoons extra virgin olive oil

$1/2$ red onion, sliced

3 garlic cloves, finely sliced

1 teaspoon sea salt

1 sour green apple, such as Granny Smith, peeled and grated

100 ml ($3^1/2$ fl oz) cider vinegar

60 g ($2^1/4$ oz/$1/3$ cup) soft brown sugar

500 ml (17 fl oz/2 cups) white wine

500 ml (17 fl oz/2 cups) vegetable or chicken stock (pages 383 and 384)

METHOD

Roughly slice the cabbage. Heat the extra virgin olive oil in a deep saucepan and sweat the onion, garlic and sea salt over low heat for 2 minutes, or until soft. Add the cabbage and continue to cook slowly for 5—7 minutes, or until it is completely soft.

Add the apple, vinegar and sugar and cook for a further 3 minutes, then add the wine and leave to simmer for about 30 minutes, stirring occasionally. Add the stock, cover and simmer for a further 1 hour. Serves 4

PEPERONATA

This is a classic Italian dish that works well on an antipasto table or as a side to roasted or barbecued food. The capsicums (peppers) are very sweet; the capers, olives and anchovies are salty; and the red wine vinegar is sour, which makes this a well-balanced dish with great flavour. At the restaurant we cut the capsicums into fine dice, which makes it more of a relish. You can also cut the capsicums into 1 cm (1/2 inch) squares if you wish. It is nice to cook and peel the capsicums before adding them to the other ingredients — you will get a different texture — and if you grill them on the barbecue you will add a smoky flavour.

Another really great thing to do with red capsicums is to stew them in olive oil. All you have to do is cut the capsicum in half lengthways, clean out all the seeds and membrane, then cut each half into quarters. Stew the capsicums in some extra virgin olive oil and sea salt until soft. Add some fresh chilli if you like and a few drops of red wine vinegar. Give a good grind of pepper and serve hot or savour later on when cold.

INGREDIENTS

1 red capsicum (pepper), julienned
1 yellow capsicum (pepper), julienned
60 ml (2 fl oz/1/4 cup) extra virgin olive oil
1 large red onion, cut into 1 cm (1/2 inch) dice
4 garlic cloves, finely chopped
1 tablespoon roughly chopped oregano
1 tablespoon salted baby capers, rinsed well and drained
2 anchovy fillets, roughly chopped
4 vine-ripened tomatoes, peeled, deseeded and finely chopped (page 66)
50 g (1 3/4 oz/1/2 cup) unpitted Ligurian olives
2 tablespoons red wine vinegar
2 teaspoons soft brown sugar

METHOD

Heat the extra virgin olive oil in a large heavy-based saucepan and add the onion, garlic and oregano. Sauté for 10 minutes, or until the onion is soft, stirring often. Add the capers and anchovy fillets and stir over medium heat for 2 minutes. Add the capsicum and tomato. Cover and simmer for 20 minutes, or until the capsicum is soft and tender. Add the olives, red wine vinegar and sugar. Uncover and simmer, stirring occasionally, for a further 10 minutes, or until slightly thickened. Serves 4

PAN-FRIED SPICY EGGPLANT

This vegetable is another great kitchen all rounder. Eggplant (aubergine) is great for dips, sauces and barbecues. It is also great in vegetarian dishes, holding many of them together, and is really yummy sautéed, as it is here. The brown caramelized exterior and the soft, warm interior makes it irresistible. The eggplant is almost chip-like and as a matter of fact you can deep-fry the pieces and just finish them off in the pan if you wish. Most eggplants that are not overmature don't really need to be salted before cooking to remove the bitterness; however, they can be salted to remove extra moisture, which I think is a good idea when simply sautéing them.

INGREDIENTS

2 eggplants (aubergines)
sea salt
extra virgin olive oil, for cooking, plus 80 ml ($2^{1}/2$ fl oz/$^{1}/3$ cup), extra
2 garlic cloves, finely chopped
2 tablespoons chopped fresh ginger
$^{1}/2$ teaspoon chilli flakes
2 tablespoons finely shredded flat-leaf (Italian) parsley
2 tablespoons finely shredded mint
lemon juice, to taste
freshly ground pepper

METHOD

Cut the eggplants into roughly 2 cm ($^{3}/4$ inch) squares. Put on a tray and season liberally with sea salt and leave for 30 minutes. The salt should draw out quite a bit of moisture. Using paper towels, wipe the eggplant, removing the salt and excess moisture.

Fill a heavy-based frying pan with extra virgin olive oil to the height of about 5 mm ($^{1}/4$ inch) and carefully heat. When hot, add the eggplant and cook for about 5 minutes on medium to high heat. Reduce the heat and cook for a further 7—8 minutes until the eggplant is brown and tender inside. Remove the eggplant from the pan and drain on paper towels. Pour off the oil and keep in a container for another use. Wipe the pan out, add the extra oil and return to medium heat. Add the garlic, ginger and chilli flakes and cook for 3 minutes. Add the eggplant and warm through. Turn off the heat and mix through the herbs. Squeeze lemon juice over to taste and give a good grind of pepper. Spoon into a serving bowl and serve. Serves 4

CREAM OF CORN

This is a wonderful summer dish, when the corn is so sweet that eating it raw is like crunching little yellow lollies. There are two ways of doing this. At Rockpool, we juice some of the corn kernels, cook the remaining kernels in that juice, then blend half the mixture, resulting in a beautiful creamy corn that has no cream in it. This is the method used below. There are only two minor drawbacks to this approach: one, you have to clean the juicer and two, you have to use more corn than normal but the flavour is intense. The other option is to add cream to the pan and then blend half the mixture; this will give you a pretty yummy result.

INGREDIENTS

8 corn cobs
60 ml (2 fl oz/$1/4$ cup) extra virgin olive oil
$1/2$ small leek, white part only, finely chopped
sea salt
30 g (1 oz) unsalted butter
freshly ground pepper

METHOD

Remove the corn kernels from the cobs with a sharp knife. The best and least messy way to do this is to stand the corn up in a bowl and run your knife down its length. Put one-third of the corn kernels through a juice extractor.

Put the extra virgin olive oil in a frying pan and set over medium to high heat. Add the leek and some sea salt. Turn the heat down to medium and sweat for 5 minutes, without colouring the leek. Add the corn kernels and corn juice and enough water to barely cover the corn, then add the butter and bring to a gentle simmer. Cover and cook for 20 minutes. Remove the pan from the heat and, with a slotted spoon, remove half the corn kernels. Tip the remaining mixture and any cooking liquid into a food processor and purée well. Return the purée and the reserved corn to the pan, season with freshly ground pepper and warm through. Spoon into a bowl and serve. Serves 4

CAULIFLOWER WITH SAFFRON, PINE NUTS AND RAISINS

I love cauliflower cooked any way: in a gratin, puréed, steamed or in a soup. This dish has a nice Spanish feel to it and is perfect with chicken.

INGREDIENTS

$1/2$ cauliflower
extra virgin olive oil
1 red onion, finely sliced
2 garlic cloves, minced
sea salt
$1/2$ teaspoon saffron threads, dissolved in 2 tablespoons boiling water
250 ml (9 fl oz/1 cup) chicken stock (page 384) or water
40 g ($1^{1}/2$ oz/$1/4$ cup) pine nuts, roasted (page 30)
30 g (1 oz/$1/4$ cup) raisins, soaked in warm water for 5 minutes
freshly ground pepper

METHOD

Cut the cauliflower into florets. Heat a little extra virgin olive oil in a saucepan. Add the onion and garlic with a pinch of sea salt and fry for a few minutes, stirring constantly over medium to high heat. Add the cauliflower florets, the saffron water and the stock or water — it should reach about halfway up the side of the cauliflower. Reduce the heat to medium–low. Leave the cauliflower for about 5 minutes to cook and allow the liquid to reduce. When the liquid is low, add the pine nuts, drained raisins and a good grind of pepper. Serves 4

BROCCOLINI WITH GARLIC AND CHILLI

Broccolini is one of those newer vegetables to Australia that have only been around for a few years. Like many green vegetables, it is great boiled and dressed with extra virgin olive oil, sea salt and lemon juice. It makes a great pasta sauce and is terrific in stir-fries.

METHOD

Bring a saucepan of water to the boil, add enough sea salt to make it taste like the sea and cook the broccolini at a rapid boil for 2 minutes. Drain and add to a sauté pan with some extra virgin olive oil, sea salt and chilli flakes and toss for about 1 minute. Add minced garlic and cook for 30 seconds. Remove from the heat and serve. Serves 4

ARTICHOKES

I love artichokes. When they are in season I have them on a couple of starters and a main course at Rockpool. We always serve some raw, some stuffed and braised as a starter and some as a sauce for meat, which we would probably top with fried artichokes. I love the idea of doubling-up on flavours, with different textures and intensity of flavours.

There are a couple of ways to prepare artichokes. You can boil or steam them whole and serve them with a dressing or a sauce like hollandaise (a classic French starter). To do this, remove the sharp points on the leaves with a pair of scissors, cut 2 cm (3/4 inch) from the top with a knife and cut the base off. Using a teaspoon, dive into the centre of the artichoke and twist. You need to remove the hairy choke. Artichoke discolours easily, so it is very important that you squeeze lemon juice over it. You should also drop your artichoke into acidulated water, which is a fancy way of saying have water with lemon juice added to it standing by. You can use that water for cooking the artichokes in; simply salt the water and simmer the artichokes for 25 minutes. Remove and drain.

To eat the artichokes, begin by tearing off a leaf, dip the fleshy end into the dressing or sauce and bite down on it. Pull the leaf through your teeth to get the yummy artichoke and discard the fibrous leaf into a side bowl. Continue leaf by leaf until you reach the centre, which you can eat with a knife and fork, if you wish. Don't forget to serve a finger bowl.

To prepare completely edible artichokes, break the stem off (this can be peeled and cooked with the artichoke) and pull off the outer leaves until you see the bright green supple flesh underneath. Lay the artichoke on a board and trim about 3 cm (1 1/4 inches) from the top. Trim around the base of the stem and carefully hollow out the core with a teaspoon to remove the choke. Rub the inside of a cut lemon over every surface of the artichoke to stop discoloration. You now have an edible artichoke. You can eat them raw, sliced thinly, with a little extra virgin olive oil, seasoning and shaved Parmesan on top, or cook them in salted water for 20 minutes until tender. They can also be stewed, stuffed and braised.

When small artichokes are available it is great to fry them whole. You just need to prepare them as described above, but leave the stem on the base and peel both. Rub with lemon juice, then cook in boiling salted water for 10 minutes. Remove and push the artichoke down on the bench to open out like a flower. Dust with flour and fry in oil, following the directions given for fried onion rings on page 338.

BARBECUED WARM VEGETABLE SALADS

There are many types of salad you can make with grilled and charred vegetables; as many salads as there are combinations of vegetables, I guess. The vegetables look attractive and taste great. Their natural flavour is enhanced through the dehydrating effect of the barbecue grill and there is also the added nuance of smokiness. Don't stop at these three salads, the options are as endless as your imagination.

BARBECUED ASPARAGUS, POTATO AND MUSHROOM SALAD

INGREDIENTS

175 g (6 oz/1 bunch) asparagus, ends snapped

60 ml (2 fl oz/^{1}/4 cup) extra virgin olive oil

^{1}/2 large red onion, cut into 1 cm (^{1}/2 inch) thick rings

4 large field mushrooms, cut into 1 cm (^{1}/2 inch) thick slices

2 garlic cloves, minced

4 pink eye or similar waxy potatoes, cooked for 20 minutes in boiling salted water, then peeled

100 ml (3^1/2 fl oz) extra virgin olive oil

juice of 2 lemons

sea salt and freshly ground pepper

METHOD

Preheat the barbecue grill to high and make sure the grill bars are clean. Season the grill plate with a little of the extra virgin olive oil. Lightly brush the asparagus with some of the oil and put on the grill. Cook for 3 minutes, turn over, and cook for a further 2 minutes. Remove from the grill and set aside.

Oil the onion and add to the grill. Oil the field mushrooms and add to the heat. Turn over after a few minutes and put the garlic on top. When the mushrooms have softened, transfer to a bowl with the onion and garlic.

Cut the asparagus in half on an angle and add to the bowl with the onions and garlic. Roughly slice the potatoes (they should still be warm) and add to the mixture. Add the remaining extra virgin olive oil, lemon juice and some sea salt and freshly ground pepper. Serves 4

PARSNIP PUREE

This is one of my favourite purées and, again, it can be made with water if you like. I love it with crumbed lamb cutlets and a little fresh mint sauce; a match made in heaven. It is also great with roast chicken. Parsnips are best in autumn and winter, as they get a little woody if available in summer, and never have as good a flavour. At their best, they are the sweetest and yummiest of vegetables. Try them roasted and, of course, they are a welcome addition to any winter stew or soup.

INGREDIENTS

6 parsnips
30 g (1 oz) unsalted butter, diced
2 tablespoons extra virgin olive oil
1 small brown onion, finely diced
2 garlic cloves, crushed
500 ml (17 fl oz/2 cups) chicken stock (page 384) or water
sea salt and freshly ground pepper
juice of 1 lemon, to taste

METHOD

Peel, core and roughly dice the parsnips. Heat the butter and extra virgin olive oil in a saucepan with a lid and add the onion and garlic. Cook slowly, without colouring, for about 8 minutes, or until soft and sweet. Add the parsnip and cook for a further 5 minutes, then add the chicken stock and slowly cook the parsnip until most of the liquid has evaporated. This will take 30—45 minutes. Season well, then blend until smooth, adding more butter if necessary. Finish by adding fresh lemon juice, to your liking. Serves 6

POTATOES

The potato was native to South America and was first brought back to Europe by the Spanish in the 1550s. Its initial acceptance was slow but by the middle of the next century it had really started to spread across Europe. It has played an important role in history and I could probably go into it in length but this is a cookbook and as such needs to focus on the culinary aspects. What started out as a small misshapen tuber has turned into the vegetable we know today, one that is the prominent vegetable in countless cuisines around the world. There are loads of varieties and many of those are good for a particular type of cooking.

THE POTATOES WE USE MOST AT ROCKPOOL ARE

• **bintje** — this potato is oval with a white to yellowish flesh. It is a great all rounder in the kitchen. We use it for gnocchi, in purées and gratins and it makes superb chips. They are so versatile and are found all over the world.

• **pink eye** — this variety has pinkish marks around the eye of the potato. It has a yellow coloured flesh and is an excellent roasting potato, delicious as a salad, and even makes good gnocchi. It is a classic waxy potato, with an incredibly sweet taste. The taste reminds me of Yukon gold potatoes in the United States.

• **kipfler (fingerling)** — these potatoes are finger shaped, with thin skin. They are fairly waxy; they boil with the skin on and roast well too. They have a similar sweetness to pink eyes, with a slightly nutty overtone.

• **pink fir apple** — this is another spud with a finger shape and blushes of pink on the skin. It is a tremendous salad and roasting potato and doesn't make a bad mash either.

• **Dutch creams** — as the name suggests, this potato variety is originally from Holland. They are great roasted and mashed but they are at their best boiled, seasoned and drizzled with extra virgin olive oil.

POTATO GRATIN

I love the taste and texture of potato cooked by this method. The layers melt together and the potato mixes with the cream and seasoning to make the whole thing extremely moreish. This gratin is incredibly easy to make but you will need a Japanese mandolin to cut the potatoes into 1 mm (1/32 inch) thick slices. It is an inexpensive tool and if you cook with this book it will come in handy on more than a few occasions. At Rockpool, we serve these gratins with beef but we also put other flavours between the layers and you can do the same. We add braised cabbage and Gruyère cheese, sometimes braised mushrooms and fresh truffles when in season. The sky is the limit and different cheeses will vary the flavour.

Potatoes can discolour. This can be prevented in a couple of ways. Firstly, you can slice them and put them in a bowl of cold water. This removes the starch from them; many people say this is a bad thing and personally I'm not a fan of removing the starch. Alternatively, you can put the slices in the cream you will use later in the gratin. This is what I recommend. It is a little messier, but if you are careful you won't have a problem. So it is up to you.

A good way to avoid the problem of oven juggling when slow-roasting meat is to cook the gratin in advance. What I do when I am working with just one oven, is put the pre-cooked gratin in the oven under the roasting rack for about 1 hour, allowing it to heat through evenly at low temperature. When I'm organizing the carving of the meat, I get Sam to sprinkle breadcrumbs, more cream and a little butter over the top of the gratin and just slide it under the grill. In a few moments, the crumbs are crispy, the gratin is golden brown and ready to serve. Yum! Roast meat and potato gratin — what a treat.

The other choice you have is what you make it in. We use beautiful copper gratin dishes that go to the table at Rockpool but there are any number of containers to cook the dish in that can go to the table, or you can just spoon out a portion and serve it next to the meat, poultry or fish.

The second recipe is a variation on the potato gratin; the celeriac brings a nice nutty flavour to the dish. When celeriac is in season throughout winter don't hesitate to make this dish, as you will be well rewarded. Again, you can make it in advance, and serve it in a dish that you can take to the table.

POTATO GRATIN

INGREDIENTS

500 g (1 lb 2 oz) bintje or other waxy potatoes
250 ml (9 fl oz/1 cup) pure (whipping) cream
sea salt and freshly ground pepper
20 g (^{3}/4 oz) unsalted butter, melted

METHOD

Peel and cut the potatoes into 2 mm (^{1}/16 inch) thick slices, covering the slices
with the cream to prevent discoloration. Season the potato slices with sea salt
and freshly ground pepper. Brush the base and sides of a shallow baking tray
or gratin dish with the melted butter. Remove the potato slices from the cream
and overlap them in lines down the dish until about 2–3 cm (^{3}/4–1^1/4 inches)
deep. If using a round dish put the slices down in a circle and cover the middle
with another circle of potato. Drizzle a little cream between each layer. Pour
any remaining cream over. Bake at 180°C (350°F/Gas 4) for 50–60 minutes, or
until lightly browned and tender.

When done, cut the gratin into four or six portions and place on the plate next
to your meat or serve in the dish in the middle of the table. Don't forget the
gratin can be made in advance and reheated. Serves 4–6

POTATO AND CELERIAC GRATIN

INGREDIENTS

250 g (9 oz) bintje or other waxy potatoes
250 g (9 oz) celeriac
250 ml (9 fl oz/1 cup) pure (whipping) cream
sea salt
20 g (^{3}/4 oz) unsalted butter, melted
freshly ground pepper

METHOD

Peel the potatoes and celeriac and cut into 1 mm (^{1}/32 inch) thick slices,
covering the slices as you work with the cream to prevent discoloration.
Season with sea salt. Brush the base and sides of a shallow baking dish with
the melted butter. Overlap the potato and celeriac slices in lines down the dish
until 2–3 cm (^{3}/4–1^1/4 inches) deep, pouring a little cream between each layer
and adding a grind of pepper. Pour any leftover cream over the gratin. Bake at
180°C (350°F/ Gas 4) for 50–60 minutes, or until lightly browned and tender.
When done, cut the gratin into four or six portions. Serves 4–6

ROAST POTATOES

This is the classic way to make crisp roast potatoes. The pre-boiling makes them a little furry on the outside, which helps to ensure a good crust. The other very important element is to not season the potatoes with salt before you roast them. Salt draws their moisture out and makes it harder for them to go crispy, so always season after.

It is also possible to get a really great result by what I call pan-roasting, but in essence you are just shallow-frying the potatoes. Boil them in the same way and toss in extra virgin olive oil. Heat a little oil in a heavy-based saucepan, add the potato and fry, turning often until crisp, then sprinkle with sea salt and pepper. This is a good way of doing it if your oven is tied up with slow-roasting. So — happy pan-roasting.

INGREDIENTS
700 g (1 lb 9 oz) bintje, pink eye or kipfler (fingerling) potatoes,
   peeled and cut into large pieces, or left whole if small
sea salt
2 tablespoons extra virgin olive oil
freshly ground pepper

METHOD
Preheat the oven to 200°C (400°F/Gas 6). Put the potato in a saucepan of cold water, add some sea salt and put over high heat for 10–12 minutes. The potato should still be slightly hard in the middle when drained. Allow the potato to cool for a few minutes, then put in a bowl and add the extra virgin olive oil and toss. Spread the potato out in a roasting tray and roast for 20 minutes, turning every 5 minutes to ensure an even golden brown colour. (The time needed will vary depending on the variety used.)

To check the potato is done, pierce with a small knife. It will glide in easily when it is cooked through. When the potato is crisp, sprinkle with sea salt and freshly ground pepper. Either place beside the meat, poultry or fish on individual plates or serve in the middle of the table. Serves 4

POTATO PUREE

Everyone loves mashed potato; however, it is impossible to get the texture that good restaurants do by just using a hand masher. You need to put the potatoes through a food mill or a potato ricer, then add the milk and butter, and if you really want the finest of textures you need to push it through a sieve. This is not as hard as it sounds and the results will get groans of enjoyment from your guests. It is also possible to make the purée 1 hour before serving and keep it warm in a little bain-marie or pan on the top of the stove. Potato purée or mash can, of course, be flavoured with many different things. Here I use garlic but you can add roast garlic, herbs, mushrooms, truffles and even other root vegetables to make a combination purée. You can follow the traditional method of boiling the peeled potatoes, but I find this makes the mash a little soggy and dilutes the flavour. If you want to boil the potatoes, boil them with the skin on and when you can handle them, peel and put through a food mill or ricer. I prefer to steam the potatoes and garlic together, as I find this makes a purée of real potato flavour. I also like to add warm milk and cold butter and season well; our little trick is to add a squeeze of fresh lemon juice, not to dominate but to just lift all the flavours.

INGREDIENTS

600 g (1 lb 5 oz) bintje potatoes, peeled and cut into 2–3 cm
   ($3/4$–$1 1/4$ inch) dice
5 garlic cloves
sea salt
150 ml (5 fl oz) milk, warmed
150 g ($5 1/2$ oz) unsalted butter, finely diced
freshly ground pepper
$1/2$ lemon

METHOD

Put the potato in a bamboo steamer. Add the garlic and steam over a saucepan of boiling water for about 1 hour, or until the potato is cooked. When done, pass the potato and garlic through a food mill or potato ricer. Put the potato and garlic in a saucepan over medium heat and stir with a wooden spoon for 1 minute until the potato begins to steam. Add a little sea salt and, while stirring continuously, pour in the warm milk. Add the butter a bit at a time, stirring until it has fully incorporated and the purée is smooth. Give a good grind of pepper, check the amount of salt and squeeze about half a lemon into the purée and stir through. It is now ready to serve and if you want to go the extra mile, push it through a sieve. You won't be disappointed. Serves 4

POTATO CHIPS

Bintje make great chips and, as with roast potato, the trick is double cooking. Peel and cut your potatoes into thick slices, then cut the slices into chips about 1 cm (1/2 inch) wide. Give them a good wash in cold water to help remove some of the starch. Wrap in a tea towel to dry and make sure you remove all the moisture, or you will have spitting chips, which is where the saying comes from, I guess. Blanch the chips in batches in a large saucepan of hot oil (or in a deep-fat fryer) using a thermometer to get a temperature of about 170°C (325°F). Cook for 5 minutes without browning, then drain on paper towels. Increase the temperature to 190°C (375°F) and cook the chips in batches until they are golden brown. Drain again on paper towels. Just before serving sprinkle the chips liberally with sea salt.

You can, of course, turn your chips into French fries with a little handy knife work. Once you taste home-made fries it is really hard to go back to the mass-produced ones that are not one hundred per cent potato. Remember that keeping the oil temperature constant is the secret to success with deep-frying; don't be tempted to overfill the pan or fryer. Do the chips in batches and keep the cooked ones warm in the oven.

FRIED ONION RINGS

Just while we are talking about deep-frying it is probably appropriate to talk about onion rings. When they are done properly they are a great complement to steak. And they are simple to do. You need only a saucepan, clean oil and a thermometer, or, even easier, a little deep-fat fryer (great invention). Fry at 180°C (350°F), don't overcrowd the pan or fryer, and you will have perfect results every time.

Slice the onions into 1 cm (1/2 inch) rings, coat in flour and dip into beer batter (page 209). Shake off any excess batter and put in the saucepan or deep-fat fryer and fry until golden brown. Carefully remove and drain on paper towels. Season with sea salt and freshly ground pepper and pile onto a steak — sensational. Don't underestimate how good onion rings are. Alternatively, try dusting some in flour, dipping in egg wash, then coating in breadcrumbs and frying until golden brown. Serve with a drizzle of aïoli and they will become a party favourite.

PUMPKIN PUREE

In many European countries pumpkin was for a long time considered food for pigs but as many know here in Australia, it makes great roasts, soups, purées and sauces.

The trick with this purée, as with all others (except potato), is to boil the pumpkin in just enough water so that when it is cooked there is only a tiny little bit of simmering water left, which will have in it all the flavours reduced and intensified. This remaining liquid is then puréed with the main ingredients, so to throw out this precious flavour would be insanity. You can steam rather than boil the pumpkin if you wish and then proceed with the recipe. As there are no starches to speak of (which turn purées to glue when you blend them), you can blend the mixture in a blender or food processor, or use a stick blender; whatever works for you. I always feel that the stick blender is easiest to clean.

INGREDIENTS
600 g (1 lb 5 oz) peeled pumpkin, cut into 2–3 cm (^{3}/4–1^1/4 inch) dice
2 tablespoons sea salt, plus 1^1/2 teaspoons, extra
50 g (1^3/4 oz) unsalted butter, diced, plus 25 g (1 oz), finely diced, extra
^{1}/2 brown onion, finely diced
freshly ground pepper

METHOD
Put the diced pumpkin in a saucepan and add enough cold water to bring the water level to just below the pumpkin. Add the sea salt and slowly simmer for about 20 minutes, or until soft. Set aside.

Meanwhile, heat the butter in a heavy-based saucepan. Add the onion and the extra sea salt and sauté over low heat for about 5 minutes, or until the onion is very soft. Add the pumpkin and cook for a further 2 minutes.

Pass the mixture through a food mill or blend in a food processor or blender. Stir in the extra butter until completely melted. Check the seasoning. Serves 6

BRAISED PUY LENTILS

I love these little French lentils. They are perfect with many of the dishes in the meat and poultry and seafood sections. The lentils need to be blanched before starting this recipe or soaked overnight. You could add water instead of chicken stock, and you could blend them and add yoghurt or cream for a wonderful soup, or reduce the soup and make a delicious sauce for barbecued fish. It is important not to cook these little treasures at too high a heat, as they will blow apart if boiled. They should retain their shape, but be very creamy.

INGREDIENTS

200 g (7 oz/1 cup) Puy lentils
1 tablespoon extra virgin olive oil
1 celery stalk, cut into 5 mm ($1/4$ inch) dice
1 carrot, cut into 5 mm ($1/4$ inch) dice
$1/2$ white onion, cut into 5 mm ($1/4$ inch) dice
$1/2$ leek, white part only, washed and cut into 5 mm ($1/4$ inch) dice
2 teaspoons finely chopped rosemary
1 tablespoon finely chopped thyme
60 ml (2 fl oz/$1/4$ cup) white wine
200 g (7 oz) can diced tomatoes
250 ml (9 fl oz/1 cup) chicken stock (page 384)
1 small handful flat-leaf (Italian) parsley, leaves only, finely chopped
1 garlic clove, finely chopped
sea salt and freshly ground pepper

METHOD

Bring the lentils to the boil in a saucepan of cold water, then refresh under cold water. (Alternatively, soak overnight and drain.)

Heat the extra virgin olive oil in a large heavy-based saucepan over low heat, add the celery, carrot, onion and leek and sweat, without colouring. Add the chopped rosemary and thyme and continue to sweat. Add the lentils and wine and simmer for 2 minutes. Add the tomato and just enough of the stock to cover the lentils. Simmer very gently for about 1$1/2$ hours, or until the lentils have cooked, adding more liquid if necessary to allow for absorption. When the lentils are ready, add the parsley, garlic and seasoning to taste. Serves 4–6

SOFT POLENTA

This is my favourite way to have polenta, soft and creamy. It is fantastic with braised dishes, pasta sauces (replacing the pasta) and simple sautées of things like mushroom, artichoke and asparagus. It has in it the classic polenta ingredients — polenta (cornmeal), water and seasoning, and is finished with cheese and butter. If you think it is too firm you can just add some more water; it should pour like porridge.

INGREDIENTS
250 g (9 oz/1^2/3 cups) polenta
sea salt
100 g (3^1/2 oz) unsalted butter
150 g (5^1/2 oz/1^1/2 cups) finely grated Parmesan
freshly ground pepper

METHOD
Bring 1.2—1.4 litres (42—49 fl oz) water to the boil in a saucepan. Add some sea salt and, while whisking, pour in the polenta until it is completely incorporated. Reduce the heat and cook for about 40 minutes at a gentle simmer, stirring from time to time with a wooden spoon. Stir in the butter and Parmesan, check for saltiness and give a good grind of pepper. The polenta is now ready to serve. Serves 4

PAN-FRIED POLENTA

This polenta dish is set in a tin and sliced, and can be pan-fried, deep-fried or barbecued, which are all really delicious options. It can be served on the side or under any braised meat or poultry and when barbecued it is a great complement to any other food cooked on that great Australian icon. It is a little more embellished than normal polenta, but it is a good variation and worth the few extra ingredients. You don't need to set it in a container, it can be simply tipped out onto a wooden board or oiled work surface, where it will form a nice circle. When it sets you can cut it into wedges and proceed with the next cooking step; this in fact is the traditional way it would be set. This dish is one we really got going for Qantas; the milk seems to make it creamier and on reheating we get a great result that is foolproof.

INGREDIENTS
100 g (3^1/2 oz/^{2}/3 cup) polenta
375 ml (13 fl oz/1^1/2 cups) milk
250 ml (9 fl oz/1 cup) chicken stock (page 384)
1 teaspoon sea salt
50 g (1^3/4 oz/^{1}/2 cup) finely grated Parmesan
50 g (1^3/4 oz) unsalted butter, finely diced
freshly ground pepper
extra virgin olive oil

METHOD
Lightly grease a rectangular loaf tin measuring 8 x 8 x 30 cm (3^1/4 x 3^1/4 x 12 inches). Line the tin with baking paper. Bring the milk, stock and sea salt to scalding point (just below boiling point) in a large saucepan. Gradually shower the polenta into the milk mixture, stirring continuously with a whisk. Simmer, still stirring, over very low heat for about 40 minutes, or until the polenta is very thick and pulls away cleanly from the side of the pan. Remove from the heat and stir in the Parmesan, butter and salt and fresh pepper to taste.

Spread the polenta immediately into the prepared loaf tin and allow it to cool slightly. Cover and refrigerate for about 3 hours, or until firm. Run a sharp knife around the edges of the tin and gently turn out the polenta. Cut into eight slices about 15 mm (5/8 inch) thick. Quickly pan-fry the polenta slices in a little extra virgin olive oil on both sides until lightly browned. Serves 4

COUSCOUS

Couscous is great with all the tagines and braises in this book, but it also makes a terrific salad. The packet of couscous will give directions to simply rehydrate the couscous, but that is not the way to make it if you want a light, fluffy result. Couscous is really like dried pasta and is better if it is cooked after rehydrating. We steam it for 20 minutes and it comes out beautifully — try it yourself. For a more elaborate couscous, try the almond couscous, below. It is great with simpler dishes.

METHOD

Combine 100 g (3¹/2 oz) butter, 2 tablespoons extra virgin olive oil and 400 ml (14 fl oz) boiling water in a bowl. Cover with foil and stand for 2 minutes. When the butter is melted, and while stirring, add 400 g (14 oz/2¹/4 cups) couscous. Leave until the liquid is absorbed, then fluff with a fork. Transfer the couscous to a tea towel or muslin-lined steamer basket. Set over a saucepan of boiling water and steam for 20 minutes, or until tender and cooked through. Serves 4–6

ALMOND COUSCOUS

INGREDIENTS

1 teaspoon jasmine tea leaves
60 g (2¹/4 oz/¹/2 cup) raisins, roughly chopped
100 g (3¹/2 oz) unsalted butter, finely diced and softened
2 tablespoons extra virgin olive oil
400 g (14 oz/2¹/4 cups) couscous
1 tablespoon finely diced preserved lemon rind (page 380)
90 g (3¹/4 oz/1 cup) flaked almonds, roasted (page 30)
1 teaspoon sea salt

METHOD

Combine the tea leaves and 250 ml (9 fl oz/1 cup) boiling water in a tea pot, and allow to stand for 30 minutes. Strain and reserve the liquid; discard the tea leaves. Combine the tea and raisins in a large bowl, cover and stand for 2 hours. Drain the raisins well, discarding the tea. Combine the butter, extra virgin olive oil and 400 ml (14 fl oz) boiling water in a large bowl, cover with foil and allow to stand for 2 minutes. When the butter has melted, and while stirring, add the couscous. Leave until the liquid is absorbed, then lightly fluff with a fork. Transfer the couscous to a tea towel or muslin-lined steamer basket. Steam for 20 minutes, or until tender and cooked through. Stir in the soaked raisins, preserved lemon rind, roasted almonds and sea salt. Serves 4

RICE PILAF

Basmati rice is a long-grain rice. The desired result with pilaf is for each of the grains to separate. This is achieved by two means. Firstly, you must wash the rice really thoroughly to rid it of the starch and secondly, the butter needs to coat each grain. We season our pilafs with sea salt, which is something you would never do with jasmine rice. Saffron pilaf, below, is simply a more sophisticated version of plain rice pilaf.

INGREDIENTS

400 g (14 oz/2 cups) basmati rice
50 g (1^3/4 oz) unsalted butter
750 ml (26 fl oz/3 cups) chicken stock (page 384)
sea salt

METHOD

Wash the rice until the water runs clear and drain well. Heat the butter in a heavy-based saucepan and add the rice. Stir over medium heat for 5 minutes. Add the stock and sea salt to taste, stirring occasionally until it comes to the boil. Reduce the heat, cover and simmer for 10 minutes. The rice should be firm to the bite but still tender. Turn off the heat and put a tea towel under the lid. Leave for 10 minutes to allow the rice to absorb all the moisture. Serves 4

SAFFRON PILAF

INGREDIENTS

500 g (1 lb 2 oz/2^1/2 cups) basmati rice
900 ml (32 fl oz) chicken stock (page 384)
^{1}/2 teaspoon saffron threads, dissolved in 2 tablespoons boiling water
30 g (1 oz/^{1}/4 cup) raisins, softened in warm water for 5 minutes, then drained
2 tablespoons slivered almonds, roasted (page 30)
1^1/2 teaspoons sea salt

METHOD

Wash the rice until the water runs clear and drain well. Put the stock in a saucepan and bring to the boil. Add the rice, saffron water, raisins, almonds and sea salt. Return to the boil, cover with a tight-fitting lid and simmer over very low heat for 10—15 minutes, or until little holes appear on the surface and the rice is tender. Stir to make sure all the ingredients are mixed through the rice. Turn off the heat and put a tea towel under the lid. Leave for 10 minutes to allow the rice to absorb all the moisture. Serves 4

STEAMED JASMINE RICE

Here is a tip for foolproof rice every time — get a rice cooker and follow the directions. It really is a fantastic piece of equipment; I would hate to have to live without mine.

This is the classic steamed rice that one would serve with Asian food, but it is also perfect for all braised dishes and saucy ones. The washing of the rice is very important and so is adding just the right amount of water to the saucepan.

INGREDIENTS

500 g (1 lb 2 oz/2^1/2 cups) jasmine rice

METHOD

Put the rice in a small saucepan and rinse by running cold water over it to cover, then pouring the water out. Do this two or three times. This rids the rice of excess starch powder and of any broken rice that will make the cooked rice mushy and sticky. Add just enough water — about 750 ml (26 fl oz/3 cups) — to cover the top of the rice by 1 cm (^{1}/2 inch). A convenient trick is to touch the top of the rice in the pan with your middle finger. The water level should be just below the first joint of your finger. No further measuring needed.

Cover the pan with the lid. Put over medium to medium–high heat and bring to the boil. Immediately reduce the heat to low. Simmer, covered, for another 10 minutes, or until the water has completely evaporated. Turn off the heat and allow the rice to sit, covered, for at least a further 5 minutes. Serve hot or at room temperature. Fluff with a fork before serving. Serves 4

SAUCES AND MORE

First let me say that this chapter is very diverse. It contains sauces; salsas (which are really only sauces in another language); dressings; butters; pastes, or what I call pastes (for example, pesto, tarator and chermoula — I make them in a mortar with a pestle, and they look like a paste at the end, so why not call them that?); simple stocks and more.

So what do they all have in common? Well, I'll tell you: like the vegetable section, I wanted to convey a strong sense of freedom. An understanding that any particular flavouring could have many uses in your day-to-day cooking, not just the one particular dish that it might have gone with in one of the other chapters. I wanted you to start thinking three-dimensionally; a recipe should be an inspiration, not a prescription. This book is a free-flowing, organic, living thing — if you choose to be inspired by it and from the two hundred odd recipes contained in it you should realize that there are actually thousands of food combinations that work together to create enjoyable everyday dishes for breakfast, lunch and dinner. This section, linked with salads and accompaniments, crossed with meat, poultry and seafood, is one of the real drivers in this book. I wanted you to come away from this chapter not just able to recreate a couple of recipes but also with skills that can be used every day to turn great produce into delicious dishes.

Sauce in the professional kitchen is a very serious thing. The saucier in a great French restaurant would be considered a magician, one who brings food to life. He or she would probably also be considered the most senior, save the executive chef. I, however, take a different view. At Rockpool we have always tried to take the approach that food is possibly cleaner and more tasty if served with light broths, vegetable garnishes or a simple salsa, or nothing at all, things that lift the taste rather than mask it. We spend more time on the sourcing, rather that the saucing, and on the effort and temperature involved in transforming raw food to cooked. The recipes here are simple things that add flavour and help pull a dish together. They will add moistness and interest to all the meat, poultry and seafood dishes. They are mostly traditional and, in the mode of classics, not only work well but are delicious too.

MAYONNAISES

This is one of the simplest and most classic French sauces and it has a hundred and one uses with food. Let me tell you why I love it so much: it tastes great. But all the available mayonnaises on the supermarket shelves are complete rubbish — that is a fact. Make it yourself and serve it to your friends and family. If they have only ever experienced the commercial variety, you will be serving something that will take them by surprise. Your sauce will taste so much better and have such a wonderful texture.

Mayonnaise is an emulsion sauce like hollandaise. It relies on the egg yolk, lemon juice and oil being perfectly suspended together. The theory is that the oil is suspended in tiny droplets throughout the egg yolk and the lemon juice mixture. If the oil is added too quickly, the droplets of oil will pool together and become large enough to fall out of the suspension with the egg mixture. If this happens you will have to take another egg yolk and some lemon juice and start over again with the broken egg and oil mixture. It will come back together if you take your time. Don't forget that it is the continuous whisking that allows this emulsion to come together.

Mayonnaise is incredibly versatile and you can add many flavours to it. Don't be shy about using it with barbecued and roasted meats and poultry; it is a real flavour enhancer. Don't believe other cookbooks that tell you to make mayonnaise out of vegetable oil — believe me, it is best when you mix half olive oil and half extra virgin. It has a wonderful rich taste that elevates the mayonnaise to a sauce worth using on more than just sandwich fillings.

A last point on adding the oil: it is important to be very gentle and slow at the beginning. Once the emulsion starts to form, you can speed up the pouring rate substantially. Khan, who is the Executive Chef at Rockpool, has a lovely way of doing it. He is such a beautiful cook to watch in action, everything is so considered and executed with real form and movement. He starts whisking the egg yolks, sea salt and lemon juice together, with the oil in a small jug, mixed and ready to go. He dips his paring knife in the oil and as it starts to drip off he moves the knife over his whisking; he does that several times, and as the emulsion starts to build up he picks up the jug and pours it more quickly. It is poetry.

CLASSIC MAYONNAISE
INGREDIENTS
3 egg yolks

sea salt

2 tablespoons lemon juice

375 ml (13 fl oz/1^1/2 cups) half olive oil, half extra virgin olive oil

freshly ground pepper

METHOD
Put a saucepan large enough to hold a stainless steel bowl on a bench. Place a tea towel around the inside edge of the pan and place the bowl on top of the pan, which will hold it steady while you whisk.

Put the eggs in the bowl and whisk. Add the sea salt and lemon juice and while whisking, drizzle in the oil very slowly. As the emulsion starts to form, add the oil in a steady stream. Don't let the oil sit on the surface as this can cause the mayonnaise to split. Add a grind of pepper and check for salt and lemon juice.

Serve immediately or keep in the refrigerator for up to one week. Makes about 400 ml (14 fl oz)

HARISSA MAYONNAISE
To make harissa mayonnaise, slowly fold 3 tablespoons hot harissa (page 374) through 250 ml (9 fl oz/1 cup) classic mayonnaise, a couple of teaspoons at a time. It will give barbecued and roasted food a real spicy lift. Makes about 300 ml (10^1/2 fl oz)

HERB MAYONNAISE
To give herb mayonnaise a really green colour, you need to add blanched spinach. It is easy to make and incredibly delicious with roasted or barbecued chicken and boiled seafood. Wash 250 g (9 oz/^{1}/2 bunch) English spinach, remove the stems and very finely chop and blanch the leaves in boiling salted water for 2 minutes. Refresh in iced water and squeeze the spinach well. Chop the spinach finely and add to 250 ml (9 fl oz/1 cup) classic mayonnaise. Add 2 tablespoons fines herbes (parsley, chives, tarragon and chervil) and mix carefully. Check the seasoning. Makes about 300 ml (10^1/2 fl oz)

TARTARE SAUCE

Home-made tartare sauce is a revelation. If you serve it with fried fish and chips that you have made yourself, you will be in heaven. But don't just limit it to seafood; it is wonderful on roasted and barbecued poultry as well. Add 1 tablespoon finely chopped cornichons, 2 teaspoons well rinsed and finely chopped salted baby capers, 2 finely chopped anchovies and 2 tablespoons roughly chopped flat-leaf (Italian) parsley to 250 ml (9 fl oz/1 cup) classic mayonnaise. Check the seasoning. Makes about 300 ml (10^1/2 fl oz)

AIOLI

This is the most wonderful of all the different types of mayonnaise that I use. It is fantastic with fish, meat and poultry — roasted, barbecued, pan-fried or braised — and is delicious on sandwiches and vegetables and in soups. It is the ultimate all rounder. There are two ways to make aïoli. The first way is to add crushed raw garlic to the egg yolk and lemon juice mixture. The second method is to add roasted garlic at the end. They are both so delicious that I make both versions often. The raw garlic version is hot and feisty, the roasted garlic version mellow and rich. Try them both; they will become indispensable on many dishes. I like to add 3 garlic cloves per 250 ml (9 fl oz/1 cup) classic mayonnaise but by all means go crazy with it if you like. Can there ever be too much garlic? For the roasted garlic version add 4 tablespoons garlic per 250 ml (9 fl oz/1 cup) classic mayonnaise.

COCKTAIL SAUCE

This sauce is really worth the effort to make. It has a fantastic taste and is so different to the commercial ones available that it's not funny. You can make it hot by adding fresh chilli but I find that Tabasco sauce sits well with the whole combination. If you can't find fresh horseradish, it's not the end of the world; you can add prepared horseradish, just avoid the relish. Add 3 tablespoons tomato ketchup, 2 tablespoons grated fresh horseradish and about 10 drops Tabasco sauce to 250 ml (9 fl oz/1 cup) classic mayonnaise. Check the seasoning. Makes about 350 ml (12 fl oz)

HORSERADISH CREAM

This sauce is perfect on roasted or barbecued meat, though it goes with just about anything. Of course, it is an absolute classic on roast beef sandwiches and I reckon it goes pretty well with pan-fried steaks or fish, as well. I use fresh horseradish here; but the freshly prepared one is a good substitute. The relish will not have the same refined flavour. You can find fresh horseradish around most of the time these days in Australia, although it is only supposed to be available in winter. If you do see some fresh horseradish get some, as it is marvellous grated on roast beef and even better on raw fish. Whip 125 ml (4 fl oz/1/2 cup) pure (whipping) cream to soft peaks and fold it gently through 125 ml (4 fl oz/1/2 cup) classic mayonnaise. Add 4 tablespoons grated fresh horseradish and fold gently through. Finish with a good grind of fresh pepper. (Alternatively, fold the freshly grated horseradish through a little whipped cream or crème fraîche and season with sea salt, freshly ground pepper and a few drops of lemon juice. This makes a lovely light sauce for fish.) Makes about 325 ml (11 fl oz)

HOLLANDAISE

The other classic French emulsion sauce is hollandaise. It is the simplest of these sauces to make. It is an emulsion of egg yolks and melted butter, using heat, and flavoured only with a little lemon juice. Use good-quality butter and add the lemon juice at the end, so that its vibrancy is not lost. I'm including hollandaise even though people probably think it a little old fashioned these days. Don't be fooled by trends, however, as it really is a wonderful accompaniment to many meat, poultry, seafood, vegetable and egg dishes. You can see just by me writing that list that the only thing I've left off is desserts — that is how versatile it is. I give a recipe for cooking whole artichokes in the vegetable section (page 324); make sure you try it with your own home-made hollandaise sauce. It is delightful to sit there dipping your artichoke leaves in the hollandaise and then pulling them through your teeth.

There are a couple of schools of thought on how to make hollandaise. What is important, however, is to cook the sauce very slowly over a gently simmering saucepan of water. This is the easiest way to stop the sauce from overcooking. By that I mean the eggs scrambling and ruining the sauce. One argument amongst chefs is whether to add clarified butter, melted butter or cubes of cold butter. Clarified butter makes a thicker sauce because it has had the water removed; standard butter is about twenty-five per cent water. But clarified butter has also lost the milk solids, so it has lost a lot of the complex flavour of butter. I prefer melted butter or butter cubes; the sauce is thinner but it has a much better flavour. As for which I use, it depends on how I feel and if I have time to melt the butter, but to be perfectly honest, it is easier to just cube the butter at home. I use a ratio of three egg yolks per 250 g (9 oz) cubed butter. Start with a little water on the egg yolks and add the lemon juice at the end.

INGREDIENTS

3 egg yolks
sea salt
250 g (9 oz) unsalted butter, cut into cubes
1 lemon, to taste
freshly ground pepper

METHOD

You need a bowl that sits comfortably on top of a saucepan of gently simmering water. Put the egg yolks, some sea salt and 2 tablespoons water in the bowl and whisk. Put the bowl over the water and start whisking. Take care that the base of the bowl does not touch the water. As it approaches the point at which it is fully cooked the mixture will thicken by doubling or tripling in size. It is very important for the egg yolks to reach this point, otherwise the sauce will fall apart when you add the butter. Once the sauce is thick, add three to four cubes of butter, whisking until they are fully incorporated before adding the next lot of butter. Repeat until all the butter is used. Don't rush this stage, as the sauce will split if you add too much butter at any one time. Also, make sure your sauce is not getting too hot; you can lift the bowl off the pan every now and again if you are having trouble.

Once the butter is fully incorporated, remove the bowl from the heat and squeeze in the juice of $1/2$ lemon and add lots of freshly ground pepper. Whisk to incorporate. Check for salt and lemon, then the sauce should be perfect. Remember that this version will not be stiff; if that is the type of sauce you are after, use clarified butter. Makes about 325 ml (11 fl oz)

BEARNAISE

This is the most popular variation of hollandaise. The egg yolks are mixed with a reduction of tarragon stems and leaves, French shallots, black pepper, white wine and tarragon vinegar. Cut 250 g (9 oz) unsalted butter into cubes, then bring to room temperature. Put 2 sliced French shallots, 2 tarragon sprigs, 5 whole black peppercorns, 125 ml (4 fl oz/$1/2$ cup) white wine and 125 ml (4 fl oz/$1/2$ cup) tarragon vinegar into a saucepan. Heat over medium to high heat and reduce until 80 ml (2$1/2$ fl oz/$1/3$ cup) remain. Put 3 egg yolks in a bowl that will sit comfortably over a saucepan. Strain the tarragon reduction and pour over the egg yolks, whisking to incorporate. Put the bowl over the saucepan of barely simmering water and start whisking. As it approaches the point at which it is fully cooked, the mixture will thicken by doubling or tripling in size. Once the sauce is thick, start adding three to four cubes of butter at a time, whisking to incorporate. When all the butter is incorporated, remove the bowl from the heat, add 2 tablespoons freshly chopped tarragon and check the seasoning. Makes about 250 ml (9 fl oz/1 cup)

BREAD SAUCE

This is another old-fashioned sauce that I feel is not only delicious but also really relevant for the home cook. Served with roast chicken, it is truly gorgeous. It also works really well with game like pheasant and guinea fowl. I remember quite vividly the first time I had it; it was back in the early eighties and I was eating at a restaurant that Anders Ousback had put together. He had a young chef by the name of Sean Moran, a gifted young cook who Anders guided to bring a menu to life at Sydney's Taylor Square restaurant — strikingly simple, but beyond words when it came to the eating of beautiful food. The menu was fixed and small; one might start with roasted capsicums (peppers) and anchovy dressing or something equally simple and exquisite and then follow with roast chook with bread sauce. What a revelation: how could something so simple taste so good (another important lesson in life)? The salad was a quarter of iceberg lettuce with some dreamy cream dressing, and for dessert, probably a slice of some fabulous pie. Since that day I have loved bread sauce but two really sad things happened. The restaurant burnt down and Anders walked away from it when it was still in its infancy; it was a great shame as I really loved it, but the biggest tragedy was that as I was writing this book, Anders himself passed away. It is a sad loss for us all in Sydney, as he had a great impact on many of us and gave lots of Sydney's, and indeed, Australia's chefs and restaurateurs happy memories and much inspiration.

Anyway, I will press on. The bread must be a day old, stale but with a good flavour. It is then mixed with milk, some aromatics added, and the mixture simmered, whisking to achieve a silky texture. Add cream or butter at the end. I'm a big fan of a good dab of butter at the end.

INGREDIENTS

80 g (2³/4 oz) day-old white bread

1 brown onion, studded with 2 cloves

sea salt

2 fresh bay leaves

1 mace blade

500 ml (17 fl oz/2 cups) milk

100 ml (3¹/2 fl oz) pure (whipping) cream

30 g (1 oz) unsalted butter

freshly ground pepper

METHOD

Remove and discard the crusts from the bread. Crumb the bread in a food processor. Put the onion, sea salt, bay leaves, mace and milk in a saucepan small enough that the milk will easily cover the onion. Bring to the boil. Stir in the breadcrumbs and reduce to a bare simmer. Cook for about 20 minutes, stirring occasionally. Remove the onion and the spices and add the cream. Cook for a further 5 minutes, then remove the pan from the heat and whisk in the butter. Finish with a grind of pepper. Makes about 600 ml (21 fl oz)

COMPOUND BUTTERS

When you add flavours to butters and melt them over fish, poultry or meat, or for that matter over vegetables, you do get a wonderful burst of flavour and moisture. Flavoured butters are really easy to make, with either the food processor or even in a mortar with a pestle. Wrap the butters up and wait for the right time to use them. The best thing is that these flavoured butters freeze well, so you always have a little zing ready to add to a barbecue, roast or sauté. You can simply place a disc over a piece of grilled fish, meat or poultry, or add it to a pan reduction and make a simple delicious butter sauce. If I'm using the butter to make a sauce, I will push it through a sieve, but otherwise I like to keep the texture on roasted and barbecued foods. Always have the butter at room temperature, but never melting, and use good-quality unsalted butter.

ANCHOVY BUTTER

This butter is great with anything that has a nice bit of crust on the outside. Anchovies and barbecued rib of beef go well together — it may seem a bit odd, but it really works. You can make roast garlic butter in the same way, just substitute the anchovies for 100 g (3^1/2 oz) roast garlic and add some sea salt.

INGREDIENTS
250 g (9 oz) unsalted butter, at room temperature
125 g (4^1/2 oz) anchovy fillets
juice of ^{1}/2 lemon
freshly ground pepper

METHOD
Put the butter and anchovies in a food processor and purée. Add the lemon juice and freshly ground pepper and process for a further minute. If making for immediate use set aside in a bowl (not in the refrigerator), ready to spoon onto your meal. Otherwise, roll the mixure in a sheet of baking paper or foil into a log shape, about 35 cm (14 inches) long and 4 cm (1^1/2 inches) in diameter. Wrap in plastic wrap and refrigerate until firm. Cut into 1 cm (^{1}/2 inch) thick slices to serve. Makes about 375 g (13 oz), or 35 portions

CURRY BUTTER

Along with anchovy butter, this would have to be my favourite on steak, especially barbecued steak, when it has a nice charred exterior and perfectly-cooked interior. It is inspired by the famous Café de Paris butter, and no one does it better than Damien Pignolet at Bistro Moncur in Sydney. I love it on beef but I used to dollop this very recipe on barbecued fish when I had the Blue Water Grill, so don't be scared to give it a bash on just about anything, it is truly yum. As I'm writing this, the thought of melting it over some peas or sugar snaps just popped into my head, perfect.

INGREDIENTS

250 g (9 oz) unsalted butter, at room temperature
$1^1/2$ tablespoons vegetable oil
$1/2$ white onion, diced
4 tablespoons Indian curry powder
2 large handfuls flat-leaf (Italian) parsley
3 garlic cloves
3 teaspoons lemon juice
$2^1/2$ tablespoons Worcestershire sauce
6 anchovies fillets
1 teaspoon salted baby capers, well rinsed and drained
$1^1/2$ teaspoons sea salt
$2^1/2$ teaspoons freshly ground pepper
1 very small handful basil
1 small handful thyme
1 tablespoon ground ginger
1 large egg yolk

METHOD

Heat the oil in a large frying pan and cook the onion and curry powder over low heat until soft and fragrant.

Put all the remaining ingredients in a food processor, add the onion mixture and process until just combined. Adjust the seasoning to taste. If making for immediate use set aside in a bowl (not in the refrigerator), ready to spoon onto your meal. Otherwise, roll the mixture in a sheet of baking paper or foil into a log shape, about 35 cm (14 inches) long and 4 cm ($1^1/2$ inches) in diameter. Wrap in plastic wrap and refrigerate until firm. Cut into 1 cm ($1/2$ inch) thick slices to serve. Makes about 400 g (14 oz), or 35 portions

HERB BUTTER

INGREDIENTS

250 g (9 oz) unsalted butter, at room temperature

3 large handfuls mixed herbs, such as parsley, chervil, tarragon and chives

4 French shallots, sliced

2 garlic cloves, finely chopped

juice of 1 lemon

sea salt and freshly ground pepper

METHOD

Blanch the mixed herbs and shallots for 2 minutes in a saucepan of boiling water. Remove and refresh in iced water, then gently wring out. Put in a food processor with the butter, garlic and lemon juice and process until combined. Adjust the seasoning to taste. Roll the mixture in a sheet of baking paper or foil into a log shape, about 35 cm (14 inches) long and 4 cm (1^1/2 inches) in diameter. Wrap in plastic wrap and refrigerate until firm. Cut into 1 cm (^{1}/2 inch) thick slices to serve. Makes about 350 g (12 oz), or 35 portions

PRAWN BUTTER

This is terrific with barbecued and pan-fried fish, but also really nice with sautéed chicken. Stockpile prawn (shrimp) shells in the freezer for use in this butter; also essential for this recipe is a drum sieve.

INGREDIENTS

250 g (9 oz) unsalted butter, at room temperature

100 ml (3^1/2 fl oz) olive oil

500 g (1 lb 2 oz) raw prawn (shrimp) shells

juice of ^{1}/2 lemon

sea salt and freshly ground pepper

METHOD

In a heavy-based frying pan, heat the olive oil and fry the prawn shells until well coloured and cooked. The oil will turn red. Remove the shells from the pan and cool. Add to a food processor with the butter, lemon juice, sea salt and some freshly ground pepper. Process to a purée, then remove and push through a drum sieve to remove all the shell. Roll the mixture in a sheet of baking paper or foil into a log shape, about 35 cm (14 inches) long and 4 cm (1^1/2 inches) in diameter. Wrap in plastic wrap and refrigerate until firm. Cut into 1 cm (^{1}/2 inch) thick slices to serve. Makes about 250 g (9 oz), or 35 portions

MARCHAND DE VIN BUTTER

This red wine butter is great on minute steak or whipped into a sauce for meat, poultry or even seafood like salmon and tuna. It is also great to use when creating a sauce from pan juices: just add a little water, scrape as you simmer, then add the compound butter, season and you have a great little flavour enhancer.

INGREDIENTS

250 g (9 oz) unsalted butter, at room temperature

500 ml (17 fl oz/2 cups) red wine

3 French shallots, finely chopped

80 ml ($2^1/2$ fl oz/$^1/3$ cup) veal glaze (page 385)

juice of $^1/2$ lemon

sea salt

2 tablespoons flat-leaf (Italian) parsley

METHOD

Put the red wine and the French shallots in a saucepan and reduce. When you are left with about 125 ml (4 fl oz/$^1/2$ cup) mixture, add the veal glaze. Continue to reduce until you have about 80 ml ($2^1/2$ fl oz/$^1/3$ cup), stirring constantly until you are left with a syrupy sauce. Towards the end take care to not burn the reduction. Remove the pan from the heat and allow the mixture to cool. Put the sauce in a food processor and add the butter, the lemon juice, some sea salt and the parsley. Process until smooth. Roll the mixture in a sheet of baking paper or foil into a log shape, about 35 cm (14 inches) long and 4 cm ($1^1/2$ inches) in diameter. Wrap in plastic wrap and refrigerate until firm. Cut into 1 cm ($^1/2$ inch) thick slices to serve. Makes about 350 g (12 oz), or 35 portions

SALSAS

Salsa is sauce in Italian and Spanish, but I think of salsas as chunkier vegetable sauces held together by extra virgin olive oil, perhaps nuts and, of course, sometimes bread. I love them for their freshness and for their suitability with all sorts of roasted, barbecued and pan-fried foods. These sauces bring beautiful fresh flavours to a dish that enhance rather than weigh it down, and like all the recipes in this book they are inspired by the true classics.

TOMATO, ALMOND AND CHILLI SALSA

This beautiful little salsa is very simple to make at home but has so much flavour and is perfect with salads, meat, fish, poultry and vegetables. It is inspired by food I have eaten in Spain and it has that lovely balance of heat and power from the chillies and garlic, sweetness from the ripe tomatoes and almonds and is finished off just perfectly with a splash of vinegar. Go easy with the pounding when you add the tomato, as you don't want to be covered in tomato juice — use a nice, steady deliberate action. Try tossing this with pasta; it is really good.

INGREDIENTS

    6 garlic cloves

    2 teaspoons sea salt

    4 long red chillies, split, deseeded and roughly chopped

    100 g (3^1/2 oz/^{2}/3 cup) almonds, roasted (page 30)

    4 large vine-ripened tomatoes, peeled, deseeded and diced (page 66)

    4 tablespoons finely shredded flat-leaf (Italian) parsley

    a splash of red wine vinegar

    80 ml (2^1/2 fl oz/^{1}/3 cup) extra virgin olive oil

    freshly ground pepper

METHOD

    Pound the garlic with half the sea salt in a large mortar with a pestle, followed by the chilli. Add the almonds and pound until well crushed, then add the tomato and remaining salt and gently crush. Add the parsley, red wine vinegar and stir through, then drizzle in the extra virgin olive oil and add a grind of fresh pepper. Makes about 800 g (1 lb 12 oz/3 cups)

ROMESCO

This is one of the great sauces of Spain! I love it served on the side of barbecued or roasted food or spooned in the pan at the end of cooking a fish fillet or tossed through sautéed prawns (shrimp). It also works well with sautéed chicken: just add it to the pan at the end and serve over the chicken. Like the tomato, almond and chilli salsa opposite, try this one tossed through penne. Romesco can be made with almonds only, or with a proportion of hazelnuts. I love the complexity of the hazelnuts, so they are added below, but if you don't have any or want to use just one nut, then by all means go ahead. This recipe is a little more complicated than the previous one as some of the ingredients are cooked before pounding. If you have the time you will get a superior result by buying nuts with the skin on, roasting them and peeling them yourself. It is a chore with a fair amount of therapy attached, but by the end you will feel calm and as one with the nuts.

INGREDIENTS

2 vine-ripened tomatoes, peeled, quartered and deseeded (page 66)

2 dried red chillies, stems removed

80 ml ($2^1/2$ fl oz/$^1/3$ cup) olive oil

4 garlic cloves

sea salt

40 g ($1^1/2$ oz/$^1/4$ cup) almonds, roasted (page 30)

30 g (1 oz/$^1/4$ cup) hazelnuts, roasted (page 30)

1 teaspoon paprika

4 tablespoons fresh breadcrumbs (page 278)

1 tablespoon red wine vinegar

125 ml (4 fl oz/$^1/2$ cup) extra virgin olive oil

freshly ground pepper

METHOD

Preheat your oven grill (broiler). Put the tomato on a tray and cook under the grill for about 5 minutes, until it dehydrates and starts to colour. Fry the chillies in the olive oil until blackened, then remove from the pan.

Put the garlic and sea salt in a mortar and crush to a paste with the pestle. Add the chillies and crush, then add the nuts and pound gently until they are completely ground. Add the tomato and paprika and pound gently, then fold through the breadcrumbs and add the vinegar. Drizzle in the extra virgin olive oil and check the seasoning, adding a generous amount of freshly ground pepper. Makes about 325 ml (11 fl oz)

SPICY MINT AND CUCUMBER SALSA

Refreshing and perfect to dollop on any barbecued food, this is one of those salsas that is a mixture of vegetables and herbs held together with a simple dressing. I love to add hot red chillies, but by all means, if you don't like it hot, leave the chillies out and it will still taste great.

INGREDIENTS

2 large handfuls mint, finely shredded
1 Lebanese (short) cucumber, cut in half, deseeded and cut into thin slices
1 red onion, finely sliced
2 garlic cloves, finely chopped
1 vine-ripened tomato, peeled, deseeded and diced (page 66)
4 small red chillies, finely sliced into thin rings
juice of 1 lemon
60 ml (2 fl oz/$1/4$ cup) extra virgin olive oil
sea salt and freshly ground pepper

METHOD

Combine all the ingredients in a bowl. Mix well and season with sea salt and freshly ground pepper. Makes about 250 g (9 oz/$1 1/2$ cups)

AVOCADO SALSA

This is delicious on barbecued fish or shellfish and works well with poultry. Again, I have added Tabasco sauce but it doesn't have to be hot. This is like a finely diced guacamole. It looks pretty and tastes great.

INGREDIENTS

1 avocado, ripe but not mushy
$1/2$ red onion, finely diced
1 vine-ripened tomato, peeled, deseeded and finely diced (page 66)
2 spring onions (scallions), cut into rings
1 red capsicum (pepper), cut in half, core removed and finely diced
2 tablespoons finely shredded flat-leaf (Italian) parsley
juice of 1 lemon
sea salt and freshly ground pepper
80 ml (2$1/2$ fl oz/$1/3$ cup) extra virgin olive oil
10 drops Tabasco sauce, to taste

METHOD

Cut the avocado in half and remove the stone by wedging your knife in and wriggling it free. Take a large spoon and scoop the avocado out of its skin, cut it into fine dice and put in a stainless steel bowl. Add the onion, tomato, spring onion and capsicum and mix. Add the parsley, lemon juice, some sea salt, freshly ground pepper and the extra virgin olive oil and stir together. Check the seasoning and add Tabasco to taste. Makes about 600 g (1 lb 5 oz/3^3/4 cups)

SAUCE VIERGE

I first came across this sauce years ago in Roger Vergé's book *Cuisine of the Sun*. It is a wonderful book and this is just one of the many gem recipes in it. It combines sun-ripened tomatoes with fresh herbs and extra virgin olive oil. It relies on the quality of the oil and the tomatoes being ripe, sweet and delicious, so file this away as a summer recipe. Make it once, however, and you'll make it time and time again. That's why it's a classic. This sauce is fantastic with cold salads, meats and fish, as well as drizzled over roasts and barbecues.

INGREDIENTS

3 vine-ripened tomatoes
2 garlic cloves, unpeeled and halved
2 tablespoons chopped chervil
2 tablespoons chopped flat-leaf (Italian) parsley
1 tablespoon chopped tarragon
8 coriander seeds, crushed
250 ml (9 fl oz/1 cup) extra virgin olive oil
sea salt and freshly ground pepper

METHOD

Remove the stalks from the tomatoes and plunge them into boiling water for several seconds. Refresh in iced water and peel the skin off with a vegetable knife. Cut the tomatoes into quarters and deseed. Scoop out the pulp with a spoon and cut into 2 cm (^{3}/4 inch) dice.

Mix the diced tomato with all the other ingredients in a bowl, then set aside for 1—2 hours for the flavours to mature. All the players must get to mingle and start to have fun; it is then that the true quality of this sauce is revealed. Makes about 500 ml (17 fl oz/2 cups)

PESTO

Pesto is one of those sauces that have been really mishandled by the great bulk of cafés and restaurants in Australia, not to mention the commercial varieties available in stores throughout the country. It is usually made in a blender, ends up tasting more of roasted nuts and garlic than it does of basil and comes out dark green. It should be made in a mortar with a pestle so that the basil leaves are creamed and their oils are released, rather than chopped and heated. It sounds hard, but it is really very simple. My daughter Josephine and I love making it at home when she feels like pasta for dinner. Although not fond of eating many green things, she really loves pesto. I don't get it, because it is really pungent, but that's JP. We make it in a mortar with a pestle; it is very quick and loads of fun for her to pound away on the leaves and see this lovely pale green creamy sauce come together. It is a simple sauce, so it is good to have all the basic ingredients in their prime. Once you have made this pesto sauce, you will find it appearing in more than just pasta. Add it to seafood and anything you barbecue; like salsa verde, it makes a great dressing on salads. You need basil leaves full of vigour, fresh pine nuts, good-quality extra virgin olive oil and very importantly a hunk of Parmesan that you can grate from. Once you have taken the step of buying the best, your pasta dishes, soups and risottos will never look back and you will make the best pesto in the world.

INGREDIENTS
125 g (4^1/2 oz/1 bunch) basil
2 garlic cloves
sea salt
2 tablespoons pine nuts
80 ml (2^1/2 fl oz/^{1}/3 cup) extra virgin olive oil
2 tablespoons freshly grated Parmesan
freshly ground pepper

METHOD
Pick, wash and dry the basil leaves. Put the garlic and some sea salt in a mortar and pound. Add the pine nuts and basil leaves and pound further. The basil will start to break up and become creamy. I don't bother to completely purée the mixture, although you can. Add a little extra virgin olive oil, followed by the Parmesan, pepper and a little more oil. Check the seasoning. You will now have a beautiful bright creamy green sauce that tastes completely different to anything you have had in the past. Use it on whatever you like and you will be making fresh pesto all the time. Makes about 250 ml (9 fl oz/1 cup)

SALSA VERDE

This is another of those wonderful, indispensable Italian sauces. I love it on barbecued food, as well as on roasts. Like pesto, it also makes a great salad dressing. I first started making this sauce back in the mid eighties at my Blue Water Grill restaurant in Bondi. It sat so nicely on top of a piece of barbecued fish and was terrific as a dressing in one of our winter salads of king prawns (shrimp), mussels and blanched fennel. At Rockpool we make it with a stick blender but it is just as easy to use a food processor.

INGREDIENTS

60 g (2^1/4 oz) sourdough bread, crusts removed, roughly chopped
60 ml (2 fl oz/^{1}/4 cup) milk
1 small handful flat-leaf (Italian) parsley, roughly chopped
2 teaspoons salted baby capers, well rinsed and drained
1 large anchovy fillet
juice of 1 lemon
1 teaspoon sea salt
125 ml (4 fl oz/^{1}/2 cup) extra virgin olive oil
^{1}/2 hard-boiled egg, finely chopped
freshly ground pepper

METHOD

Combine the bread and milk in a bowl and set aside for 5 minutes for the milk to be absorbed. Combine the soaked bread with the parsley, capers, anchovy, lemon juice and sea salt in a bowl, if using a stick blender, or in a food processor. Process until well combined. Gradually pour in the extra virgin olive oil while processing, emulsifying as you would with a mayonnaise (page 350) until well combined. Stir in the egg and freshly ground pepper. Makes about 325 ml (11 fl oz)

TARATOR

Tarator is another simple sauce that is easy to make and as versatile as the rest. I use it on the side of barbecued and roasted meats, poultry and fish and it is great on vegetables. I also love it tossed with mussels just after they have been opened, or mixed through pasta. Tarator is a Middle Eastern sauce that is used a lot in Turkey, mostly in conjunction with fish. It can be made with walnuts, hazelnuts, almonds or pine nuts, or a combination of a couple at a time. I like this one, which is all walnut, but by all means experiment, as you will get distinctive flavour results through the combination of the different nuts.

INGREDIENTS

50 g ($1^3/4$ oz/$^1/2$ cup) walnuts, roasted (page 30)
sea salt
2 garlic cloves
40 g ($1^1/2$ oz/$^1/2$ cup) fresh breadcrumbs (page 278)
freshly ground pepper
juice of 1 lemon
125 ml (4 fl oz/$^1/2$ cup) extra virgin olive oil

METHOD

Put the walnuts, salt and garlic in a mortar and pound to a paste with the pestle. Add the breadcrumbs and a dash of water and pound to mix through. Add some freshly ground pepper and the lemon juice, then slowly add the extra virgin olive oil, a little at a time, pounding to a creamy consistency. Makes about 250 ml (9 fl oz/1 cup)

GREMOLATA

Gremolata is a very simple mix of aromatics that the Italians use to bring braises back to life. When I say that, I mean that it just adds a bit of freshness that may be missing after long cooking. But because garlic with herbs and citrus peel is such a wonderful combination, I like to use it sprinkled on roasts, barbecues and pan-fried foods as well as traditional braises. Gremolata is great mixed with extra virgin olive oil and drizzled over food or just mixed with a little butter and put on top of a gorgeous steak as it rests by the side of the barbecue. This simple little mix will help bring lots of food to life. Here are three versions; the first is the classic and loves to mingle with osso bucco.

GREMOLATA NO. 1 THE ORIGINAL

INGREDIENTS

2 large handfuls flat-leaf (Italian) parsley, roughly chopped
finely grated zest of 2 lemons, without any pith
1 garlic clove, minced

GREMOLATA NO. 2

INGREDIENTS

finely grated zest of 2 lemons, without any pith
finely grated zest of 2 oranges, without any pith
50 g (1^3/4 oz/^{1}/3 bunch) flat-leaf (Italian) parsley, finely chopped
2 garlic cloves, minced

GREMOLATA NO. 3

INGREDIENTS

finely grated zest of 2 lemons, without any pith
1 large handful flat-leaf (Italian) parsley, finely chopped
1 large handful mint, finely chopped
1 teaspoon salted baby capers, well rinsed and drained
2 teaspoons Ligurian olives, pitted and finely chopped

METHOD

For all three versions, simply put the ingredients in a bowl and mix well.
Sprinkle over any food you like. Makes about 300 ml (10^1/2 fl oz)

ROAST GARLIC SAUCE

I adore roast garlic, as a matter of fact any garlic will do, I just love the taste of it. I really love the way it tastes so different depending on how you treat it. The volatile oils in garlic are driven by a number of enzymes that have to be ruptured to cause the strong smell and taste of garlic, so a whole bulb of garlic has very little smell. If you slice a single clove, the smell and taste is released, and if you mince it, it becomes even stronger. If you roast it, you see another change: the oils are converted to sugars and the garlic becomes mellow and caramelized.

INGREDIENTS

15 whole garlic bulbs
sea salt
125 ml (4 fl oz/^{1}/2 cup) chicken stock (page 384)
60 ml (2 fl oz/^{1}/4 cup) crème fraîche
juice of 1 lemon
freshly ground pepper

METHOD

Preheat the oven to 150°C (300°F/Gas 2). Slowly roast the garlic for about 1^1/2–2 hours, or until very soft and caramelized. When cooked, remove from the oven and leave to cool. Once cool, cut the garlic through the equator and squeeze the garlic bulbs to release the flesh. Discard the skins. Put the garlic, sea salt, chicken stock and crème fraîche in a small saucepan and warm over medium heat. Blend with a stick blender, then add the lemon juice and freshly ground pepper. Check the seasoning and it's ready. If you don't have a stick blender, use a blender or food processor. Makes about 500 ml (17 fl oz/2 cups)

ROAST GARLIC DRESSING

This is a fantastic little dressing that relies on the wonderful taste of mellow sweet garlic. I love it drizzled over roast chook or barbecued tuna steak. It is also delicious on freshly boiled leeks or artichokes. Slowly roast 2 whole garlic bulbs as instructed in the above recipe. When cool enough to handle, cut the garlic through the equator and squeeze out the flesh, discarding the skin. Blend with 125 ml (4 fl oz/^{1}/2 cup) extra virgin olive oil, 2 tablespoons sherry vinegar, 1 tablespoon red wine vinegar, the juice of ^{1}/2 lemon, some sea salt and freshly ground pepper in a blender or food processor, or use a stick blender. Makes about 125 ml (4 fl oz/^{1}/2 cup)

SKORDALIA

This is a great sauce with roast lamb but I have used it at Rockpool on everything from pasta to fish, so go for broke. This sauce has big flavours; get them in balance and you'll make it all the time. The sauce should be garlicky, but with a tangy edge, so add more lemon juice if necessary. The texture should be creamy and you should serve it warm.

INGREDIENTS
4 whole garlic bulbs
2 pink eye potatoes
2 tablespoons ground almonds
1 teaspoon sea salt
freshly ground pepper
juice of 1 lemon
60 ml (2 fl oz/¼ cup) extra virgin olive oil

METHOD
Slowly roast the garlic as instructed in the recipe for roast garlic sauce. When cool enough to handle, cut the garlic through the equator and squeeze out the flesh. Discard the skin. Peel the potatoes and steam for 15–20 minutes, or until tender. Put through a potato ricer or food mill. Put the potato and garlic in a bowl and mix thoroughly. Add the almonds, sea salt, freshly ground pepper and lemon juice and mix until incorporated. Add the oil in a thin stream, whisking all the time. Check the seasoning. Makes about 425 ml (15 fl oz)

GARLIC YOGHURT

This is a wonderful sauce to make, and it is so easy. Buy good-quality yoghurt to get the best result. I love to use sheep's milk yoghurt, as it is a little sharper and more interesting than many commercial yoghurts. The sauce is fantastic drizzled on any meat, poultry or seafood, makes a great dip at the start of a meal with good bread and is fabulous mixed with steamed pink eye potatoes, creating a delicious Middle Eastern potato salad. You can also add finely sliced mint leaves to the yoghurt. If you then add grated cucumber, which has been salted and squeezed out, you end up with the famous Greek sauce tzatziki. Add more garlic if you like — I like it really fiery hot, and will add up to 5 cloves at home. To make, crush 2 garlic cloves and 1 teaspoon sea salt in a mortar with a pestle. Transfer to a bowl and stir through 250 g (9 oz/1 cup) plain yoghurt, the juice of 1 lemon and a grind of pepper. Makes about 250 g (9 oz/1 cup)

CHERMOULA

Chermoula is the paste that gives Moroccan cooking its great flavour. I have provided three versions here, but think of them as your servants, you are not a slave to this recipe, it is a movable feast and you are in control. The first version is the most complex in terms of flavour. The important thing with all three options is to use very fresh spices, so don't buy large amounts of them. Take these thoughts and experiment with adding different flavours and ingredients, as well as changing the proportions. You can have it hot, full of different spices, or with different herbs. I sometimes make what I call free-form chermoula, that is, I just chop everything and fry it with the main ingredient; if it is slow-cooking, the flavours will infuse and the texture will be interesting. I add julienne of ginger to some of the dishes and so on. I also like the flavour of lemon grass in these pastes, as it is aromatic and fresh, like many of the other flavours. I guess what I'm saying is go for it, experiment and have fun with it, all these flavours go together, so you won't have a disaster. As a starting point you should think about this: a simple chermoula could be flat-leaf (Italian) parsley, coriander (cilantro), garlic and red onion. From that simple marinade you can build anything you like.

CHERMOULA NO. 1
INGREDIENTS
1 red onion, roughly chopped

4 garlic cloves, roughly chopped

90 g (3^1/4 oz/1 bunch) coriander (cilantro), including stalks, washed and roughly chopped

150 g (5^1/2 oz/1 bunch) flat-leaf (Italian) parsley, including stalks, washed and roughly chopped

1 heaped teaspoon sea salt

1 tablespoon ground cumin

1 tablespoon ground coriander

1^1/2 tablespoons ground chilli

1 tablespoon ground turmeric

2 teaspoons sweet paprika

1^1/2 tablespoons ras el hanout

185 ml (6 fl oz/^{3}/4 cup) extra virgin olive oil

juice of 1 lemon

CHERMOULA NO. 2
INGREDIENTS

1 red onion, roughly chopped

4 garlic cloves, roughly chopped

70 g (2^1/2 oz/^{1}/2 bunch) flat-leaf (Italian) parsley, including stalks, washed and chopped

40 g (1^1/2 oz/^{1}/2 bunch) coriander (cilantro), including stalks, washed and roughly chopped

1 tablespoon ground cumin

1 tablespoon ground turmeric

1 tablespoon ground chilli

2 teaspoons paprika

1 teaspoon sea salt

150 ml (5 fl oz) extra virgin olive oil

juice of 1 lemon

CHERMOULA NO. 3
INGREDIENTS

1 red onion, roughly chopped

2 garlic cloves, roughly chopped

150 g (5^1/2 oz/1 bunch) flat-leaf (Italian) parsley, including stalks, washed and chopped

90 g (3^1/4 oz/1 bunch) coriander (cilantro), including stalks, washed and chopped

1 tablespoon ground ginger

1 tablespoon sweet paprika

sea salt

150 ml (5 fl oz) extra virgin olive oil

METHOD

Put all the ingredients in a food processor, except the extra virgin olive oil and lemon juice. Process for 1 minute, then slowly pour in the oil until a thick paste forms. Stir through the lemon juice, if making the first or second version. If making ahead of time, refrigerate the chermoula until ready to use. Makes about 500 ml (17 fl oz/2 cups)

HARISSA

I love this spicy Moroccan chilli paste. It sits in the middle of the table whenever I'm eating Moroccan style at home. Actually, it ends up on a lot of food and is a great marinade as well as a fantastic flavour booster for braises. It is great with tagines and barbecued fish, poultry or meat, or just on a roast chicken sandwich. It is hot, so check how you handle it before you spread it all over your food. The original is made with dried chillies, so if you want to tone it down a bit you can add fresh large red chillies, which are not that hot. The second version will be hot, but not as incendiary as the first one, and it will taste fresh, as it is not made with dried chillies. The barbecued red capsicums (peppers) make it a bit smoother and also add a nice charred flavour. You can blend it if you wish, although I think these first two versions should be fairly rustic.

The original harissa inspired me to create the third sauce included here. It is smooth and warm, but not too hot, with lots of wonderful spice taste. I couldn't help but use two of my favourite ingredients, fish sauce and palm sugar. We use this harissa to dress all sorts of food. Prawns (shrimp), squid and fish straight off the barbecue are yummy. We also make salads with it; try mixing it with spiga (Tunisian toasted couscous), mint, orange segments and dates. Don't forget we are looking for a smooth consistency in this one. All three versions will last for about one week in the refrigerator.

HARISSA NO. 1 THE ORIGINAL
INGREDIENTS
    8 dried long red chillies, soaked overnight
    1 teaspoon cumin seeds
    1 teaspoon coriander seeds
    4 garlic cloves
    1 teaspoon sea salt
    80 ml (2^1/2 fl oz/^{1}/3 cup) olive oil

METHOD
    Remove the chillies from the water and reserve the water. Cut the core off the tops of the chillies and roughly chop. Remove the seeds if you want. Roast the cumin and coriander in a saucepan until fragrant. Put in a spice grinder or mortar and grind or pound to a fine powder. Put in a blender with the chilli, garlic, sea salt and oil and 2 tablespoons of the reserved water. Blend to a rough paste and spoon into a sterilized jar (page 376) and cover with a layer of oil. Makes about 80 ml (2^1/2 fl oz/^{1}/3 cup)

HARISSA NO. 2

INGREDIENTS

2 red capsicums (peppers), barbecued and skinned (page 76)

2 teaspoons cumin seeds

1/2 teaspoon coriander seeds

2 garlic cloves

sea salt

60 ml (2 fl oz/1/4 cup) extra virgin olive oil

5 hot red chillies, thinly sliced

METHOD

Preheat the oven to 150°C (300°F/Gas 2). Chop the capsicums, retaining the seeds. Put the cumin and coriander in the oven and slow-roast for 10 minutes. Allow to cool, put into a spice grinder or mortar and grind or pound to a fine powder. Put the capsicum, capsicum seeds, ground spices, garlic and some sea salt in a mortar. Pound to a paste and add 1 tablespoon extra virgin olive oil. Add the chillies and pound to mix. Add the remaining oil. Spoon into a sterilized jar (page 376) and cover with a layer of oil. Makes about 250 ml (9 fl oz/1 cup)

HARISSA NO. 3

INGREDIENTS

2 tablespoons fennel seeds

2 tablespoons cumin seeds

2 tablespoons coriander seeds

6 red capsicums (peppers), cut into strips

2 teaspoons sea salt

500 ml (17 fl oz/2 cups) extra virgin olive oil

6 garlic cloves, sliced

70 g (2 1/2 oz) palm sugar, grated

2 tablespoons fish sauce

1 tablespoon ground medium-strong chilli

1 tablespoon lemon juice

METHOD

Slow-roast the fennel, cumin and coriander in the oven at 150°C (300°F/Gas 2) for 10 minutes. Allow to cool, then grind to a fine powder in a spice grinder. Put the capsicum, sea salt and oil in a large frying pan. Cook over low heat for 1 1/2–2 hours, then add the garlic and cook for 2 minutes. Add the palm sugar, fish sauce, chilli and ground spices. Simmer for 5 minutes, then blitz in a food processor until smooth. Add the lemon juice. Spoon into a sterilized jar (page 376) and cover with a layer of oil. Makes about 500 ml (17 fl oz/2 cups)

TOMATO JAM

This is another basic recipe that we always have on hand at Rockpool. It really adds a wonderful taste to ratatouille or a simple pasta dish. It is also delicious just on the side of roasts or barbecues. We often mix it with red capsicums (peppers) that have been barbecued and skinned, and we would then add some olives and flat-leaf (Italian) parsley and serve it cold on top of slices of raw tuna or hiramasa kingfish. Oil will come out of the jam after it stands; make sure you serve some of it with the tomato jam itself, as it is really delicious. This lasts for two weeks.

HOW TO STERILIZE A JAR — Preheat the oven to 170°C (335°F/Gas 3). Wash the jars and lids in hot soapy water. Rinse and dry them, then put in the oven for 10 minutes to sterilize. Turn the oven off, but leave the jars in the oven to keep warm. You can put them through the dishwasher if you wish, but you must use them while they are still warm.

INGREDIENTS

15 vine-ripened tomatoes
1 red onion, diced
10 garlic cloves, crushed
2 large knobs of fresh ginger, peeled and chopped
400 ml (14 fl oz) olive oil
1 tablespoon fennel seeds, roasted and ground (page 330)
1 tablespoon coriander seeds, roasted and ground (page 330)
1 teaspoon cumin seeds, roasted and ground (page 330)
70 g ($2^1/2$ oz) palm sugar, grated
80 ml ($2^1/2$ fl oz/$^1/3$ cup) fish sauce
125 ml (4 fl oz/$^1/2$ cup) red wine vinegar

METHOD

Preheat the oven to 180°C (350°F/Gas 4). Core the tomatoes, put in a roasting tin and roast for 20–30 minutes. Remove the tomatoes and pass them through a food mill. Put the onion, garlic, ginger and 100 ml ($3^1/2$ fl oz) of the olive oil in a blender and purée. Add the fennel, coriander and cumin. Purée to a paste.

Put a heavy-based saucepan over low heat and add the remaining oil. Add the paste and cook for 30 minutes. Add the palm sugar and allow to caramelize. Add the fish sauce and cook to reduce slightly. Add the vinegar and cook for 1 minute, then add the tomato purée and stir through. Cook slowly for 2 hours, stirring regularly and checking that it doesn't stick to the pan. You should be left with a thick, sweet jam with no liquid. Put in a sterilized jar, cover with a layer of oil and refrigerate. Makes about 750 ml (26 fl oz/3 cups)

TOMATO RELISH

This is a simple, tasty relish that is much easier to make than the tomato jam. It is great with pies and sandwiches and is delicious on eggs for breakfast. It lasts for about two weeks.

INGREDIENTS

10 vine-ripened tomatoes
1 brown onion, finely diced
2 garlic cloves, finely diced
150 ml (5 fl oz) olive oil
100 ml (3^1/2 fl oz) red wine vinegar
55 g (2 oz/^{1}/4 cup) sugar
sea salt

METHOD

Preheat the oven to 180°C (350°F/Gas 4). Core the tomatoes and mark a crisscross at the bottom. Put the tomatoes in a roasting tin and roast for about 30 minutes, or until soft. Remove the skin with a pair of tongs and discard. Pass the tomatoes through a food mill. In a heavy-based frying pan, cook the onion and garlic in the olive oil over low heat. Do not allow it to colour. Add the tomato purée, vinegar, sugar and sea salt. Cook for about 1 hour, reducing the mixture slowly to a jam consistency. Remove from the heat and when cool put into a sterilized jar (page 376), cover with a layer of oil and refrigerate. Makes about 600 g (1 lb 5 oz)

TOMATO AND CHILLI RELISH

This sauce goes the whole nine yards. You can make it as hot as you like, just subtract or add chillies to achieve your desired level. You can use it as a sauce for just about anything you like. It lasts for one week. Peel, deseed and chop 15 vine-ripened tomatoes (page 66). Put a saucepan on the stove and add 2 finely chopped brown onions, 4 chopped garlic cloves, 1 finely chopped small knob of fresh ginger, 2 finely diced red capsicums (peppers), 125 ml (4 fl oz/ ^{1}/2 cup) olive oil and 1 tablespoon sea salt. Cook over medium heat until syrupy. Add the chopped tomato, 375 ml (13 fl oz/1^1/2 cups) cider vinegar, 225 g (8 oz/1 cup) caster (superfine) sugar, 175 g (6 oz/1 cup) soft brown sugar, the juice of 3 lemons, 2 cloves, 1 cinnamon stick and 8 finely chopped small red chillies. Simmer for 1^1/2 hours, or until reduced to a jam consistency. Remove from the heat and when cool put in a sterilized jar (page 376), cover with a layer of oil and refrigerate. Makes about 1.25 litres (44 fl oz/5 cups)

ROAST TOMATO SAUCE

INGREDIENTS

10 vine-ripened tomatoes, cores removed
150 ml (5 fl oz) extra virgin olive oil
100 ml (3$^{1}/_{2}$ fl oz) red wine vinegar
10 g ($^{1}/_{4}$ oz/$^{1}/_{2}$ bunch) tarragon, finely chopped
10 g ($^{1}/_{4}$ oz/$^{1}/_{2}$ bunch) thyme, finely chopped
sea salt and freshly ground pepper

METHOD

Preheat the oven to 150°C (300°F/Gas 2). Put the tomatoes on a baking tray with the extra virgin olive oil, red wine vinegar, herbs and seasoning. Roast for 30–40 minutes, or until the skin starts to blister and peel. Remove the tomato skin with a pair of tongs and discard. Pass the tomato through a food mill with the herbs and any residual liquid. Put the sauce in a saucepan and reduce for 45 minutes over very low heat. Check the seasoning. If the tomato is a little tart, add a pinch of sugar and more salt. Makes about 500 ml (17 fl oz/2 cups)

RED CAPSICUM PUREE

This is a welcome relief for those who don't like the taste of chillies. It is important to burn the capsicums (peppers) without totally destroying them as that will give the sauce its great taste. This is a beautiful sauce to just pour on the plate and top with a perfectly barbecued piece of fish or even some roast chicken.

INGREDIENTS

4 red capsicums (peppers)
125 ml (4 fl oz/$^{1}/_{2}$ cup) extra virgin olive oil
balsamic vinegar
sea salt and freshly ground pepper

METHOD

Barbecue the capsicums over a hot barbecue until the skins are blackened and blistered on all sides (or roast in the oven). Put them in a bowl and cover with plastic wrap. When cool enough to handle, skin the capsicums and remove the seeds. Purée the cleaned flesh with the extra virgin olive oil and balsamic vinegar, to taste. You want the flavour of the balsamic to be there but not to dominate. Season to taste. Makes about 750 ml (26 fl oz/3 cups)

BARBECUE SAUCE

This is a classic American-style barbecue sauce. I use it at home in a couple of ways. Firstly, as a sauce on the side with any barbecued meat or poultry, and secondly, as a marinade. It is great with pork ribs: poach the ribs for one hour in salted water, marinate them in this sauce, then barbecue until caramelized and serve with some extra sauce on the side. Any of you who have been lucky enough to have barbecue from the deep south in the United States would have fond memories of this taste. You can do the same with chicken or lamb; just cook the meat until three-quarters cooked, perhaps rub with a spice mix and then brush the sauce on and caramelize, again serving more sauce on the side. This sauce lasts for up to three weeks.

INGREDIENTS

2 x 400 g (14 oz) cans Italian tomatoes

80 ml (2^1/2 fl oz/^{1}/3 cup) vegetable oil

1 brown onion, finely diced

2 garlic cloves, minced

1 tablespoon sea salt

125 ml (4 fl oz/^{1}/2 cup) tomato ketchup

60 ml (2 fl oz/^{1}/4 cup) Worcestershire sauce

2 tablespoons honey

185 ml (6 fl oz/^{3}/4 cup) red wine vinegar

140 g (5 oz/^{3}/4 cup) soft brown sugar

1 tablespoon smoky sweet paprika

2 teaspoons chilli powder

2 teaspoons freshly ground pepper

125 ml (4 fl oz/^{1}/2 cup) orange juice

METHOD

Roughly chop the tomatoes, reserving the juice. Heat the oil in a pan and add the onion, garlic and sea salt. Sweat for 5 minutes until soft. Add the tomato and juice and the remaining ingredients and bring to the boil, then reduce to a simmer and cook gently for 2–2^1/2 hours, or until thick. Purée with a stick blender or use a food processor to blend. Makes about 500 ml (17 fl oz/2 cups)

PRESERVED LEMONS

These are indispensable to have in the pantry. Not only do they bring life to braises but they can be used in salads and with barbecued meats and poultry. They are perfectly at home with seafood and are just as good with raw fish. I have also included the quick version because I don't want you to get caught short and think you have to wait six weeks. The quick version will not have the complexity of flavour that the ones preserved with spices have, but they are really yum and make a great salsa (see opposite). I find preserved lemons an essential ingredient at home. Serve them on fish, meat and poultry, roasted or barbecued, and you will love it. Remember only use the rind, all the rest is discarded.

INGREDIENTS

12 ripe lemons
20 tablespoons sea salt
1 tablespoon coriander seeds
3 cinnamon sticks, broken up
3–4 lemons, juiced, extra

METHOD

Thoroughly wash the lemons in cold water to remove the waxy coating, then pat them dry with paper towels. Cut the lemons into quarters, leaving the last 1 cm ($1/2$ inch) uncut. Put 1 tablespoon sea salt in the middle of each lemon and close the lemon. Take a large sterilized jar (page 376) big enough to snugly fit the lemons and push the lemons down as you go, fitting as many as possible. Intersperse the lemons with the coriander seeds and broken pieces of cinnamon. Add the remaining salt and enough lemon juice to just cover. Make sure all the lemons are covered or they will not cure properly at the top and will go mouldy. Seal the jar and put it in a cold dark place for at least six weeks.

To use the lemons, wash the preserved lemon and remove all the pith with a sharp knife. Discard. Dice or slice the rind finely and use in an array of dressings, sauces and dishes. Makes 12 preserved lemons

QUICK PRESERVED LEMONS

INGREDIENTS

4 ripe lemons
1 large handful sea salt

METHOD

Thoroughly wash the lemons in cold water to remove the waxy coating. Put
enough water to cover the lemons in a large saucepan and bring to the boil.
Add the lemons and sea salt. Boil the lemons for 30—40 minutes, or until soft,
then remove from the water and set aside to cool. They are now ready for use.
Makes 4 preserved lemons

PRESERVED LEMON SALSA

INGREDIENTS

1 whole preserved lemon
1 garlic clove
80 ml ($2^1/2$ fl oz/$^1/3$ cup) extra virgin olive oil
juice of 1 lemon
sea salt and freshly ground pepper

METHOD

Quarter the preserved lemon, remove the pith and finely chop the rind. Crush
the garlic in a mortar with a pestle. Put the crushed garlic in a bowl and add
the extra virgin olive oil, lemon juice, preserved lemon rind, sea salt and freshly
ground pepper. Mix well. Makes about 250 ml (9 fl oz/1 cup)

RED WINE REDUCTION

Make this reduction with good-quality full-bodied red wine; don't use wine that is not pleasant to drink or you will end up with something that is not rich enough. Cook the reduction with some meat scraps, bacon or pancetta, as they add flavour and help remove any bitter and sour flavours from the wine.

Once you have your reduction you can add veal stock to it and reduce it further. When it is ready to serve you may want to add a little butter at the end. Alternatively, you can just add butter and leave the stock out. This will make a really beautiful, rich butter sauce for roasted meats or fish like salmon and tuna.

INGREDIENTS

500 ml (17 fl oz/2 cups) full-bodied red wine
olive oil
1 small carrot, peeled and finely diced
$1/2$ red onion, finely diced
2 garlic cloves, chopped
2 field mushrooms, chopped
150 g ($5^1/2$ oz) meat trimmings, chopped
100 ml ($3^1/2$ fl oz) balsamic vinegar
$2^1/2$ tablespoons red wine vinegar
150 ml (5 fl oz) port
2 thyme sprigs

METHOD

Put a little olive oil in a small saucepan and add the carrot, onion, garlic, mushrooms and meat trimmings. Cook until they are lightly coloured and the meat well sealed. Add the two vinegars and reduce to barely $2^1/2$ tablespoons. Add the port and again reduce to barely $2^1/2$ tablespoons. Add the red wine and thyme and reduce to 150 ml (5 fl oz), then strain and reserve for use. Makes about 150 ml (5 fl oz)

STOCKS

VEGETABLE STOCK

This stock gives water a good flavour for making vegetarian risottos and soups. It is quick to make and you can add other ingredients if you wish such as carrots or cabbage and, of course, lots of herbs. This is the only stock to which we add salt. This stock will last for up to four days in the refrigerator.

INGREDIENTS

2 tablespoons olive oil

1 brown onion, finely chopped

2 garlic cloves, finely chopped

1 leek, white part only, washed and finely chopped

2 celery stalks, finely chopped

70 g (2^1/$_2$ oz/^{1}/$_2$ cup) finely chopped fennel

1 vine-ripened tomato, finely chopped

1 fresh bay leaf

sea salt

METHOD

Put the olive oil in a large saucepan and add the onion, garlic and leek. Sweat for 5 minutes over medium heat. Add the remaining vegetables and cook for 10 minutes over low heat. Add 4.5 litres (157 fl oz) water and the bay leaf and bring to the boil; simmer for 20 minutes, skimming off any impurities if necessary. Strain twice through a muslin-lined fine strainer and season. Cool slightly and refrigerate. Makes about 3 litres (105 fl oz)

CHICKEN STOCK

This is the most used stock at Rockpool. It has a well-balanced and clean flavour; it has body and tastes of chicken. That may sound funny, but it's not, just an observation that many chicken stocks taste like vegetables or have a cloudy and confused taste. We wanted purity and a clean flavour because in many cases it is used in seafood dishes. It has no added flavourings, not the vegetables and herbs of the French, or the ginger and spring onion (scallion) of the Chinese; I believe it has the right clarity of taste and texture for my cooking, so try it. You can make stock with chicken bones, but if you try it with whole chicken you will taste the difference. It will last for up to four days in the refrigerator.

METHOD

Wash a 1.6 kg (3 lb 8 oz) corn-fed chicken and remove the fat from the cavity. Set the chicken on a chopping board and with a large cook s knife or a cleaver cut off the legs at the point where the thigh and drumstick meet. Make a few slashes into the flesh with a sharp knife. Cut the wings off where they meet the breast, then cut down the side of the chicken so the back comes off the breast. Cut the back and breast in half, and again, cut into the flesh slightly.

Put 3 litres (105 fl oz) water in a large saucepan and add the chicken pieces. Bring to the boil, then reduce the heat to the barest simmer and cook, uncovered, for about 4 hours. Remove any impurities from the surface during the cooking process. Carefully strain the stock twice through a muslin-lined fine strainer and discard the chicken pieces. Cool to room temperature, then refrigerate; remove the layer of fat before using. Makes about 2.5 litres (87 fl oz)

VEAL STOCK

I have put this stock in just in case you want to make a classic red wine sauce or other veal-stock-based sauce. It is also used to braise a couple of meats in the meat chapter. It is funny but at Rockpool these days the only dish that has a veal stock base is the tuna. It has a red wine as well as a garlic sauce served with it. This veal stock is like all things at Rockpool, a little different to the norm, but we have developed it as we believe it gives us the best result. I would urge you to try it. Remember, don't boil the stock vigorously or you will cloud it; skim it regularly and strain at least twice through muslin — this applies to all stocks.

INGREDIENTS

5 kg (11 lb) veal shanks, cut into rounds

15 garlic cloves

2 small or 1 large red onion, finely diced

1 carrot, peeled and finely diced

500 ml (17 fl oz/2 cups) vegetable oil

3 thyme sprigs

3 fresh bay leaves

6 vine-ripened tomatoes, peeled, deseeded and diced (page 66)

METHOD

Preheat the oven to 220°C (425°F/Gas 7). Put the veal bones in a roasting tin and roast until golden brown, turning once during the cooking time. Transfer the bones to a saucepan large enough to fit them snugly, pour a little water into the roasting tin and with a wooden spoon scrape the residue off the bottom. Add this to the pan with enough water to just cover the bones. Put the pan on the stove over high heat and bring to the boil. Turn down to a gentle simmer and skim continuously for 30 minutes.

Put the garlic and onion in a mortar with a pestle and crush for 5 minutes until you have a rough paste. Add the carrot and continue for a further 2 minutes. Put the vegetable oil in a wok and put it on the stove. Add the vegetable paste and stir from time to time to stop it from burning. Fry until dark brown, then strain the oil into a container and add the vegetables to the stock that has been skimmed and simmering for 30 minutes. It is very important that the vegetables are very dark but not burnt, as that will cause the stock to be bitter.

Add the herbs and tomato to the stock and simmer very slowly, skimming occasionally, for 5 hours. Once cooked, remove the pan from the stove and cool. As it cools, more fat will come to the top. Skim well before straining.

Very carefully ladle the stock out of the pan and pass through a muslin-lined strainer. Lift the strainer and allow the stock to freely run out; don't squeeze or push against the bones, as this will allow sediment to run into the stock, thus risking the clarity. Strain the stock a second time through the muslin and allow to cool before refrigerating. It will last five to six days in the refrigerator. After that time, boil it again to kill any bacteria and it will keep for another few days. It also may be frozen until required. Makes about 2 litres (70 fl oz/8 cups)

NOTE

To make veal glaze, reduce the strained stock in a wide saucepan over high heat. When it is reduced to about 5 mm ($1/4$ inch) deep and beginning to thicken, re-strain into a smaller, shallow pan. Continue to reduce until it is syrup-like. Pass through a fine strainer. Cool and refrigerate until needed.

DESSERTS

A special meal always needs a special dish to finish with, that little bit extra that holds the company, extends the enjoyment of the moment and lets everyone finish their wine. Because, let's face it, it can't be because you're still hungry. Haven't you just eaten enough to make your doctor worry? No, it's not hunger, it's the desire to finish the meal with grace and hospitality, to show the extra care that is a part of looking after one's friends and family. In any case, we all know that the dessert stomach is another stomach altogether and that this one hungers for something sweet. No matter how much savoury food you have managed, a little sweet something is always good at the end. I quite like to end a meal with a plate of cheese and another of fruit... some fruit may go with the cheese, other fruit is just on the plate to be eaten by itself; this makes everyone at the table happy, no matter what diet they are on, and a little sweet fruit often provides satisfaction enough. One reason I don't make many desserts at home is that I have such a wonderful pastry chef working in my restaurant. Whenever I need a really sophisticated sweet taste, I have it at work. Anyway, meal endings at home should be simple; it is informal eating at home that we all love. Dessert making in top restaurants is the preserve of the true technician: if cooking is a craft, then pastry making is a science. These chefs, the devotees of the religion of turning sugar, butter, flour, eggs, chocolate and fruit into wonderful dreams, have an exacting taskmaster. The science that drives them fails them in an instant the moment they deviate from the path.

These are formulas, not recipes, and these formulas are absolute. It is not only about exact weights and measures; it is about the science that causes these ingredients to interact in precise ways. Only with all these things in perfect balance does the ordinary become the sublime. These formulas behave either like angels or, in the worst case scenario, like devils. To create the beautiful desserts that Catherine Adams, the head pastry chef at Rockpool does, one must possess the skills and determination of a saint. It is lucky for us mere mortals that there are a number of delicious, simple things we can cook at home to satisfy the sweet tooth of friends and family. The following are the only desserts you will see me cooking at home. All of them are classics, and they are classics because one, they are simple, and two, they taste fantastic. They also have a skill attached: baking a cake, making custard, dealing with gelatine and so forth. These skills will allow you to take these basics and reach for the stars. If you decide that you're ready to study the science of the restaurant pastry chef, when that day comes, good luck. Several of these recipes have been flying around the world with Qantas for a few years now. We know that not only are they incredibly delicious but the recipes are also really solid and work every time.

As I said before, I love to serve cheese after the main course. The reason is that good-quality cheese in peak condition is a pure food. When well made and properly looked after, it is the food of angels. There is something about simplicity combined with great flavour and texture that increasingly appeals to me, the more I cook, the more I dine around the world and the older I get. Things such as beautiful cheeses, a ripe piece of fruit, a slice of aged Spanish ham, a perfectly mature glass of wine; these are the things I love more and more, and feel most satisfied with these days.

A QUICK WORD ON CHEESE

As with all things in life, there is cheese... and there is cheese. There are a number of quality cheeses, and these are the ones I suggest you try to find, being the perfect end to the perfect meal. Look for those made by small producers who would consider their cheese hand-made; ones by larger producers who care for the old traditions fiercely, such as the producers of Parmigiano Reggiano; and some of the larger producers from France who make Camembert, Brie and blue cheeses of great quality. An English Cheddar made to traditional farmhouse methods and aged is one of the great tastes in the world. Try to avoid mass-produced cheeses that lack flavour, character and balance. Unfortunately, this is the great majority of cheeses in the world today, so search hard for the best-quality cheese you can find; it isn't as easy as you think. Cheese is simply preserved milk, so it makes sense that the quality of the milk and the way it is handled will really make not just a difference, but a huge difference. Think of cheese as you do wine. It's not always true, but a lot of the time you get what you pay for. Also, don't waste money by having mounds of cheese on the table. About 60–100 g (2 1/4–3 1/2 oz) cheese per person will be more than enough, so buy quality not quantity.

I usually serve three cheeses: a soft one like a Brie, washed rind or triple cream; a blue cheese, either firm or soft; and a hard cheese like Parmigiano Reggiano, Gruyère, Beaufort or Cheddar. I would serve a fruit plate full of seasonal fruit, but also some dried fruit like dates and apricots and nuts such as almonds and pecans. You can, of course, just serve one beautiful cheese, which is a sophisticated way to do it. I like a mixture of bread and crackers. After that, it's all up to the cheese.

A QUICK WORD ON FRUIT

Fruit is not only healthy but, when perfectly ripe and in season, is also one of the best ways to finish a meal. Perhaps it isn't cooking but, as with selecting the best cheese, selecting the best fruit in season can by itself elevate the end of a meal to something special. The other essential thing about seasonal fruit is that it all seems to go well together, so try working with fruit that is not imported and is in its natural season. The next simplest dessert to prepare after selecting fruit and putting it on the table is to make a fruit salad; again, make it a seasonal celebration. It can make a marvellous centrepiece, served in a beautiful large glass bowl and set in the middle of the table. A little sugar syrup mixed with passionfruit, or the juice of one of the fruits you are serving, or a mixture of vanilla, fruit juice and a little sugar syrup is also a great dressing for the salad. At the restaurant we will sometimes cut all the fruit into very fine dice; this is time consuming, but very impressive visually. You need to make sure that each of the fruits can be tasted individually as well as collectively. Serve with fresh granita, ice cream or a little clotted cream, or au naturel, in beautiful martini glasses.

A QUICK WORD ON BAKING

Baking is relatively easy as long as you are organized and make sure you follow the recipe. This means you must have the oven at the right temperature, and the best way to do that is to check with an oven thermometer. For fan-forced ovens, as a general rule, set the oven temperature to 20°C (36°F) lower than indicated in the recipe. Make sure the board you are using is free from odours of other cooking (such as garlic and onion). Also, unlike pasta, cakes and puddings need soft flour, so invest in cake flour when starting these recipes. When blind baking, do not fill the flan tin all the way to the top as this will hinder the cooking process and some parts may be raw and others brown.

DATE, ORANGE AND MINT SALAD WITH ORANGE GRANITA

This is a refreshing way to end a meal. The little salad combines spice, the sticky sweetness of the dates and the gentle, sweet acid of the orange granita to bring a cold refreshing feel to the mouth. Granitas can be easily produced at home with no special equipment, and there is no end to the number of flavours you can produce, using either fruit purées or flavoured waters. You will need a container which fits in the freezer and allows the granita base to be 5 cm (2 inches) deep, a freezer and a fork. All of these things are easily found in the home. The granita base needs to taste strongly of the main ingredient and be of a sweetness that balances with all the other flavours. Coffee, chocolate, wine and all berry fruit make good granitas. You need to fork the granita as it starts to set; regularly doing this makes for a lighter, fluffier granita, so it is worth the effort. Other than that, this fruit-driven dessert is easy, tastes great and is incredibly refreshing.

INGREDIENTS

16 fresh dates, soaked in hot water for 10 minutes, skins removed and pitted
4 oranges, segmented (page 246)
8 mint leaves, very finely sliced

FOR THE GRANITA
550 ml (19 fl oz) freshly squeezed orange juice
115 g (4 oz/$1/2$ cup) caster (superfine) sugar
$1/2$ teaspoon ground cinnamon
pinch of ground cardamom
5 drops of orange blossom water (optional)

METHOD

To make the granita, strain the orange juice through a fine sieve and put into a bowl with the sugar, spices, orange blossom water, if using, and 125 ml (4 fl oz/$1/2$ cup) water. Stir for about 3 minutes until the sugar dissolves. Strain the mixture through a fine strainer into a container that allows the mixture to be 5 cm (2 inches) deep. Put in the freezer. Using a fork, stir it every 30 minutes, scraping the edges and breaking up any chunks until the granita is slushy and frozen. This will take 4—5 hours.

Cut the dates into quarters. Gently mix the dates, orange segments and mint together, then divide among eight glasses. Add the granita to each of the glasses and serve immediately. Serves 8

PANNACOTTA WITH FRESH RASPBERRIES

This is a wonderful Italian dessert that has swept the world in the last two decades and why not? It is easy to make, has a wonderful affinity with fresh fruit and, even if you put all that aside, it simply tastes divine. 'Panna' in Italian means cream and 'cotta' means cooked. Therefore, it is cooked cream and, unlike many French desserts of the same ilk, it doesn't contain eggs. It is only the gelatine that holds the dish together. It has quite a different texture to custards and bavarois as there is no trapped air, so the texture is dense; however, dense doesn't mean firm. This is a 'set' dessert, yet good pannacotta should melt in your mouth, and it is critical to correctly estimate the amount of gelatine needed to hold the mass. So, try this and if it is a little firm or soft, adjust the amount of gelatine you use next time to make it perfect. We use leaf gelatine of medium strength. Types of gelatine do vary, and if you use powdered gelatine, that will behave a little differently again. It is worth trying to get it perfect; the pannacotta should just stand up of its own accord, and delicate is best. When using leaf gelatine, always soak it in cold water to soften it first, then make sure that whatever you are adding it to is warm, so that it melts. Any fresh, ripe summer fruit will work well here, especially berries, mangoes, peaches and cherries. In winter, serve with poached quinces or pears and, as spring approaches, segment blood oranges for a real treat. Although cream should be the dominant taste, it is also easy to give these little creams different flavour. I love buttermilk for one, and you can flavour them with citrus peel or nut-flavoured milk.

INGREDIENTS

125 ml (4 fl oz/^{1}/2 cup) milk
250 ml (9 fl oz/1 cup) pure (whipping) cream
1 vanilla bean, split lengthways and seeds scraped out
2 tablespoons caster (superfine) sugar
8 g (^{1}/6 oz) leaf gelatine (about 1–2 sheets)
125 ml (4 fl oz/^{1}/2 cup) thick (double/heavy) cream
300 g (10^1/2 oz/2 punnets) raspberries

METHOD

You will need four 125 ml (4 fl oz/^{1}/2 cup) plastic dariole moulds. Put the milk, cream, vanilla bean and seeds and half the sugar in a saucepan. Bring to the boil, stirring, then gently simmer for 1 minute. Soften the leaf gelatine in a little cold water, then squeeze out. Remove the pan from the heat and stir in the remaining sugar and softened leaf gelatine.

Strain the mixture into a bowl and chill over ice. It will start to set around the edges so, while chilling, keep stirring, making sure you scrape the bottom of the bowl. This will help to keep an even distribution of the vanilla seeds and ensure that they are suspended throughout the entire dessert. When the mixture reaches a gelatinous appearance, similar to the thickness of thick cream, remove the bowl from the ice.

Stir some mixture into the cream to break it down, then add back to the remaining mixture. Strain again and pour into the moulds to set. Leave for 1–2 hours in the refrigerator.

To release the pannacotta, pour some boiling water into a bowl and submerge the moulds halfway down in the water for about 10 seconds. Gently place a small knife down the inside edge to create an air pocket and separate the pannacotta from the mould. Turn the pannacotta out onto four plates and serve with fresh raspberries. Serve immediately. Serves 4

PINEAPPLE AND GINGER PUDDINGS

I love crystallized ginger and it is worth getting a good-quality brand for these puddings. If you don't like munching on it all by itself, then it's not good enough for this dish. These little baked puddings are very easy to make. They have a heavy texture, although the batter is made light by self-raising flour and baking powder. You could, I suppose, add the egg yolks separately to the whites, then fold the whites through afterwards to create a soufflé effect, but part of the charm of this dish is its firmer texture, which makes it more like a pudding than a cake. In baking, when the word 'cream' is used in relation to the butter and sugar, it is very important that the sugar completely dissolves, as whole crystals will burn out during the baking process and create little air bubbles in the pudding. As this particular recipe has a heavy texture it wouldn't be the end of the world, but it would be if you were trying to create a light sponge. These little puddings are great served with vanilla or honey and cassia ice cream or with some lightly whipped cream or a little warm crème anglaise.

INGREDIENTS

200 g (7 oz) unsalted butter

115 g (4 oz/^{1}/2 cup) caster (superfine) sugar

4 eggs

1 teaspoon baking powder

25 g (1 oz/1/4 cup) ground almonds

60 g (2^1/4 oz/1/2 cup) self-raising flour

125 g (4^1/2 oz) crystallized ginger, roughly sliced

FOR THE TOPPING

100 g (3^1/2 oz/1/2 cup) brown sugar

6 slices fresh pineapple, about 5 mm (^{1}/4 inch) thick, cut in circles the same size as the moulds

METHOD

Line a baking tray with greaseproof paper. Butter and lightly flour six individual bottomless moulds, about 5 cm (2 inches) high and 7 cm (2³/4 inches) in diameter. Put the moulds on the tray and set aside.

To make the topping, dissolve the brown sugar in 60 ml (2 fl oz/¹/4 cup) water and bring to the boil. Add the pineapple slices to the syrup and simmer for 5 minutes until tender, turning the slices over once. Remove the pineapple and leave to dry on a tray. Retain the syrup for later.

Preheat the oven to 190°C (375°F/Gas 5). To make the pudding batter, cream the butter and sugar together. Add the eggs. The mixture may appear to split at this point but keep beating and it will come back together. Mix together the baking powder, almonds and flour and add to the batter. Finally, thoroughly mix through the ginger. Place a pineapple round in the base of each mould, fill the moulds two-thirds full with batter and bake for about 25 minutes, or until golden and springy.

Run a small knife gently around the inside of a mould and upturn onto a white plate. Remove the mould and repeat the process with the remaining moulds. Drizzle some of the reserved syrup over the top. Serves 6

FOLLOWING PAGES pineapple and ginger pudding, served with vanilla ice cream (page 430), left, and crème caramel, right

CREME CARAMEL

Crème caramel is vanilla custard that is baked in a mould that has been first ringed with caramel. It is a self-saucing dessert that is, quite simply, a classic beauty. Don't even think about serving something with this, it needs nothing save a good glass of dessert wine to accompany it. When the texture is right and the taste of the caramel has that tiny hint of bitterness, it is nearly impossible to beat. But, as with all simple things, it is one of the easiest desserts to muck up. If the texture is not perfect, all is lost. The two things that affect the texture are the ratio of egg yolks to egg whites — too much egg white and it will be tough, too little and it will fall apart — and the heat. If cooked for too long or at too high a heat it will have little air bubbles through it, which will destroy the glacial texture that makes a crème caramel great, and, again, it will be too firm. You must cook this in a bain-marie half filled with water, and you need to have a cloth or tea towel on the bottom to stop the bottom of the moulds feeling direct heat; this can cause air bubbles to form as well.

This particular custard is flavoured with vanilla but you can add different flavours to the custard such as orange or lemon and still sauce with the caramel. If you would like to, make custards by this method and leave the caramel out: try chocolate or coffee crème caramels, or flavour the custard with wine or nut-infused milk.

INGREDIENTS

1 litre (35 fl oz/4 cups) milk

115 g (3^{3}/4 oz/^{1}/2 cup) caster (superfine) sugar

1 vanilla bean pod, split lengthways and seeds scraped out

6 eggs

6 egg yolks

FOR THE CARAMEL

225 g (8 oz/1 cup) caster (superfine) sugar

METHOD

Combine the milk, sugar and vanilla bean and seeds in a saucepan and bring slowly to the boil. Remove the pan from the heat and leave to stand for 1 hour to infuse.

Meanwhile, to make the caramel, bring the sugar and 125 ml (4 fl oz/^{1}/2 cup) warm water to a gentle simmer, stirring briefly to dissolve the sugar. Do not stir once it is simmering. Watch the sugar and water carefully, and simmer only until it starts turning a deep caramel colour. Immediately remove the pan from the heat and carefully pour equal amounts of the caramel into six 250 ml (9 fl oz/1 cup) metal dariole moulds. Hold the moulds at the top of the rim (the metal will be hot lower down) and swirl to coat the moulds halfway up their sides with the caramel. Set aside.

Preheat the oven to 190°C (375°F/Gas 5). Lightly mix the eggs and yolks in a bowl. Strain the cooled milk mixture into the egg mixture, slowly whisking. Strain again and pour into the moulds. Lay a tea towel on the bottom of a roasting tin or bain-marie that is deeper than the moulds. Put the moulds in and half fill the tin with hot water. Cover the tin with foil and place in the centre of the oven to cook for 30–55 minutes, or until set. (The time will vary depending on the oven.) Allow to cool, then store in the refrigerator.

Pour some boiling water into a bowl and place a mould in the water for about 15 seconds. Carefully run a knife around the inside of the mould. Place the serving plate on top and quickly upturn the crème caramel and slowly remove the mould, allowing the caramel to gently spill down the edges of the dessert. Repeat with the remaining moulds. Serve immediately. Serves 6

BREAD AND BUTTER PUDDING WITH CREME ANGLAISE

Bread features in many desserts. I think it safe to say that, originally, there would have been the need to simply use up stale bread, and then a number of bright young folk recognized that it could be used in sweet things. This is a version of the classic baked bread and butter pudding. These days in restaurants, stale bread is not used. Indeed, in many cases, bread is baked especially for the pudding — brioche, panettone and raisin bread are all finding their way into this great dessert. In its simplest form, it is simply bread baked with a custard that is set with eggs. It has only become complex with our desire to throw more and more things into it. Anyway, try this recipe and I'm sure you will be hooked. It is served cold, but it is also really good served warm with ice cream. You can put the pudding in the oven and serve it as soon as it comes out, or cool it and just rewarm in the oven at a low temperature for about 15 minutes.

INGREDIENTS

400 g (14 oz) brioche loaf

125 g (4^{1}/2 oz/1 cup) sultanas

100 ml (3^{1}/2 fl oz) apple juice

1 vanilla bean, split lengthways and seeds scraped out

100 g (3^{1}/2 oz) unsalted butter, softened

^{1}/2 teaspoon ground cinnamon

^{1}/2 teaspoon ground nutmeg

55 g (2 oz/^{1}/4 cup) caster (superfine) sugar

5 eggs

1 egg yolk

185 ml (6 fl oz/^{3}/4 cup) milk

185 ml (6 fl oz/^{3}/4 cup) pure (whipping) cream

crème anglaise (page 419)

METHOD

Lightly grease a rectangular ceramic baking dish, about 12 x 22 cm (4^1/2 x 8^1/2 inches) in size, 4 cm (1^1/2 inches) high. (It will also work in dishes with different dimensions, or in a round dish, as long as the dish has a 900 ml (32 fl oz) capacity.) Remove the crust from the brioche and cut the loaf into slices about 1 cm (^{1}/2 inch) thick.

Preheat the oven to 170°C (325°F/Gas 3). Combine the sultanas, apple juice and vanilla bean and seeds in a small saucepan. Bring to the boil, then reduce the heat and simmer, uncovered, for about 5 minutes, or until the liquid has been absorbed. Remove the pan from the heat and allow to cool.

Mix together the butter, cinnamon, nutmeg and 1 teaspoon of the sugar until well combined. Spread a thin layer over both sides of each brioche slice. Lay a slice of brioche in the prepared dish at a slight angle, so that about one-third of the slice is sticking out of the dish. Scatter with 1 tablespoon of the sultana mixture and repeat the process until the dish is full.

Whisk together the eggs, egg yolk, milk, cream and remaining sugar until well combined. Slowly pour the egg mixture over the dish, a third at a time, giving the mixture a chance to be soaked up by the bread. You should be able to use the entire amount. Stand for 10 minutes to allow the egg mixture to be fully absorbed. Put the dish in a deep roasting tin and pour in enough hot water to come halfway up the outside of the baking dish. Bake, uncovered, for about 40–45 minutes, or until the pudding is just set and the top is lightly browned and puffed.

Remove the dish from the roasting tin and allow to stand for 30 minutes, or until cooled. Cover and refrigerate for 8 hours, or until cold and firm. Carefully turn the pudding out of the baking dish onto a clean cutting board and cut into slices using a serrated knife. Serve each slice with crème anglaise. Serves 6–8

LIME SYRUP CAKE

Syrup cakes are great because although they have a fairly dense texture they are always very moist. This cake has a lovely sweet-sour nature. You can serve it with cream; however, I like it with finely diced fresh fruit. There are two things you must make sure you do right here: don't make the syrup too sweet; and, very importantly, pour the hot syrup over the cake while it is also hot.

INGREDIENTS

350 g (12 oz/1^1/2 cups) caster (superfine) sugar
300 g (10^1/2 oz/2^1/2 cups) self-raising flour
90 g (3^1/4 oz/1 cup) desiccated coconut
zest of 1 lime
250 g (9 oz) unsalted butter, melted
2 eggs
250 ml (9 fl oz/1 cup) milk

FOR THE LIME SYRUP
225 g (8 oz/1 cup) caster (superfine) sugar
zest of 1 lime
juice of 5 limes

METHOD

Preheat oven to 180°C (350°F/Gas 4). Lightly grease a 22 cm (8^1/2 inch) round cake tin or a 19 cm (7^1/2 inch) square cake tin. Line the base and side of the tin with baking paper that extends 2 cm (^{3}/4 inch) above the side. Sift together the sugar and flour and mix with the coconut and lime zest in a bowl. Stir in the butter. Combine the eggs and milk and add to the bowl. Mix until smooth.

Spoon the mixture into the prepared tin and bake on a tray for 1 hour, or until a skewer put into the centre comes out completely dry. If the top of the cake starts to brown before it is baked through, cover with some foil and continue cooking. Meanwhile, make the syrup. Put the sugar and 185 ml (6 fl oz/^{3}/4 cup) water in a heavy-based saucepan and stir over low heat until the sugar is fully dissolved. Add the lime zest and juice, bring to the boil, reduce the heat and simmer uncovered for 8 minutes, then strain.

Remove the cake from the oven and use a skewer to poke a few holes evenly over the cake. Slowly pour the hot syrup over the cake. Let it stand for about 20 minutes, or until the syrup has soaked into the cake, then turn the cake out onto a wire rack lined with baking paper and allow to cool. To serve, simply slice and serve on its own or with a fresh fruit salad. Serves 10

SUMMER PUDDING

This is a classic English dessert. Like bread and butter pudding, it is another great dessert that uses bread, this time to corral a mixture of summer berries. It is usually made as one large pudding, but can be made in individual moulds as well. The key to this dessert is to cook the berries with the sugar just long enough to release most of their juices; it is these juices that soak into the bread and help hold it together. Without their juices, the fruit is compressed into a more dense form; a weight is placed on the pudding overnight or during the day to further press the whole thing together. It is important that you have a tray under the bowl, as lots of juice will come out. You must catch this juice, as it sauces the pudding afterwards, making it another self-saucing pudding.

There are two very important things to get right with this pudding: the bread must be a fairly good-quality sliced white sandwich bread; and it must be stale, or the bread will become mushy. It is also essential to serve this pudding reasonably fresh; by that I mean make it in the morning for that night, or the night before for the following day's lunch. The pudding is at its best when between eight and sixteen hours old. To serve, simply unmould, cut and serve with lightly whipped cream, pouring the juices over.

INGREDIENTS

500 g (1 lb 2 oz/2 punnets) strawberries, stemmed and quartered
600 g (1 lb 5 oz/4 punnets) raspberries
150 g (5^1/2 oz/1 punnet) blueberries
225 g (8 oz/1 cup) caster (superfine) sugar, plus extra
1 loaf stale sliced white bread, crusts removed
whipped cream

METHOD

Combine the berries, sugar and 60 ml (2 fl oz/$1/4$ cup) water in a medium saucepan. Gently stir over low heat without boiling, until the sugar has completely dissolved. Simmer, without stirring, for about 5 minutes until the juices are released from the fruit. Strain the juices from the fruit in a sieve and put aside for later use. Leave the fruit and juices to cool.

Lightly butter a 1 litre (35 fl oz/4 cup) glass bowl, sprinkle with a little extra caster sugar and shake away the excess. Cut two-thirds of the bread slices into triangles, leaving the rest in squares. Reserving some triangular pieces for the top of the pudding, lightly soak the remaining bread triangles in the prepared berry juices, then line the bottom of the sugared bowl, making sure the bread is firmly packed and the base is totally covered. Soak enough of the bread squares to line the side of the bowl, overlapping them slightly.

Put the strained fruit into the centre of the bowl and add just enough juice to nearly cover the fruit, about 125 ml (4 fl oz/$1/2$ cup), but don't use it all. Soak the remaining bread triangles in the last of the fruit juices and cover the top of the fruit with the bread, overlapping the pieces to completely cover the top.

Place the bowl in a larger tray that can catch any spilt juices. Put a flat plate that fits the bowl perfectly on top with something else heavy on that to weigh the pudding down. Refrigerate for between 8 and 16 hours.

Remove the pudding from the mould, slice and place on white plates, pour any juice collected over the pudding and serve with whipped cream. Serves 6

STRAWBERRY AND MASCARPONE CAKE

This is a classic meringue-based cake. The filling of sweetened mascarpone is lightened with whipped egg whites much in the same way you lighten mascarpone when making tiramisu. You can change the fruit without too much trouble to reflect the season. The important thing to remember when making meringue is to not overbeat the egg whites, as they will lose their energy and end up flopping instead of holding a good form — essential to making the cake look really good.

Make sure the egg whites are free of any egg yolk, and the bowl and whisk you are using are really clean. Having even the smallest drop of water in the bowl can end in disaster. Some mascarpone brands can be quite salty; make sure you use a good-quality unsalted one.

INGREDIENTS

500 g (1 lb 2 oz/2 punnets) strawberries, hulled and sliced
icing (confectioners') sugar, for dusting

FOR THE COCONUT MERINGUES
35 g ($1^1/4$ oz/$^1/3$ cup) ground almonds
150 g ($5^1/2$ oz/$1^3/4$ cups) desiccated coconut
7 egg whites
80 g ($2^3/4$ oz/$^1/3$ cup) caster (superfine) sugar
175 g (6 oz/$1^1/3$ cups) icing (confectioners') sugar, sifted

FOR THE MASCARPONE FILLING
500 g (1 lb 2 oz) good-quality mascarpone
70 g ($2^1/2$ oz/$^1/3$ cup) caster (superfine) sugar
2 eggs, separated

METHOD

Preheat the oven to 150°C (300°F/Gas 2). Mark two 25 cm (10 inch) circles on baking paper and use to line two baking trays (or one tray if big enough). To make the coconut meringues, combine the ground almonds with the coconut in a bowl. Using an electric mixer, whisk the egg whites, in two batches if necessary, until soft peaks form. Gradually add the sugar, about 1 tablespoon at a time, whisking until the mixture is thick and glossy and firm peaks form. Using a metal spoon, gently fold the icing sugar into the egg white mixture until just combined, then fold in the coconut mixture, again in batches, until just combined.

Using a spatula, divide the mixture between the two circles on the trays, spreading it out to a thickness of 1 cm ($1/2$ inch). Bake the meringues for about 30 minutes, or until golden, and allow to cool on the trays.

To make the mascarpone filling, use a hand-held whisk to whisk the mascarpone, two-thirds of the sugar and both the egg yolks until very thick. Using an electric mixer, whisk the egg whites until soft peaks form, then gradually add the remaining sugar and whisk until firm peaks form. Fold half the egg white mixture into the mascarpone mixture to lighten it, then gently fold in the remaining egg white mixture.

Using a 25 cm (10 inch) springform cake tin or cake ring, place a meringue disc in the base, top with half the mascarpone filling, then cover with the strawberries. Top with the remaining mascarpone filling. Finish with the final meringue disc, placed crispy side up. Cover and refrigerate overnight.

When ready to serve, run a knife around the inside of the tin or ring and remove the cake. Dust with icing sugar. This cake will keep refrigerated, in an airtight container, for up to three days. Serves 12

BRANDIED FIG AND FRANGIPANE TART

This may seem complicated at first glance, but it is quite easy. You make the pastry, marinate the figs and then make the frangipane paste. It is then just a matter of putting all the elements together. The frangipane mix is really versatile: you can fill tarts with it, as I have here; you can spread it over the tart base and put the fruit on top; or you can pour it around the fruit. Peaches, nectarines, apricots, pears and cherries work really well. A note on the figs: don't use tenderized figs (often packaged as dried), as they won't soak up the alcohol. Make sure you rest the pastry for at least one hour before rolling out, so that it can relax and you won't have to work with tough dough.

INGREDIENTS

250 ml (9 fl oz/1 cup) apple juice
125 ml (4 fl oz/^{1}/2 cup) brandy
280 g (10 oz) dried figs, about 18 in total
150 g (5^1/2 oz/^{1}/2 cup) good-quality plum jam
icing (confectioners') sugar, to dust
mascarpone

FOR THE PASTRY
250 g (9 oz/2 cups) plain (all-purpose) flour
70 g (2^1/2 oz) unsalted butter, cubed
pinch of sea salt
90 g (3^1/4 oz/^{3}/4 cup) icing (confectioners') sugar
60 ml (2 fl oz/^{1}/4 cup) milk
2 egg yolks

FOR THE FRANGIPANE
125 g (4^1/2 oz) unsalted butter, softened
125 g (4^1/2 oz/1 cup) icing (confectioners') sugar
125 g (4^1/2 oz/1^1/4 cups) ground almonds
3 eggs
25 g (1 oz/^{1}/4 cup) plain (all-purpose) flour

METHOD

You will need a round, fluted, loose-bottomed flan tin, 24 cm ($9^1/2$ inches) in diameter and 2.5 cm (1 inch) deep.

To make the pastry, put the flour, butter, sea salt and icing sugar in a food processor and process for 20 seconds. Add the milk and egg yolks and process for a further 30 seconds until a dough forms.

Turn the dough out on to a lightly floured bench and knead gently for a few moments. Flatten on the bench and form into a ball, then wrap in plastic wrap and refrigerate for 1 hour.

Lightly butter and flour the flan tin. Roll out the pastry until it is about 2–3 mm ($^1/16$–$^1/8$ inch) thick. Cut out a circle that is about 5 cm (2 inches) wider than the tart case base. Roll the pastry round over the rolling pin and gently ease it into the tart case, pushing the sides in gently. Allow to rest in the refrigerator for 30 minutes.

Cut off any excess pastry and prick the base a few times with a fork to prevent blistering and rising. Line the tart case with foil, add raw rice and bake blind for 20–25 minutes. Remove from the oven and lift out the rice and foil (the foil should come away easily; if not, bake for a few more minutes). Return the pastry case to the oven and bake for a further 5–10 minutes, or until the base has dried out.

Combine the apple juice and brandy in a saucepan, bring to the boil, then add the figs and simmer, uncovered, for 10–15 minutes, or until the figs have plumped up and softened. Drain and reserve the liquid for the frangipane and mascarpone (there should be about 100 ml ($3^1/2$ fl oz) liquid remaining).

To make the frangipane filling, use an electric mixer to beat the butter in a large bowl until light and creamy. Add the sugar and mix until well combined. Add the ground almonds and mix until well combined. Gradually add the eggs, one at a time, mixing well after each addition. Gently stir in the flour and 25 ml (1 fl oz) of the reserved apple brandy mixture and mix well. Cover and refrigerate for 30 minutes. Preheat the oven to 180°C (350°F/Gas 4).

Spread the plum jam over the base of the tart shell, top with the drained figs and gently spoon enough of the frangipane mixture — about 500 g (1 lb 2 oz) — over the jam and figs to cover. Bake for 35–40 minutes. Cool until just warm, then dust with icing sugar.

Serve the tart with the mascarpone. Try folding the remaining apple brandy mixture through the mascarpone for added flavour. Serves 10–12

INDIVIDUAL PASSIONFRUIT CURD TARTS

These yummy little tarts are simple to put together and you can change the flavours if you wish. Lemon or lime curd is just as easy to make as passionfruit; simply swap the passionfruit juice for lemon or lime juice and proceed as per the recipe. I fold whipped cream through the curd to lighten it and take the edge off the big flavour. That isn't common practice, but try it and I'm sure you'll appreciate it. Just don't boil the curd as it will scramble and you will have to throw the whole thing out. These individual tart cases are great. Instead of filling with curd, you can make a crème pâtissière, lighten it with whipped cream, fill the cases with it and top with seasonal fruit. At this stage, you can serve the tarts as they are, or glaze with a little melted jam.

INGREDIENTS

FOR THE PASSIONFRUIT CURD

10 passionfruit

150 g (5^1/2 oz) unsalted butter

300 g (10^1/2 oz/1^1/3 cups) caster (superfine) sugar

12 egg yolks, lightly beaten

1 tablespoon lime juice, strained

125 ml (4 fl oz/^{1}/2 cup) pure (whipping) cream

FOR THE PASTRY

185 g (6^1/4 oz/1^1/2 cups) plain (all-purpose) flour

100 g (3^1/2 oz) cold unsalted butter, cubed

1^1/2 tablespoons caster (superfine) sugar

1 teaspoon natural vanilla extract

1 egg, lightly whisked

1 egg, whisked, extra, for the egg wash

METHOD

To make the passionfruit curd, scoop out the seeds and pulp from the passionfruit and strain through a fine sieve. Rinse the seeds separately and return 1 tablespoon of the seeds to the juice; discard the rest.

Heat the butter and sugar in a saucepan over low heat until the butter has melted and the sugar has dissolved. Remove the pan from the heat and add the passionfruit seeds and juice, followed by the egg yolks. Stir well and return the pan to the heat. Stir over low heat for 15–18 minutes, or until the mixture has thickened. Be careful to not let it curdle at this point.

Remove the pan from the heat and stir in the lime juice. Scrape the curd into a bowl, cover closely with plastic wrap to avoid a crust forming on the curd and leave to cool before refrigerating for a couple of hours to allow the curd to set. When cold, whip the cream to soft peaks and fold through the curd. This can all be done a day in advance.

To make the pastry, process the flour, butter and sugar together in a food processor until the mixture resembles fine breadcrumbs. Add the vanilla extract to the whisked egg and combine. Add to the food processor and process until the mixture just comes together. Form the mixture into a ball, then divide into eight equal pieces. Roll each piece into a ball, wrap in plastic wrap and refrigerate for 1 hour.

Butter and flour eight individual tart cases, about 8 cm (3 1/4 inches) in diameter and 2 cm (3/4 inch) deep. Generously flour your workbench and rolling pin, and roll out the first ball until it is very thin — about 1 mm (1/32 inch) thick — then lightly ease it into a tart case, pushing the side in gently. Repeat with the other pastry balls. Rest the tart cases in the refrigerator for 30 minutes. Preheat the oven to 180°C (350°F/Gas 4).

Once rested, cut off any excess pastry and prick the bases a few times with a fork to prevent blistering and rising. Line the tart cases with foil, add raw rice and blind bake for 10 minutes. Remove from the oven, lift out the rice and foil (the foil should come away easily; if not, bake for a few more minutes) and brush the base with egg wash. Cook for a further 10 minutes, or until golden brown. Allow to cool. When ready to serve, spoon the passionfruit curd into the tart cases and serve. Serves 8

HOT CHOCOLATE SOUFFLE

This soufflé, like all soufflés, is really just flavouring and egg whites, and so makes a dessert that chocolate lovers will adore. I cook these in cups, which I think is an easy way of dealing with the soufflé, but if you have soufflé bowls, by all means use them. Make sure you butter and sugar the moulds, as this helps the soufflés to rise evenly.

The egg whites can be whisked in a copper bowl if you have one; not only do the whites become fluffier, but the whole process looks so good. Make sure that whatever you intend to whisk the whites in, it is meticulously clean, and that no egg yolk gets into the whites. Fat stops the whites from becoming as light as they can be. Also, don't overwhip them, as they won't rise as well. For all soufflé making, it's important to know your oven temperature accurately — you may want to do a practice run before making these soufflés for guests.

INGREDIENTS

melted butter and sugar, for lining
175 g (6 oz) good-quality dark chocolate, finely chopped
4 eggs, separated
1 teaspoon lemon juice
50 g ($1^3/4$ oz/$1/4$ cup) caster (superfine) sugar
icing (confectioners') sugar, for sprinkling
pure (whipping) cream, whipped to soft peaks, to serve

METHOD

Preheat the oven to 200°C (400°F/Gas 6). Brush the insides of six 200 ml (7 fl oz) coffee cups with a thin coating of melted butter, then dust with sugar. Melt the chocolate in a stainless steel bowl on top of a saucepan of slowly simmering water. Make sure the bowl fits snugly in the saucepan; at the same time the bottom of the bowl should not touch the water. The bowl mustn't be too deep or the water level too high. You want just a gentle steam, so keep the heat very low. If it is too high the chocolate will split, and the fat content will leach out. If a film of oil appears on top, there is no choice other than to start again. Once the chocolate has melted, remove the bowl from the pan and set aside to cool slightly.

Using an electric mixer, beat the egg whites with the lemon juice until soft peaks form and slowly add the sugar. Whisk together on high speed until the mixture is quite glossy and moderately stiff.

Stir the yolks into the melted chocolate. Whisk in one-quarter of the egg whites to help form a paste. Fold the remaining egg whites into the chocolate mixture. Use a metal spoon when you do this to ensure that only a minimal amount of air is knocked out. And whatever you do, don't knock the side of the bowl or the volume of air will dramatically decrease and the mixture may not rise.

Ladle the soufflé mixture into the prepared soufflé dishes and bake in the centre of the oven for 14–16 minutes. The soufflés should be well risen and have a nice firm crust on top when done. The inside will be moist and fluffy but cooked through. If the tops start to brown, remove the soufflés immediately.

Immediately upon removing from the oven, sprinkle each soufflé with icing sugar and serve with a bowl of whipped cream. This dessert cannot be cooked in advance, as the soufflés will collapse a few minutes after coming out of the oven. However, the mixture can be placed in the prepared moulds and will hold in the refrigerator for up to three days. Serves 6

CREME ANGLAISE

This is a very simple sauce that is a great accompaniment to desserts. Use a 0–100°C (32–212°F) thermometer and you will never fail.

INGREDIENTS

250 ml (9 fl oz/1 cup) milk
1/2 vanilla bean, split lengthways and seeds scraped out
3 egg yolks
2 tablespoons caster (superfine) sugar

METHOD

Put the milk in a saucepan with the vanilla bean and seeds and heat until almost boiling. Remove the pan from the heat and discard the bean. Whisk the egg yolks and sugar together until creamy. While whisking, pour the warm milk over the egg mixture. Tip the mixture back into the pan and stir over very low heat until it thickens and coats the back of a spoon or reaches 86°C (187°F). Strain and cool over a bowl of ice, then refrigerate. Makes about 300 ml (10 1/2 fl oz)

CREME PATISSIERE

INGREDIENTS

500 ml (17 fl oz/2 cups) milk
125 g (4 1/2 oz/heaped 1/2 cup) caster (superfine) sugar
1 vanilla bean, split lengthways and seeds scraped out
6 egg yolks
40 g (1 1/2 oz/1/3 cup) plain (all-purpose) flour
150 ml (5 fl oz) pure (whipping) cream, whipped to soft peaks

METHOD

Put two-thirds of the milk into a saucepan and add half the sugar and the vanilla bean and seeds. Bring to the boil, then stand for 10 minutes. Whisk the egg yolks and the remaining sugar in a bowl until pale. Mix the remaining milk with the flour, then strain through a chinois or fine sieve into the egg mixture.

Remove the vanilla bean and strain the milk infusion into the egg mixture. Add to a saucepan and return to the heat. Bring to the boil, then reduce to a gentle simmer and cook out the mixture for at least 2 minutes, whisking regularly until it is thick and coats the back of a wooden spoon. Pour the mixture into a large shallow bowl to cool and whisk every 5 minutes. Press plastic wrap onto the surface of the crème pâtissière to prevent a film forming and refrigerate. When completely cold, fold in the whipped cream. Makes about 1 kg (2 lb 4 oz)

INDIVIDUAL PRUNE TARTS

These are little baked custard tarts, flavoured with prunes and alcohol. Be careful to not overcook the custard and don't have the heat too high or the custard will have little bubbles through it and be tougher than it should be. Like all these tart recipes, you can use any dried or fresh fruit you like, just start experimenting. I reckon cherries in season with some Kirsch would be pretty smart.

INGREDIENTS

FOR THE PASTRY
175 g (6 oz/1^1/2 cups) plain (all-purpose) flour
100 g (3^1/2 oz) cold unsalted butter, cubed
1^1/2 tablespoons caster (superfine) sugar
1 egg, lightly whisked
1 teaspoon natural vanilla extract
1 egg, whisked, extra, for the egg wash

FOR THE FILLING
60 ml (2 fl oz/^{1}/4 cup) Armagnac or cognac
16 pitted prunes, quartered
100 g (3^1/2 oz/heaped ^{1}/3 cup) caster (superfine) sugar
1 egg
3 egg yolks
1^1/2 vanilla beans, split lengthways and seeds scraped out
300 ml (10^1/2 fl oz) pure (whipping) cream

METHOD

To make the pastry, process the flour, butter and sugar together in a food processor until the mixture resembles fine breadcrumbs. Combine the whisked egg and vanilla extract and add to the processor. Process until the mixture just comes together. Form the mixture into a ball, then divide it evenly into eight pieces. Roll into individual balls and wrap with plastic wrap. Refrigerate the dough for 1 hour.

Meanwhile, to make the filling, combine the alcohol and prunes in a small saucepan, bring gently to the boil, simmer for 1 minute, then cover. Remove from the heat and cool to room temperature. Reserve.

Butter and flour eight individual tart cases, about 2 cm (3/4 inch) high and 8 cm (3^1/4 inches) in diameter. With a generously floured workbench and rolling pin, roll out the first ball until it is very thin — about 1 mm (^{1}/32 inch) — then gently ease into a tart case, pushing the side carefully. (Roll out the pastry between sheets of baking paper if that is easier.) Repeat with the other balls of pastry. Rest in the refrigerator for 30 minutes. Preheat the oven to 180°C (350°F/Gas 4).

Once rested, cut off any excess pastry and prick the bases a few times with a fork to prevent blistering and rising. Line the tart cases with foil, add raw rice and blind bake for 10 minutes. Remove the tarts from the oven, lift out the rice and foil (the foil should come away easily; if not, bake for a few more minutes) and brush the base with egg wash. Cook for a further 8 minutes, or until lightly golden. Allow to cool. Reduce the oven temperature to 160°C (320°F/Gas 2–3). Place a baking tray in the oven to heat.

Drain the reserved prunes over a bowl and reserve the liquid. Place the prunes in concentric circles in the tart shells, leaving some space in between. Whisk together the reserved liqueur, sugar, egg, egg yolks and vanilla seeds until the sugar dissolves. Add the cream and whisk lightly by hand (to avoid bubbles on the top of the tart) until just combined, then pour over the prunes, filling right to the top. Place the tarts on the hot baking tray and bake for 25–30 minutes, or until just set.

Stand the tarts for at least 20 minutes before serving warm or at room temperature. Serves 8

CHOCOLATE CAKE

This is my and my daughter Josephine's favourite chocolate cake. It has a heavenly texture. It is like a chocolate soufflé — and it behaves like one, as it rises and falls. So don't freak out as it drops in the middle, because it has no flour to hold it up. It keeps well for two days, as long as it isn't put in the refrigerator; this will result in it becoming hard and unpalatable.

INGREDIENTS

400 g (14 oz) good-quality dark chocolate, broken up

6 eggs, separated

150 g (5^1/2 oz/^{2}/3 cup) caster (superfine) sugar

2^1/2 tablespoons Cointreau

300 ml (10^1/2 fl oz) pure (whipping) cream, plus extra, whipped, to serve

icing (confectioners') sugar, to serve

METHOD

Preheat the oven to 175°C (345°F/Gas 3). Cut a piece of greaseproof paper to fit a 20 cm (8 inch) round cake tin, with a double layer for the side and a single layer for the bottom. Spray the tin with cooking oil and fit the greaseproof paper in snugly.

Melt the chocolate in a stainless steel bowl set over a saucepan of hot water. Don't let the water in the saucepan boil, as you can scald the chocolate. Remove the chocolate from the heat and allow to return to room temperature.

In a large bowl, beat the egg yolks and two-thirds of the sugar until pale and creamy. Add the Cointreau and continue to beat until well combined. Add the chocolate to the egg yolk mixture and stir until completely incorporated, then slowly stir in half the cream. Set aside. Whip the remaining cream until soft peaks form. Set aside. Start whisking the egg whites in a very clean bowl. When soft peaks start to form, slowly add the remaining sugar and whip until very firm. Fold the whipped cream into the chocolate mixture. Finally, fold in the whipped egg whites.

Pour into the cake tin, put the tin in a bain-marie or on a baking tray and add enough hot water to come about 2.5 cm (1 inch) up the outside of the tin. Bake for 45 minutes. Turn the oven down to 150°C (300°F/Gas 2) and bake for a further 45 minutes. Turn the oven off and leave the cake in the oven for 20 minutes. Cut around the edge of the tin, turn it over onto a plate and the cake should slide out easily. Cut slices using a knife dipped in hot water and clean the knife after each cut. Place on white plates. Sprinkle with icing sugar and serve with lightly whipped cream. Serves 10

THREE CHOCOLATE SEMIFREDDO

The Italian semifreddo is a flavoured mousse that sets in the freezer. It has a texture that is icier than ice cream or sorbet, but is at the same time very light. The best thing is that you need no special equipment to make it. It tastes delicious and, if you don't have an ice-cream machine (which, by the way, is a reasonably inexpensive purchase these days), is the best thing to make at home, along with granitas. The French also make a version called parfait, so if you see a recipe, dive in, as again they need a freezer only.

INGREDIENTS

    5 large egg yolks

    6 tablespoons caster (superfine) sugar

    $1/4$ teaspoon salt

    375 ml (13 fl oz/$1^1/2$ cups) milk

    1 teaspoon natural vanilla extract

    70 g ($2^1/2$ oz) good-quality milk chocolate, finely chopped

    375 ml (13 fl oz/$1^1/2$ cups) pure (whipping) cream

    200 g (7 oz) good-quality white chocolate, finely chopped

    60 g ($2^1/4$ oz) good-quality dark chocolate, finely chopped

METHOD

Take a rectangular loaf tin or terrine dish, measuring about 20 x 10 x 7 cm (8 x 4 x $2^3/4$ inches), with a liquid capacity of about 1.3 litres ($45^1/2$ fl oz), and line the inside with a few layers of plastic wrap, allowing some excess to hang over the edges. This will make it easy to remove the semifreddo from the container once it has frozen.

Whisk the egg yolks in a medium stainless steel bowl with half the sugar and the salt. Whisk until the sugar has dissolved. Set aside.

Fill a saucepan one-third full with water and bring to a simmer. In a heavy-based saucepan, heat the milk to just below boiling point over medium to high heat but do not let it boil. Whisk the milk slowly into the egg yolk and sugar mixture. Set the bowl over the saucepan of simmering water. Make sure the bowl fits snugly in the saucepan; at the same time the bottom of the bowl should not touch the water. Remember that the bowl mustn't be too deep or the water level too high. Cook the milk mixture for about 4 minutes, stirring constantly and scraping the bottom of the bowl, until it has thickened slightly. Stir in the vanilla extract. Strain the mousse base through a medium sieve and refrigerate until cold.

Melt the milk chocolate in a double boiler or a stainless steel bowl set over hot water, making sure the water does not touch the bottom of the pan holding the chocolate. Take care to melt the chocolate over very low heat. Whisk until smooth. Slowly whisk one-third of the cold mousse base into the chocolate. Allow to cool.

In a small bowl, whip 125 ml (4 fl oz/^{1}/2 cup) of the cream with 1 tablespoon of the remaining sugar until soft peaks form. Fold the cream into the chocolate mixture. Pour into the prepared pan and place in the freezer.

Prepare the white and dark chocolate mousses in the same way, melting the white and dark chocolate as described above. Put the white and dark chocolate mixtures in the refrigerator for about 40 minutes. When the milk chocolate layer is firm to the touch, spread the white chocolate mousse on top. Once the white chocolate layer is firm to the touch, after about 50 minutes, spread the dark chocolate layer over. Freeze the semifreddo for at least 4 hours until hard.

To serve, unmould the semifreddo and remove the plastic wrap. Cut into even slices and serve. Serves 6–8

FOLLOWING PAGES three chocolate semifreddo, left, and rhubarb ice cream and vanilla ice cream, right

ICE CREAM

Small ice-cream machines have become more and more affordable and practical for the home user. Try these recipes and I promise you won't be sorry. The difference between home-made ice cream and commercially available ones is chalk and cheese. Don't boil the milk when making the custard, or you will have sweet scrambled eggs. The rhubarb ice cream, opposite, is very simple. It is made without eggs, and you will be surprised how creamy it is.

VANILLA ICE CREAM

INGREDIENTS

10 egg yolks
200 g (7 oz/heaped $3/4$ cup) caster (superfine) sugar
500 ml (17 fl oz/2 cups) milk
2 vanilla beans, split lengthways and seeds scraped out
300 ml ($10^1/2$ fl oz) pure (whipping) cream

METHOD

Whisk the egg yolks and sugar until pale and creamy. Bring the milk to the boil with the vanilla bean and seeds. Remove the milk from the heat as soon as it boils and pour it onto the egg and sugar mixture, whisking all the time.

Pour the combined mixture into a saucepan and stir over low heat for about 20 minutes until the temperature reaches 72°C (162°F), or coats the back of a wooden spoon. Strain the mixture into a bowl through a fine sieve and cool over an ice bath.

Once cool, add the cream and churn in an ice-cream machine. Transfer the ice cream to a tub and freeze. This may take about 4–6 hours. Serves 8

RHUBARB ICE CREAM

INGREDIENTS

500 g (1 lb 2 oz) trimmed rhubarb

115 g (4 oz/^{1}/2 cup) caster (superfine) sugar

200 ml (7 fl oz) pure (whipping) cream

METHOD

Wash the rhubarb and cut it into small pieces. Put in a saucepan, cover with the sugar and gently simmer for about 30 minutes until it is very soft and the bulk of the liquid has evaporated. The rhubarb should still be a vibrant colour. Remove the pan from the heat and allow to cool.

Purée the cooled rhubarb in a blender or food processor until fine, then put in a bowl and stir in the cream. Churn in an ice-cream machine, then transfer to a tub and freeze. This may take about 4–6 hours. Serves 8

HONEY AND CASSIA ICE CREAM

INGREDIENTS

500 ml (17 fl oz/2 cups) milk

30 g (1 oz) cassia bark, roasted and roughly crushed in a mortar (page 330)

10 egg yolks

150 g (5^1/2 oz/^{2}/3 cup) caster (superfine) sugar

1^1/2 tablespoons honey

300 ml (10^1/2 fl oz) pure (whipping) cream

METHOD

Put the milk in a saucepan and bring to the boil. Add the cassia and remove the pan from the heat. Leave to infuse for 2 hours, then strain the milk through a fine sieve. Whisk the egg yolks and sugar until pale and creamy.

Return the milk to the heat. As soon as it comes to the boil, remove from the heat, add the honey and allow to melt through. Add the milk to the creamed eggs and sugar. Pour the combined mixture into a saucepan and stir for about 20 minutes over low heat until the temperature reaches 72°C (162°F), or coats the back of a wooden spoon. Strain the mixture through a fine sieve into a bowl and cool over an ice bath. Once cool, stir through the cream and churn in an ice-cream machine. Transfer to a tub and freeze. This may take between 4 and 6 hours. Serves 8

POACHED PEARS

These pears are great to make and have with things like muesli in the morning, or with ice cream for a dessert. They would be perfect with the honey and cassia ice cream.

INGREDIENTS

4 whole pears, such as William, Beurre Bosc or Josephine
500 ml (17 fl oz/2 cups) sweet white wine
175 g (6 oz/3/4 cup) caster (superfine) sugar
zest of 1/2 lemon

METHOD

Make sure your saucepan will hold the pears quite snugly. Combine the wine, sugar, lemon zest and 375 ml (13 fl oz/1 1/2 cups) water in the saucepan. Put over low heat and stir until the sugar dissolves. Add the pears and cover with a round of baking paper. Bring slowly to the boil, then simmer for 10—15 minutes, or until the pears are soft yet still a little firm. Remove the pan from the heat and cool the pears in the poaching liquid.

Once cool, remove the pears from the pan using a slotted spoon and serve. The poaching liquid can be strained and used later in a variety of ways. Serves 4

POACHED QUINCES

These are wonderful with vanilla ice cream or crème anglaise. They also go really well with Bircher muesli. Cook the quinces at the barest of simmers; they seem to go a deeper colour if cooked slowly. It is also very important to cook the skin and core with the quinces, as they too affect the colour. We often just roast them in the oven on a very low heat for a couple of hours.

INGREDIENTS

2 large quinces
600 g (1 lb 5 oz/2^2/3 cups) caster (superfine) sugar
500 ml (17 fl oz/2 cups) good-quality red wine
1 piece cassia bark
2 cloves
zest of 1 orange
^{1}/2 vanilla bean, split lengthways and seeds scraped out

METHOD

Peel the quinces and slice them lengthways into quarters — do not remove the core. Put the quinces and peelings in a large, heavy-based saucepan. Add the remaining ingredients and 500 ml (17 fl oz/2 cups) water and bring slowly to the boil. Reduce the heat to a simmer and cook the quinces until they are soft yet still slightly firm. They should turn a lovely red colour.

Remove the pan from the heat and leave the quinces to cool in the liquid. Once cool, remove with a slotted spoon and serve. Remove the core before serving, if you wish. The poaching liquid can be strained for use in a number of dishes or reduced to a syrup consistency and poured over the quinces. If too sweet, adjust the taste with a little lemon juice. Serves 4

INDEX

BIBLIOGRAPHY

Bertolli, Paul. *Cooking by Hand.* Clarkson Potter, 2003.

Bertolli, Paul and Waters, Alice. *Chez Panisse Cooking.* Random House, 1994.

Gray, Rose and Rogers, Ruth. *The River Cafe Cookbooks (Boxed set 1 & 2).* Ebury Press, 1998.

Hazan, Marcella. *Essentials of Classic Italian Cooking.* Knopf, 1992.

McGee, Harold. *On Food and Cooking.* Scribner, 1997.

Morse, Kitty. *Come with me to the Kasbah: A Cook's Tour of Morocco.* Editions SERAR, 1989.

Rodgers, Judy. *The Zuni Cafe Cookbook.* W. W. Norton & Company, 2002.

Time-Life Books, various Editors. *Good Cook Series.* Time-Life Books.

Waters, Alice. *Chez Panisse Café Cookbook.* HarperCollins, 1999.

Published by Murdoch Books Pty Limited.

AUSTRALIA
Murdoch Books
Pier 8/9
23 Hickson Road
Millers Point NSW 2000
Phone: 61 (0)2 8220 2000
Fax: 61 (0)2 8220 2558

UK
Murdoch Books UK Ltd
Erico House, 6th Floor North
93–99 Upper Richmond Road
Putney, London SW15 2TG
Phone: + 44 (0) 20 8785 5995
Fax: + 44 (0) 20 8785 5985

Concept and art direction: Marylouise Brammer

Project manager and editor: Margaret Malone

Photographer: Earl Carter

Styling and direction: Sue Fairlie-Cuninghame

Assistants to Neil Perry and food preparation:
Sarah Kodicek and Kate Barker

Second stylist: Sonia Greig

Chief executive: Juliet Rogers

Publisher: Kay Scarlett

Editorial director: Diana Hill

Food editor: Katy Holder

Production: Megan Alsop

National Library of Australia Cataloguing-in-Publication Data
Perry, Neil, 1957- .
The food I love.
Includes index.
ISBN 1 74045 717 X.
1. Cookery, Mediterranean. I. Title
641.591822

Printed by 1010 Printing Limited. PRINTED IN CHINA. First printed 2005.

IMPORTANT: Those who might be at risk from the effects of salmonella poisoning (the elderly,
pregnant women, young children and those suffering from immune deficiency diseases) should
consult their doctor with any concerns about eating raw eggs.

CONVERSION GUIDE: You may find cooking times vary depending on the oven you are using.
For fan-forced ovens, as a general rule, set the oven temperature to 20°C (36°F) lower than
indicated in the recipe. We have used 20 ml (4 teaspoon) tablespoon measures. If you are using a
15 ml (3 teaspoon) tablespoon, for most recipes the difference will not be noticeable. However,
for recipes using baking powder, gelatine, bicarbonate of soda, small amounts of flour and
cornflour (cornstarch), add an extra teaspoon for each tablespoon specified.